TM

References for the Rest of Us! ®

BESTSELLING BOOK SERIES FROM IDG

Are you intimidated and confused by computers? Do you find that traditional manuals are overloaded with technical details you'll never use? Do your friends and family always call you to fix simple problems on their PCs? Then the *...For Dummies*® computer book series from IDG Books Worldwide is for you.

...For Dummies books are written for those frustrated computer users who know they aren't really dumb but find that PC hardware, software, and indeed the unique vocabulary of computing make them feel helpless. *...For Dummies* books use a lighthearted approach, a down-to-earth style, and even cartoons and humorous icons to diffuse computer novices' fears and build their confidence. Lighthearted but not lightweight, these books are a perfect survival guide for anyone forced to use a computer.

> *"I like my copy so much I told friends; now they bought copies."*
>
> — Irene C., Orwell, Ohio

> *"Quick, concise, nontechnical, and humorous."*
>
> — Jay A., Elburn, Illinois

> *"Thanks, I needed this book. Now I can sleep at night."*
>
> — Robin F., British Columbia, Canada

Already, millions of satisfied readers agree. They have made *...For Dummies* books the #1 introductory level computer book series and have written asking for more. So, if you're looking for the most fun and easy way to learn about computers, look to *...For Dummies* books to give you a helping hand.

IDG BOOKS WORLDWIDE ™

NETSCAPE COMMUNICATOR™ 4.5 FOR DUMMIES®

NETSCAPE COMMUNICATOR™ 4.5 FOR DUMMIES®

by Paul E. Hoffman

IDG Books Worldwide, Inc.
An International Data Group Company

Foster City, CA ♦ Chicago, IL ♦ Indianapolis, IN ♦ New York, NY

Netscape Communicator™ 4.5 For Dummies®

Published by
IDG Books Worldwide, Inc.
An International Data Group Company
919 E. Hillsdale Blvd.
Suite 400
Foster City, CA 94404
www.idgbooks.com (IDG Books Worldwide Web site)
www.dummies.com (Dummies Press Web site)

Library of Congress Catalog Card No.: 96-88794

ISBN: 0-7645-0324-3

Printed in the United States of America

10 9 8 7 6 5 4 3 2 1

1O/RQ/RS/ZY/IN

Distributed in the United States by IDG Books Worldwide, Inc.

Distributed by Macmillan Canada for Canada; by Transworld Publishers Limited in the United Kingdom; by IDG Norge Books for Norway; by IDG Sweden Books for Sweden; by Woodslane Pty. Ltd. for Australia; by Woodslane (NZ) Ltd. for New Zealand; by Addison Wesley Longman Singapore Pte Ltd. for Singapore, Malaysia, Thailand, and Indonesia; by Norma Comunicaciones S.A. for Colombia; by Intersoft for South Africa; by International Thomson Publishing for Germany, Austria and Switzerland; by Distribuidora Cuspide for Argentina; by Livraria Cultura for Brazil; by Ediciencia S.A. for Ecuador; by Ediciones ZETA S.C.R. Ltda. for Peru; by WS Computer Publishing Corporation, Inc., for the Philippines; by Contemporanea de Ediciones for Venezuela; by Express Computer Distributors for the Caribbean and West Indies; by Micronesia Media Distributor, Inc. for Micronesia; by Grupo Editorial Norma S.A. for Guatemala; by Chips Computadoras S.A. de C.V. for Mexico; by Editorial Norma de Panama S.A. for Panama; by Wouters Import for Belgium; by American Bookshops for Finland. Authorized Sales Agent: Anthony Rudkin Associates for the Middle East and North Africa.

For general information on IDG Books Worldwide's books in the U.S., please call our Consumer Customer Service department at 800-762-2974. For reseller information, including discounts and premium sales, please call our Reseller Customer Service department at 800-434-3422.

For information on where to purchase IDG Books Worldwide's books outside the U.S., please contact our International Sales department at 317-596-5530 or fax 317-596-5692.

For information on foreign language translations, please contact our Foreign & Subsidiary Rights department at 650-655-3021 or fax 650-655-3281.

For sales inquiries and special prices for bulk quantities, please contact our Sales department at 650-655-3200 or write to the address above.

For information on using IDG Books Worldwide's books in the classroom or for ordering examination copies, please contact our Educational Sales department at 800-434-2086 or fax 317-596-5499.

For press review copies, author interviews, or other publicity information, please contact our Public Relations department at 650-655-3000 or fax 650-655-3299.

For authorization to photocopy items for corporate, personal, or educational use, please contact Copyright Clearance Center, 222 Rosewood Drive, Danvers, MA 01923, or fax 978-750-4470.

is a trademark under exclusive license to IDG Books Worldwide, Inc., from International Data Group, Inc.

About the Author

Paul E. Hoffman has written more than a dozen computer books, many of them about the Internet (including IDG Books Worldwide's *The Internet,* the official book of the Public Television presentation *The Internet Show*). In fact, he's been active on the Internet for almost 20 years. As the director of the Internet Mail Consortium, he is responsible for letting the world know how wonderful e-mail is and how well it works with the Web. He is also the author of *Perl For Dummies,* which explains how to program with the Perl language. For ten years, he was the News Editor at *MicroTimes,* the largest regional computer magazine in the United States.

ABOUT IDG BOOKS WORLDWIDE

Welcome to the world of IDG Books Worldwide.

IDG Books Worldwide, Inc., is a subsidiary of International Data Group, the world's largest publisher of computer-related information and the leading global provider of information services on information technology. IDG was founded more than 30 years ago by Patrick J. McGovern and now employs more than 9,000 people worldwide. IDG publishes more than 290 computer publications in over 75 countries. More than 90 million people read one or more IDG publications each month.

Launched in 1990, IDG Books Worldwide is today the #1 publisher of best-selling computer books in the United States. We are proud to have received eight awards from the Computer Press Association in recognition of editorial excellence and three from Computer Currents' First Annual Readers' Choice Awards. Our best-selling ...*For Dummies*® series has more than 50 million copies in print with translations in 31 languages. IDG Books Worldwide, through a joint venture with IDG's Hi-Tech Beijing, became the first U.S. publisher to publish a computer book in the People's Republic of China. In record time, IDG Books Worldwide has become the first choice for millions of readers around the world who want to learn how to better manage their businesses.

Our mission is simple: Every one of our books is designed to bring extra value and skill-building instructions to the reader. Our books are written by experts who understand and care about our readers. The knowledge base of our editorial staff comes from years of experience in publishing, education, and journalism — experience we use to produce books to carry us into the new millennium. In short, we care about books, so we attract the best people. We devote special attention to details such as audience, interior design, use of icons, and illustrations. And because we use an efficient process of authoring, editing, and desktop publishing our books electronically, we can spend more time ensuring superior content and less time on the technicalities of making books.

You can count on our commitment to deliver high-quality books at competitive prices on topics you want to read about. At IDG Books Worldwide, we continue in the IDG tradition of delivering quality for more than 30 years. You'll find no better book on a subject than one from IDG Books Worldwide.

John Kilcullen
Chairman and CEO
IDG Books Worldwide, Inc.

Steven Berkowitz
President and Publisher
IDG Books Worldwide, Inc.

Eighth Annual
Computer Press
Awards ≥1992

Ninth Annual
Computer Press
Awards ≥1993

Tenth Annual
Computer Press
Awards ≥1994

Eleventh Annual
Computer Press
Awards ≥1995

IDG is the world's leading IT media, research and exposition company. Founded, in 1964, IDG had 1997 revenues of $2.05 billion and has more than 9,000 employees worldwide. IDG offers the widest range of media options that reach IT buyers in 75 countries representing 95% of worldwide IT spending. IDG's diverse product and services portfolio spans six key areas including print publishing, online publishing, expositions and conferences, market research, education and training, and global marketing services. More than 90 million people read one or more of IDG's 290 magazines and newspapers, including IDG's leading global brands — Computerworld, PC World, Network World, Macworld and the Channel World family of publications. IDG Books Worldwide is one of the fastest-growing computer book publishers in the world, with more than 700 titles in 36 languages. The "...For Dummies®" series alone has more than 50 million copies in print. IDG offers online users the largest network of technology-specific Web sites around the world through IDG.net (http://www.idg.net), which comprises more than 225 targeted Web sites in 55 countries worldwide. International Data Corporation (IDC) is the world's largest provider of information technology data, analysis and consulting, with research centers in over 41 countries and more than 400 research analysts worldwide. IDG World Expo is a leading producer of more than 168 globally branded conferences and expositions in 35 countries including E3 (Electronic Entertainment Expo), Macworld Expo, ComNet, Windows World Expo, ICE (Internet Commerce Expo), Agenda, DEMO, and Spotlight. IDG's training subsidiary, ExecuTrain, is the world's largest computer training company, with more than 230 locations worldwide and 785 training courses. IDG Marketing Services helps industry-leading IT companies build international brand recognition by developing global integrated marketing programs via IDG's print, online and exposition products worldwide. Further information about the company can be found at www.idg.com. 10/8/98

Author's Acknowledgments

The Web is a big place, and hundreds of thousands of people have put millions of hours into making it enjoyable. The vast majority of those folks haven't made any money from their work yet, and many did it for the joy of starting something new. These people deserve the most thanks for this book because there'd be no Web for me to write about — and for you to read about — without them.

Writing for computer novices is always easier if you have a few of them around asking you questions. My close circle of novices and ex-novices keeps me on my toes and reminds me of what is not obvious, how frustrating it can be when the system is designed by know-it-all dweebs, and what parts are fun. I'd particularly like to thank Morgan and Zoriah Tharan for their help in this area. I'd also like to thank my grandfather, Oscar Hoffman, for instilling in me a healthy mistrust of computer jargon.

Of course, this book also wouldn't exist without the work of the people at IDG Books Worldwide, Inc. Take a glance at the Publisher's Acknowledgments page to see the names of the people who worked specifically on getting this book into your hands. I thank them all.

Publisher's Acknowledgments

We're proud of this book; please register your comments through our IDG Books Worldwide Online Registration Form located at http://my2cents.dummies.com.

Some of the people who helped bring this book to market include the following:

Acquisitions, Editorial, and Media Development

Project Editor: Nate Holdread

Acquisitions Editor: Joyce Pepple

Media Development Technical Editor: Heather Heath Dismore

Associate Permissions Editor: Carmen Krikorian

Senior Copy Editor: Christine Meloy Beck

Technical Editor: Keith Underdahl

Editorial Manager: Mary C. Corder

Editorial Assistant: Alison Walthall

Production

Project Coordinator: E. Shawn Aylsworth

Layout and Graphics: Daniel Alexander, Lou Boudreau, Linda M. Boyer, Angela F. Hunckler, Jane E. Martin, Brent Savage, Jacque J. Schneider, Kate Snell, Brian Torwelle

Proofreaders: Vickie Broyles, Michelle Croninger, Nancy Price, Ethel M. Winslow, Janet M. Withers

Indexer: Johnna Van Hoose

General and Administrative

IDG Books Worldwide, Inc.: John Kilcullen, CEO; Steven Berkowitz, President and Publisher

IDG Books Technology Publishing: Brenda McLaughlin, Senior Vice President and Group Publisher

Dummies Technology Press and Dummies Editorial: Diane Graves Steele, Vice President and Associate Publisher; Mary Bednarek, Director of Acquisitions and Product Development; Kristin A. Cocks, Editorial Director

Dummies Trade Press: Kathleen A. Welton, Vice President and Publisher; Kevin Thornton, Acquisitions Manager

IDG Books Production for Dummies Press: Michael R. Britton, Vice President of Production and Creative Services; Cindy L. Phipps, Manager of Project Coordination, Production Proofreading, and Indexing; Kathie S. Schutte, Supervisor of Page Layout; Shelley Lea, Supervisor of Graphics and Design; Debbie J. Gates, Production Systems Specialist; Robert Springer, Supervisor of Proofreading; Debbie Stailey, Special Projects Coordinator; Tony Augsburger, Supervisor of Reprints and Bluelines

Dummies Packaging and Book Design: Robin Seaman, Creative Director; Kavish + Kavish, Cover Design

♦

The publisher would like to give special thanks to Patrick J. McGovern, without whom this book would not have been possible.

♦

Contents at a Glance

Introduction 1

Part I: Wild, Wild Web 9
Chapter 1: Welcome to Too Many Ws 11
Chapter 2: The Web: A Concerto in Three Parts 23
Chapter 3: Getting Caught in the Web 37

Part II: Knowing Your Navigator 59
Chapter 4: Getting into Navigator 61
Chapter 5: Making Navigator Work for You 75
Chapter 6: Searching High and/or Low 93
Chapter 7: Playing Favorites 101
Chapter 8: It May Be Broken 107

Part III: Your E-Mail Messenger 115
Chapter 9: Starting Up Your Messenger 117
Chapter 10: There's Something in Your Mailbox 135
Chapter 11: Getting the Word Out with Messenger 147
Chapter 12: Making Mail Even Better 155

Part IV: Who's Webbing Now? 169
Chapter 13: Starting in the Library 171
Chapter 14: Finding Fun, Fun, Fun 187
Chapter 15: Web Ways to Shop 203
Chapter 16: Self-Reference: Computers on Computers 219
Chapter 17: Your Government: At Work? 235

Part V: Your Name in Lights 251
Chapter 18: So You Want to Be a Producer 253
Chapter 19: That's Why They Call It Composer 265
Chapter 20: The Best Parts: Hypertext and Graphics 281
Chapter 21: In Case You Need HTML 289

Part VI: The Part of Tens 299
Chapter 22: Ten Things Communicator and the Web Won't Do for You . . . Yet ... 301
Chapter 23: Ten Ways to Have Fun with Communicator 307
Chapter 24: Ten Charming Places on the Web 313

Glossary 323

Index 339

Book Registration Information .... Back of Book

Cartoons at a Glance

By Rich Tennant

page 115

page 169

page 9

page 251

page 299

page 59

Fax: 978-546-7747 • E-mail: the5wave@tiac.net

Table of Contents

Introduction *1*

About This Book 1
Conventions Used in This Book 1
Foolish Assumptions 2
What's a Netscape? 3
How to Get Communicator 4
  Get it from the source 4
  Get it elsewhere 5
  Updating from earlier versions 5
  Free source code 5
How This Book Is Organized 6
  Part I: Wild, Wild Web 6
  Part II: Knowing Your Navigator 6
  Part III: Your E-Mail Messenger 6
  Part IV: Who's Webbing Now? 6
  Part V: Your Name in Lights 7
  Part VI: The Part of Tens 7
  The Glossary 7
Icons Used in This Book 7
Where to Go from Here 8

Part I: Wild, Wild Web *9*

Chapter 1: Welcome to Too Many Ws **11**

The Internet of Today 11
  The Internet as a network 13
  The Internet for humans 13
The World Wide Web: Not a Thing, Not a Place 15
Hang On, It's about to Shift 16
What You Need to Start Using the Web 19
  The starting point: A computer 19
  Someone to connect with 20
  Modems: Paying for speed 20
  Minimal Internet connection 21
  Modern Internet connection 21
What's This about Netscape? 22

Chapter 2: The Web: A Concerto in Three Parts **23**

It Is Written: Content 24
    Topics on the Web 25
    The many media of the Web 26
    We interrupt this Web for a commercial announcement 27
    Web content is still mostly free 29
    Netscape gets into the content business 29
Your End of the Deal: Client Software 30
They Give It All to You: Servers 33
Tying It All Together 35

Chapter 3: Getting Caught in the Web **37**

Overview of Internet Services 38
The Center of the Web: HTTP 41
    A bit hyper about hypertext 41
    Why hypertext is popular 43
    What hypertext looks like 44
    How to hypertext: HTML 45
A Little Farther Out: Other Services on the Internet 47
    Internet mail 47
    FTP 48
    Usenet news 49
    Gopher 50
    WAIS 51
    Telnet 51
The Internet outside the Web 52
    Other non-Web Internet services 52
    Gateways: On and not on the Web at the same time 53
You Need URL in That Engine 53
    Service names in URLs 54
    Host names 55
    URL requests 57

Part II: Knowing Your Navigator **59**

Chapter 4: Getting into Navigator **61**

Where Does It All Begin? 61
Starting on the Same Page 62
Windows 3.1? Windows 95? Windows 98? Macintosh? Who Cares! 65
Click-O-Rama: Following Links 65
    Backward and forward 67
    Knowing where you've been 67
    Who says you can't go home again? 68
    Stop right there 68
    Get it again 69
Entering Links Instead of Clicking Them 69

Filling In Forms 70
Save That Web Page! 71
    Saving pages on disk 72
    Printing Web pages 72
    Downloading files that you can't see 73
Use What You Have: Opening Local Files 73
Many Windows to the Web 73
So Go Out and Have Fun 74

Chapter 5: Making Navigator Work for You 75
What More Could You Prefer? 75
Appearance 77
    Fonts 78
    Colors 79
Navigator 79
    Languages 80
    Applications 80
    Smart Browsing 80
Mail and Newsgroups 80
Roaming Access 81
Composer 81
Offline 81
Advanced 82
    Cache 83
    Proxies 84
    SmartUpdate 84
Customizing Your Toolbars 85
The Best Commands at Your Fingertips 85
Finding Text 86
Plug-ins and Helper Applications 87
Security Preferences 88
    Personal certificates 90
    Site certificates 90
    Certificate authorities 90
Onward to the Web! 91

Chapter 6: Searching High and/or Low 93
Web Catalogs 94
Get Smart with Smart Browsing 97
    Internet keywords 97
    What's related 98
Guessing How to Get What You Want 99

Chapter 7: Playing Favorites 101
Getting Acquainted with Your Bookmarks 102
Adding a Web Page to Your List 103
Organizing Your Life — Or At Least Your Bookmarks 103
    Folders are your friends 104
    Moving things around 104

Changing Your Bookmarks 105
Getting Bookmarks from Other Places 106

Chapter 8: It May Be Broken 107

The Errors of Your Ways 108
    The URL doesn't exist 108
    The server name is wrong 110
    Sometimes very busy and very dead look the same 110
Hmmmm, Nothing Happened 111
Surviving Netstorms 113
Fixing Broken Pictures 114

Part III: Your E-Mail Messenger 115

Chapter 9: Starting Up Your Messenger 117

The Marvelous World of Mail 118
    In and out are different 118
    Messages are amazingly flexible 120
Usenet Isn't Really News 121
Setting It All Up in Messenger 121
    General 121
    Identity 123
    Mail Servers 123
        Incoming servers 124
        Outgoing server 125
    Newsgroup Servers 125
    Addressing 125
    Messages 126
    Window Settings 127
    Copies and Folders 128
    Formatting 128
    Return Receipts 129
    Disk Space 129
It's Not Little, and It's Not Black, but It's Your Address Book 130
    No more crossed-out entries! 130
    Automating entries with vCard 132
    Accessing an LDAP directory for addresses 132
    Making mailing lists 132

Chapter 10: There's Something in Your Mailbox 135

Getting to Know the Messenger Window 135
Getting Your Mail 137
    Looking through a folder 137
    Following threads through the cloth 139
    Reading the message 140
    Reading mail offline 140

Organizing Your Messages in Folders 142
    Moving messages 142
    Creating folders 142
    Copying messages to other folders 142
    Deleting folders 143
Handling Attachments 144
Starting Up with Usenet News 145
    Finding your groups 145
    Reading Usenet messages 146

Chapter 11: Getting the Word Out with Messenger 147

Creating an E-Mail Message 147
    Where is it going? 148
    Adding the subject and body of the message 149
    You've written it: Now send it! 150
Going Back and Forth: Replying to and Forwarding Messages 150
Attaching Files to a Message 151
Checking Your Spelling 152
Creating Usenet Messages 153

Chapter 12: Making Mail Even Better 155

Getting Organized by Filtering Messages 155
    Defining filters 156
    Filtering incoming mail and Usenet news 158
Securing Your Mail 158
    Getting your key pair and certificate 159
    Using your digital signature 163
    Sending and receiving private e-mail 164
Receiving and Sending Mail Receipts 165
Making the Most of Instant Messages 166

Part IV: Who's Webbing Now? 169

Chapter 13: Starting in the Library 171

Getting In When There's No Front Door 171
    Collecting because it's there 173
    Picking the best 174
Virtual Libraries 174
    World Wide Web Virtual Library 174
    Yahoo! 175
    Argus Clearinghouse 177
    Inter-Links 178
Anointers of Pointers 180
    WebRing 180
    Business Web 182
    Microsoft Library 182
    Larry's InfoPower Pages 183

Chapter 14: Finding Fun, Fun, Fun 187

All This and People, Too! 187
     Who's who on the Internet 188
     Going other places 189
     Making things 190
     Yahoo! People Search 192
     AnyWho 192
Names of the Games 194
     Games Domain 195
     Sport Virtual Library 196
Funky Web Groove Thang 197
     Internet Underground Music Archive 197
     Listening to Indigo 197
TeeVee via TCP 199
     Star Trek: Voyager 199
     The Tonight Show 200

Chapter 15: Web Ways to Shop 203

Doing the Mall Crawl 204
     DealerNet 204
     The Internet Mall 205
     WebAuction 206
One Shop Towns 207
     Music Boulevard 207
     Internet Shopping Network 208
     Computer Literacy Bookshops 209
     Amazon.com 210
     Wits' End Antiques 211
Services with a Smile 212
     Homebuyer's Fair 213
     BookWeb 214
The Business of Business 215
     CommerceNet 215
     CEO Express 215

Chapter 16: Self-Reference: Computers on Computers 219

Emergency Road Crews for Your Computer 219
     Capital PC User Group 220
     PC questions 221
     MacInTouch 222
Support in Your Court 222
     Microsoft 223
     Apple 224
     Novell 224
Dweeb Talk 225
     Seidman's Online Insider 226

HotWired 227
Perl 228
The Internet in the Mirror 229
IETF 230
Usenet Info Center 231
Security Reference Index 233
Consummate Winsock Apps List 234

Chapter 17: Your Government: At Work? 235

The Feds Are Ahead 235
U.S. House of Representatives 236
Federal legislation 237
FedWorld 238
National Science Foundation 239
U.K. Government Information Service 240
State and Local Folk 241
California 241
Oregon 242
K through 12 through the Web 243
Web66 244
ERIC 245
Change That Law: Advocates Get the Word Out 246
NRA and NOW 247
Tibet liberation 248
Computer Professionals for Social Responsibility 249

Part V: Your Name in Lights *251*

Chapter 18: So You Want to Be a Producer 253

Home Sweet Home Pages 254
Personal Webtop Publishing 254
The teeny cost of gigantic storage 255
Communications cost more than storage 256
Administration can be cheap or expensive 256
You may get it for free 257
Business Publishing on the Web 257
That professional look 258
Selling it 258
Getting people in the front door 259
Where to Hang Your Shingle 260
Think Twice, Then Think Again 260
When the Web Is Slow, Small Is Fast 261
Just Because It's Cool Doesn't Mean It's Good 262
Pay Attention to the Law 263

Chapter 19: That's Why They Call It Composer **265**

It's Just Like a Word Processor — But Completely Different 266
HTML WYSLCDFWYG (Say What?) 267
What HTML looks like 268
HTML documents 268
Getting into Composer 270
Levels of Formatting 272
Formatting characters 273
Formatting paragraphs 274
Learning to love lists 275
Formatting pages 276
Adding Horizontal Lines 277
Fun with Tables 277
You Created a Web Page: Now What? 280

Chapter 20: The Best Parts: Hypertext and Graphics **281**

Thinking about Linking 281
The name of the link 282
Choosing good link targets 283
Linking to the Outside World 284
Linking within a Document 285
Mixtures with Pictures 285
Where images go on the line 286
Images as links 287
Where do images come from? 287

Chapter 21: In Case You Need HTML **289**

What Does Composer Compose? 289
< and > Are Your Friends 290
Starts and stops 291
Capitals don't count 291
Where does the line end? 291
Adding Your Own Tags in Composer 292
Top of the Doc 293
Other Bits and Pieces 294
Comments 295
Special characters 296

Part VI: The Part of Tens *299*

**Chapter 22: Ten Things Communicator and the Web Won't Do
for You . . . Yet** **301**

Publish Software That Never Gets out of Date 301
Put the Content Close to You 302
Use Names instead of Locations 302

Let People Write Content Reviews 303
Send You the Daily News 304
Enable Whole-Web Searching 304
Tell You Where the Problems Are on the Internet 304
Bring You High-Quality, Inexpensive Telephone Service 305
Build Real Communities 305
Bring Everyone into the Tent 306

Chapter 23: Ten Ways to Have Fun with Communicator 307

See What It's Like Around the World 307
Get Free Things in the Mail Every Day 308
Listen to Radio Outside Your City 308
Say What You've Always Wanted to Say 308
Collect Pictures for an Electronic Scrapbook 309
Discover Different Kinds of Music 309
Watch What Other People Are Searching For 310
Share Your Instant Poems 310
Play the Stock Market 310
Wander Around Aimlessly 311

Chapter 24: Ten Charming Places on the Web 313

Bill's Lighthouse Getaway 313
Zen Page 313
Exploratorium 315
Plugged In 316
The Peace Page 317
Positive Vibrations 318
Crossword Puzzles 319
GardenNet 320
Bird Watching 321
Pete's Pond Page 322

Glossary *323*

Index *339*

Book Registration Information .... *Back of Book*

Introduction

The World Wide Web is a big place. It had better be: The hype for it is already so great that people have high expectations about what they'll find when they get there. The Web (I'll drop the "World Wide" stuff for now) is a new kind of online place where you can find all sorts of interesting people and information. The Web is part of the Internet, which is part of the overall online world. But you can find plenty to do without straying far from the Web.

About This Book

Netscape Communicator is one program that enables you to use the World Wide Web. Imagine that you see a book about Excel and spreadsheets. You know that Excel is a kind of spreadsheet program. Any book about Excel should discuss spreadsheets in general and how to use Excel in particular. Well, this book is similar. Some of the book is about the World Wide Web, and some of the book is about how to use what is currently the most popular program for the World Wide Web — namely, Communicator.

This book isn't meant to be read from front to back. It's more like a reference, with each chapter divided into sections describing some aspect of Communicator or the World Wide Web.

You don't have to remember anything in this book. Again, this book is meant to be a reference, and you're not expected to "learn" anything here. The information in this book enables you to get by; you can look up the information you need and then move on.

Conventions Used in This Book

This book functions as a reference: You start by looking up the topic that interests you in either the table of contents or the index. Then you go the specific section of the book where the topic is covered and read about the topic.

As you know, computer books look different from other books. One of the methods used to make things in the text clearer is to use different type styles to mean different things.

If you've read other computer books, you know that figuring out which text in a sentence is text that you are seeing on the computer screen isn't always easy. In this book, such text is shown in a special typewriter-like type style `that looks like this`. This style is also used for addresses on the Web or the Internet because these addresses are most often what you type into Communicator and other programs and thus see on-screen.

The computer field is full of jargon and unfamiliar words. In this book, the first time a word or phrase is used, it appears in italic type, *like this*. (Remember, too, that at the end of the book is a very complete glossary in which most of these new words are fully defined. If you see an unfamiliar word or abbreviation that isn't in italic type and isn't explained — and you don't remember it from what you've read so far — check the glossary; you're likely to find it right there.)

You also find sprinkled throughout the book short sections in yet a different typeface with a gray-shaded background. These are *sidebars* that contain interesting information (I think) that isn't essential to the flow of the main text. You can stop and read them where they appear or go back and read them after you finish the section, chapter, or even the entire book. (You'll recognize these sidebars when you see them.)

Foolish Assumptions

You are not a dummy. And if you can read this sentence, you're certainly not stupid. (This book's title comes from the name of a best-selling book that started the entire series: *DOS For Dummies*. The book and the series are quite popular. Regardless of how you or I feel about the word "dummy," these books have introduced tens of millions of readers to new computer concepts.)

You are, however, probably a novice at using Communicator. If you weren't a novice, you probably would have grabbed a different book from the shelf in the bookstore. Advanced users of Communicator may find much (although not all) of the information in this book comfortably familiar because they already know it.

You're probably not a Web expert; this book is perfect for novices and even intermediate Web users. It assumes that you already know a little bit about your computer and a bit about the Internet, but not much. It is definitely written with the beginner, particularly the frustrated beginner, in mind.

Here are the assumptions that I've made about you, the reader:

- ✔ You want to connect to the Internet to use the Web, e-mail, and other Internet services.

- ✔ You want to use Netscape's Communicator software. Maybe you have heard how easy it is, or maybe you just don't like using the other popular Internet program, Microsoft's Internet Explorer.

- ✔ You want to know what's on the Web and why everyone seems so excited about it.

- ✔ You may or may not already have an Internet account; if you do, you're not yet a "net.weenie."

- ✔ Besides getting information from the Web, you may also want to put your own information out for others to see.

Again, you are not a dummy; the fact that you've picked up this book shows that you're actually quite intelligent. You simply have yet to master the Web and Communicator. Read this book and you'll know everything you need to go cruising around the Web like a pro.

What's a Netscape?

Good question, and the answer is a bit harder than it should be. Netscape is all the following:

- ✔ The first part of the name of a company: Netscape Communications.

- ✔ The first part of the name of the software that millions of people now use to access the Web: Netscape Communicator.

- ✔ The first part of the name of other software made by the same company (but you don't need to worry about this additional software in this book).

Netscape Communications has created a program called Netscape Communicator, and that's part of what this book is about.

Just to make things more confusing, Netscape's Web browser goes by two names: *Communicator* and *Navigator.* The first few versions of the browser were called *Navigator,* although most people just called it *Netscape* because it was the software for which the company was famous. In recent years, Netscape changed the name of the package to *Netscape Communicator,* with the Web browser part of the package being called *Navigator.*

How to Get Communicator

As I state earlier, you don't need to use Communicator to get plenty out of this book. In fact, if for some reason you are dead set *against* becoming a Communicator user, you'll find many chapters that relate to any Web software. But if you're like most Internet users, you'll want to get Communicator.

Communicator is free. Communicator is also really, really good. Other Web browsers are available, and some of them are free, too. Communicator's only serious competition is Microsoft's Internet Explorer, which is also free, but Netscape has a tendency to make better software than Microsoft.

If you follow the news, you may know that Communicator wasn't always free. Until early 1998, Netscape charged around $50 for Communicator, although the company let people try it for free and gave it away to many people in special deals. However, the pressure of Microsoft giving away Communicator's competitor, Internet Explorer, for free forced Netscape to offer Communicator for the same price: nothing.

Communicator is available for PCs running Windows (3.1, 95, 98, and NT), for Macs, and for some UNIX systems running XWindows. This book covers only Communicator for Windows and Macintosh. (UNIX users can probably figure out the differences on their own.)

Get it from the source

Netscape Communications, the folks who make Netscape Communicator, knew that it would be hard to get millions of people to fork out $50 for a product they weren't sure about, particularly if it competes against other products that are, in fact, free. For the first few years, the company let individuals try out Communicator for as long as they wanted; corporate users evaluating Communicator could do so for free for up to 90 days before buying the product. Now everyone can get it for free.

If you already have access to the Internet, you can download your copy of Communicator from Netscape's Web server or FTP server. For example, most people who have Windows 95 already have a copy of a Web browser, namely Internet Explorer. If you want to switch to Communicator (and tens of millions of people have), all you need to do is go to Netscape's home page at `home.netscape.com` and follow the links to the software download area. Or, if you prefer, you can go to its FTP server at `ftp.netscape.com` and download from there. The methods for doing this are discussed a few chapters further into this book.

Get it elsewhere

Because Communicator is free, some Internet service providers (ISPs) give it away to new customers. Thus, you can often find it on CD-ROMs that ISPs give you when you sign up. Communicator also sometimes comes on CD-ROMs that come with computer hardware such as modems. Heck, these CD-ROMs sometimes even get handed out to airline passengers with their meager snacks.

Updating from earlier versions

If you already have a copy of Communicator, it may not be up to date. This book covers Communicator Version 4.5, but many people are still using copies from Versions 4.0, 3, 2, and even Version 1. Of course, Netscape allows you to update your software for free.

To get the updated version, use your current version to go to Netscape's Web site (this procedure is described in Chapter 4, if you're patient). The first page on the site usually contains a link to getting the most recent version of the software. Follow that link, and away you go.

Free source code

When Netscape started giving away Communicator, it also did something amazing: It started giving away the source code for the program as well. Anyone with the right programming tools can change the way the program works and recompile it to make a different program. The main restriction that Netscape puts on the source code is that any changes made to it have to also be made available to Netscape so that the company can distribute those changes to its users.

It's unlikely that many people want to compile the source code because few people have the right tools. Still, you benefit from the free source code. How? Well, as Netscape hoped, many people started making changes to the source code and giving Netscape copies of their changes. Netscape plans to take the best of the changes and roll them into Communicator Version 5 and beyond. If you're a programming guru, you can go get the source code now (but it's unlikely that the folks reading this book are programming gurus. . .).

How This Book Is Organized

Yes, yes, you see this in the introduction of almost every computer book: a description of what you'll find in the rest of the book. This particular convention may seem a tad silly, given that all the headings are listed in the lovely table of contents. Yet every book does it, and so must this one, given the incredible bad luck that may befall the author if the Universal Rule of Introductions is broken.

Part I: Wild, Wild Web

The first three chapters of this book give you an overview of what the Web is and what it isn't. You also find a discussion of how to get connected to the Internet if you aren't already — or how to get a better connection if you already have one. By the time you finish with these chapters, you should have a solid foundation in using the Web with Communicator.

Part II: Knowing Your Navigator

The next five chapters describe the "how" of the Web: how to use Communicator, how to search for things, and how to get around problems. These chapters get you up to speed with understanding how Navigator and the Web work together.

Part III: Your E-Mail Messenger

The Internet is much more than just the Web. Many people like mail and Usenet news more than the Web, and the four chapters in this part show you how Messenger, another part of Communicator, lets you, well, communicate with other Internet users. By the time you're done with these chapters, you'll probably use both Navigator and Messenger and be a regular Internet pro.

Part IV: Who's Webbing Now?

Most of the glowing descriptions of the Web talk about how much is out there to experience. The five chapters in this part show you dozens of great examples of what's on the Web today. Even though the Web is still in its infancy, these examples can give you a pretty good feel for what you may see there next year as well.

Part V: Your Name in Lights

If you find the material in Part IV interesting enough to entice you to create your own Web information, you need to read the four chapters in this part. Putting information on the Web isn't that difficult, but it isn't terribly easy either. You must find out a bit about how to make your information look good, and you also need to know how to avoid the many pitfalls of publishing. This part helps you do all that — and more.

Part VI: The Part of Tens

Yep, you've gotten to the end of the main part of the book. To bring things to a close, this part contains a few short chapters, each containing ten items of interest to all Web users. These are things that didn't really fit in the rest of the book and make a nice closing.

The Glossary

Finally, what's a computer book without a glossary? You can use this book's glossary to find quick definitions for all kinds of techie terms.

Icons Used in This Book

If you flip through this book, you should notice that some paragraphs have little round pictures — called *icons* — next to them. These icons are used to make important information stand out, just in case you're one of those readers who skims just a bit too quickly.

The icons you find in this book — and what they represent — are as follows:

This icon flags handy information that is just a bit more useful than everything else around it. A Tip icon is like a gold star for some of the best information in the book.

Hey, not everything on the Web is all fun and games. You may need to pay extra attention to a few things so that they don't come back and bite you later. Warnings tip you off to these potential pitfalls.

Most beginners like a bit of technical jargon once in a while. Technical Stuff sections, which you can feel free to skip, go into more detail than really needs to appear in a book such as this. Still, they can give you that special "propeller-head" (also known as techno-geek) understanding.

A Remember icon provides a friendly reminder of information you don't want to forget (even if you already have).

This book is part of the ...*For Dummies* series of books on many computer-related topics. (In fact, the series now includes many non-computer books as well!) Of course, this one book can't cover everything in the entire computer universe, so you often spot plugs for other books in the series that go into greater depth on particular subjects not covered in detail here.

Where to Go from Here

My, you are quite the reader, aren't you? You even read the obligatory end-of-introduction exhortation to start Chapter 1. Well, get to it! Zip through the first few chapters, get on the Web, and start exploring. You'll find an amazing wealth of information, a fair amount of fun, and who knows what else out there. As a novice, you're in good company on the Web; this book can help make you a seasoned Web user in no time.

Part I
Wild, Wild Web

The 5th Wave   By Rich Tennant

"Would you like Web or non-Web?"

In this part . . .

Welcome to the Web! In the three short chapters of this part, you can gain a solid understanding about what the Web is, its parts, and how to use it. This part also uncovers and dymystifies the hardware and software you need to get started using the Web.

Chapter 1
Welcome to Too Many Ws

In This Chapter

▶ A first attempt at defining the World Wide Web

▶ Separating the Web from the rest of the Internet

▶ Getting a feel for how much is out there

▶ Describing what you need to start using the Web

*U*nless you don't read the newspaper and never watch TV, you have probably heard about the so-called "Information Superhighway." Politicians and businesspeople are promising you a rosy future filled with entertainment, information, and communications right in your home. Soon you can buy high-tech gadgets that give you access to more than everything in your local library and the neighborhood video store combined.

Yeah, right. No problem.

This is a great time to take a few steps back and look more closely at what people are promising, what already exists today, and what you really want. The Information Superhighway (or whatever silly name computer pundits are now calling whatever it is) won't be running through your living room for many years, and you want to get going with the best of what's available right now.

The Internet of Today

One important component of today's version of the Information Superhighway is known as the *World Wide Web*. Understanding the World Wide Web without knowing the context in which it lives is impossible. The Web is part of the *Internet,* which is an international network of computers linked by certain rules and guidelines. You may already be a user on the Internet, or you may be coming to the Web and the Internet at the same time; it really doesn't matter.

Note: Just as the Internet has numerous names, so do the parts of the Internet. The World Wide Web goes under many names, such as *the Web, WWW,* and even *World Wide Web.* They are all the same thing, and this book usually uses the term *the Web* as the preferred name. Feel free to pick any of them — or even make up one of your own.

Describing the Internet is a bit like describing a city, in that doing a good job of it in less than a paragraph is impossible. Think, for example, about the many ways by which you may describe a city to someone who hasn't been there:

- Its location on a map
- The terrain
- Its architecture
- The kinds of people who live there
- The kinds of people who don't live there but just work there
- Its politics
- The business climate
- Some major tourist attractions
- Its history

Similarly, you can't simply describe the Internet as a particular place, the kind of information available, the people you may find there, and so on. You're unlikely, however, to be happy with the nondescription of "Gosh, it's hard to describe." Instead, the following sections provide a too-short description that should help demystify that which everyone likes to babble on about.

When you found this book, it was probably on the shelf near a bunch of other books about the Internet. If you want to know about the Internet in general, not just the Web in particular (that's why you're reading *this* book!), take a look at *The Internet For Dummies*, 5th Edition and *MORE Internet For Dummies,* 4th Edition, both from IDG Books Worldwide, Inc.

The Internet as a network

The Internet is a collection of millions of computers that communicate through certain methods that have been agreed on for many years. The Internet started about 25 years ago with a small handful of computers run by a few people as an experiment. The initial results were successful; the network was useful, so it grew.

In fact, the Internet was partially intended to be an experiment for how to design a network that could grow easily, with very little central control. That concept is still considered radical today, and you find few networks as loose as the Internet.

If you use a computer on a network in your office, you are probably familiar with how you must ask some central administrator for help getting access to other computers or for permission if you want to add a computer to the network. One of the big experiments of the Internet (one that is still evolving) is how to make such growth as easy as possible.

Another experimental aspect of the Internet that was unique when it was created was the concept that messages passed between two computers may travel over a variety of paths. The idea mimics the highway system. Think of the different routes you could use to drive from Los Angeles to New York, all of which take about the same amount of time.

On the Internet, a message between two computers may go on one path the first time you send it and on a different path the next time you send it. Even stranger, if the message is split into smaller parts, the parts may travel along different routes.

The Internet for humans

In the last ten years, some of the most interesting experimentation has revolved around the best ways for humans (that's you and me) to access information stored on computers that are on the Internet. Some of the questions arising from these experiments include:

- How do you find information if you don't know what you're looking for?
- If you find something interesting, how do you find other, related material?

✔ How do you get information from a computer that isn't always connected to the Internet?

✔ How should different kinds of information be presented?

✔ What's this all going to cost, and how is the cost to be determined?

To use the World Wide Web, you don't need to know many technical details of the Internet. In fact, only a tiny percentage of Internet users know more than a smattering of the *protocols* (a fancy term for rules and regulations), *standards groups* (the folks who define the rules), and so on. I'm not saying that knowing technical details won't help you; I can tell you, however, that absorbing the little bit of technical information that you do need in order to deal with the World Wide Web is fairly painless.

So a reasonably non-technical summary of the Internet may include the following facts:

✔ It is a network of millions of computers.

✔ These computers communicate with each other in a consistent fashion.

✔ Users on one computer can access services from other computers.

✔ You can access a wide variety of these services, most of which are free.

✔ Each service can give you many kinds of information.

The trickiest part of this summary is the word *services*. On the Internet, you can use many methods to communicate with a computer somewhere else on the Internet. These methods are called *services* because they service your requests. A few of the most popular Internet services that you may have heard of are the following:

✔ Mail

✔ The World Wide Web

✔ FTP (for getting files)

✔ Usenet news

If you haven't heard of these services, fear not: They and other services are described in Chapter 3.

Figure 1-1 shows a document that is a semiofficial introduction to the Internet for beginners. This document, at `ftp://ftp.isi.edu/in-notes/fyi/fyi20.html`, gives a great overview of what you may find, and it contains pointers to other interesting documents on the same topic.

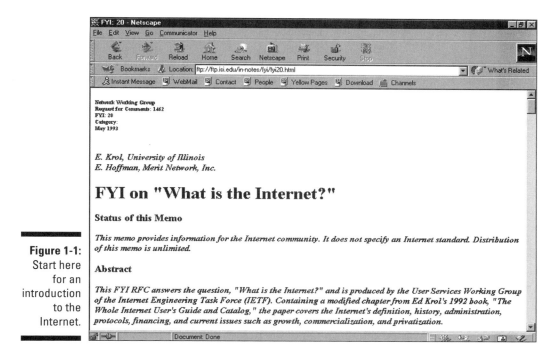

Figure 1-1:
Start here
for an
introduction
to the
Internet.

The World Wide Web: Not a Thing, Not a Place

Given the somewhat vague definition of the Internet that I present in the preceding pages, you're probably wondering where this much-touted World Wide Web fits in. The Web is primarily a service — a method for obtaining information from a variety of computers on the Internet. If you think of the Internet as a supermarket, the Web is one section, such as the produce section. While you're in the market, you can go to other sections, and you don't need to go to the frozen foods section at all if you don't want to.

The analogy can actually be extended a bit without stretching it too far. Have you noticed that, even in the produce section of most supermarkets, you can find lots of non-vegetables being sold? Depending on where you shop, you often find items such as salad dressing, charcoal, flowers, holiday cards — you name it. The Web is like that, in the sense that you can locate other kinds of information — not just things that are made expressly for the Web — while using the Web. Convenient, yes?

This mixing of Webish and non-Webish information is due not to the structure of the Web itself but to the creativity on the part of those who write the software you use whenever you access the Web. Most Internet software programs enable you to access one (and only one) Internet service. With mail software, you use only mail; with Usenet software, you use only Usenet; and so on. Most Web software, on the other hand, enables you to access many services without switching to a different piece of software.

This mixing of services is a great help to users but tends to confuse even advanced users a bit. You often hear computer novices use phrases such as "I'm in Lotus 1-2-3" or "I'm in WordPerfect." If you use Web software to access Usenet news, for example, are you "in" the Web or "in" Usenet? The answer is that you are really never "in" any service; you are "in" your software. The more flexible your software is (and Web software is the most flexible on the Internet today), the more you can do with that software.

As you can see, the vocabulary used for the Internet is often less than clear. Remember that just because you hear people use a phrase (such as "in Usenet") doesn't mean that the phrase is correct. In fact, many of the commonly misused phrases can be quite confusing. On the other hand, feel free to make up your own vocabulary if doing so enables you to keep things straight more easily; the term *Webish* a couple of paragraphs ago is an example of something you may say to mean "things that pretty much pertain to the Web."

Chapters 2 and 3 describe in much more detail what is and isn't on the Web from different perspectives. Chapter 2 describes the Web in terms of its functional parts, and Chapter 3 describes the services that are part of the Web.

Hang On, It's about to Shift

This is probably not your first computer book, and if you're like most people, you've become used to the unfortunate fact that computer books sometimes become outdated. The bad news is that the book in your hands is probably one of those that will become outdated because the Web is changing even as you read this very sentence.

Fortunately, even the swift changes occurring on the Web are unlikely to make anything in this edition of this book totally wrong. More likely is that you'll discover that some new features on the Web aren't covered in the book at all. A year from now, for example, you can expect to find at least three times as many great places to visit and things to see on the Web as currently exist. In fact, after you've read this book, you, too, can publish your own (interesting, I hope) information on the Web.

The Web is growing in other ways, too. The folks at Netscape Communications, for example, keep adding features to their Netscape Navigator software so that users can access a new Internet service they couldn't before. For example, Netscape added the capability to read and send electronic mail when it released Version 2 of Netscape Navigator. (Such a change doesn't make any of the old services act differently, and it certainly doesn't make those old services any less interesting.) In Version 3, they added many multimedia features, and in Version 4, they added a slew of nifty geegaws like conferencing and desktop management. In the newest edition, Version 4.5, they added even more improvements. They also changed the name to *Communicator* in Version 4 and (thankfully!) kept the name in 4.5. As the Web grows and becomes more diverse, you are sure to find more things that aren't covered in this book. But all the information here will still be valid and correct.

As you can see, the Web is quite a bit different than, say, a word processing package. If you buy a book for ZowieWord Version 3, you may find that some of the commands in the book are no longer valid after ZowieWord Version 4 comes out. That's not the case with the Web, however, because there are no "versions" of the Web. The Web changes slowly, and it almost always changes simply by adding new information providers and Internet services, leaving the older features essentially the same as they've always been.

You may, however, run across one possible problem as you read this book. Sometimes the locations of some Web spots discussed in this book change, similar to when companies move and change their mailing addresses. If the people or companies that maintain these interesting Web sites are nice, they leave a forwarding address at their old location so that you can then hop to their new one. Some people, however, aren't that conscientious of things and just up and split with no forwarding information. This problem is discussed in more detail in Chapter 8.

Another way the Web is about to change may be more important to you than either new places to visit or new services: *You*'ll be there. Your presence on the Web, even if you just poke around a bit, is going to be noticed by those who put their own information on the Web. The more people who are using the Web, the more likely is it that those service providers will put more effort into their sites.

In the past year or so, for example, the number and types of commercial services on the Web have expanded incredibly. This increase is mostly a result of companies realizing the potential for using the Web to reach the growing number of Web users. A publisher who didn't think that putting its magazine on the Web was worthwhile only a year ago may today be scrambling to publish it there, now that so many more users — such as you — are climbing the Web.

The industry group known as the World Wide Web Consortium (also called W3C) coordinates the various companies that sponsor technical advancement, new standards, and other activities that help the Web grow. You can get a sneak preview of its home page at `www.w3.org/` in Figure 1-2.

Some of the sites on the Web are community-based interactive sites, meaning that you can read something, respond to it, and have other people see your responses. As you may imagine, anything that is interactive and even barely interesting gets busier as more and more people start using the Web. Some of the fastest-growing services on the Internet are so popular, in fact, because people can say what they want to a small or large audience. As more of these services are encompassed by the Web, the Web itself will become that much more active.

Nothing in this section should worry you or make you think, "Ahhh, maybe I'll just wait until *next year* to start using the Web." Come on — face it: You'd rather be using something that is adding new and interesting parts than something that's stuck in one place, wouldn't you?

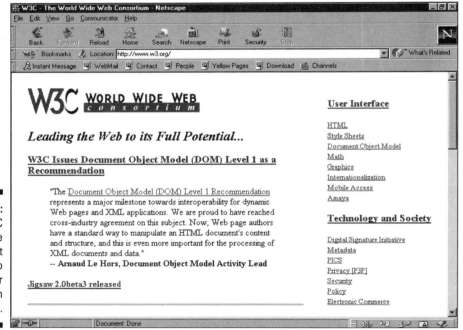

Figure 1-2:
The W3C home page is a great place to start your exploration of the Web.

In this sense, the Web is somewhat like a good cable TV service: It's adding channels all the time. Some are really interesting and just what you've been waiting for, while others are worth about ten seconds of viewing time before you decide to skip right over them. Either way, most people would rather be hooked up to a cable system that is always adding channels than one that isn't (especially one that's always raising its prices for the same old thing).

What You Need to Start Using the Web

Just like kids in the back seat of the family car on a long trip, you may be yelling: "Are we there yet? Are we there yet?" One important subject still needs to be covered before you jump onto the Web: What it takes to get going.

The starting point: A computer

First, you need a computer. That's obvious, you say? Not really. In fact, by the time the next edition of this book comes out, that sentence may not be in it. Today, most people need a computer; in only a few years, however, you may need only a good local cable provider or phone company, a *cable converter box* (also called a *set-top box*), and a television.

As I write this edition of the book, the first Web-to-television systems are being sold, although they aren't doing very well in the market. The most widely known system, WebTV, got plenty of initial interest but still has made very few sales. The device is interesting, but I'm skeptical as to how well it will do over time. However, the folks at Microsoft have much more faith in WebTV than I do, because they just paid hundreds of millions of dollars for the company. Go figure.

Okay, for now, you still need a computer to get to the Web. To be specific, you need a computer that can communicate with the Internet. Today that kind of communication takes place through one of the following two vehicles:

- ✔ A modem
- ✔ A *local-area network* (LAN)

The majority of people use a modem to access the Internet because many companies have yet to install Internet links to their LANs, but that's changing. I expect that most white-collar workers — and plenty of others — will have constant Internet connections at their desks at work within a couple of years.

Someone to connect with

Next, you need an *Internet service provider (ISP)* that offers Web access. These providers are companies that offer access to the Internet, usually for a fee. That is, you need to connect to some computer that is already on the Internet, and that computer also must enable its users to access the Web. Be sure to get an ISP that has modems in your local area so that you can keep down your phone costs when calling them.

If you're using a modem, you also need communications software so that your computer can use your modem. Windows 95 and Windows 98 come with this software, as does the Macintosh operating system and most flavors of UNIX. If you are using Windows 3.1 or an older version of MacOS, you can get free Internet communications software.

Modems: Paying for speed

If you read the ads in computer magazines, you are probably under the impression that the faster the computer you own, the better off you are. That's true for many things, but not for Internet connections. Even a slow computer can keep up just fine with a 28,800-bps (bits per second, which used to be called *baud*) modem installed. (I use the term *bps* instead of *baud* because "baud" hasn't meant anything for almost ten years; if you read "baud" some other places, assume that the writers mean "bits per second.")

On the other hand, having a faster *modem* does make a big difference in how enjoyable and useful your Internet connection is. These days, you have basically three choices in modem speeds: 9600/14,400; 28,800/33,600; and 56K (which have variable speeds that are all less than 56,600 bps). Many 9600/14,400-bps modems cost less than $50; the prices on 28,800/33,600-bps modems are around $70 to $150; the prices on 56K modems are around $120 to $250, but dropping quickly.

And now you can get faster than fast. In the past year or two, superfast modems called *ISDN* modems have started to become popular. ISDN modems run at about four times the speed of 28,800-bps modems and only cost about twice as much. However, you need to get special phone lines to use them, and many local telephone companies are charging ridiculous prices for these lines. By mid-1999, ISDN should be cheaper and more useful, but if you can't wait that long, be prepared to spend lots of money for the faster speed.

 Modems are a topic unto themselves, and not a pretty one at that. Even for computer experts, modems can be a terrible headache. Given how "standard" modems are supposed to be, you'd be amazed at how different they really are from one another. If you're happy with your modem and have no problems using it, great! If not, you probably want to check out *Modems For Dummies,* 3rd Edition, by Tina Rathbone (IDG Books Worldwide, Inc.).

Minimal Internet connection

Rest assured that all common computers made in the past 15 years or so can be used to access the Internet. You can even use a clunky old 286-based PC or a Mac Classic with a 2400-bps modem to connect to the Web, although you may not be terribly impressed with the results. (In fact, some people still use even older computers with no problems at all.) If your Internet provider uses a character-based connection, almost any old thing will do.

For character-based Internet connections, you probably need to supply your own communications software. This software is usually called a *terminal emulation program,* a *terminal program,* or sometimes a *modem program.* For example, some popular terminal emulation programs you may have heard of include ProComm, SmartComm, and MicroPhone. These programs are usually very simple and don't do much other than dial your modem, display characters sent from the remote computer, and enable you to type to the remote computer.

If you are running under MS-DOS or on a Macintosh, you can use many freeware, shareware, and commercial communications systems. If you are running Windows 3.1 or Windows 3.11 on your PC, you already own such a program: Terminal. You may want to buy a shareware or commercial communications program that is better than Terminal, however, because Terminal has very few features of its own. On Windows 95, the HyperTerminal program has even more features that aid in a minimal Internet connection, but it is still far from complete.

Modern Internet connection

Although you can get by with a minimal Internet connection, you may want to spend more money to get a better system. Such a system must run *TCP/IP software,* which has come with all new computers in the past three years. In fact, to use Netscape Communicator, you must have a TCP/IP connection. Communicator requires a TCP/IP connection because such a connection enables it to perform many neat tricks that the other kinds of connections don't.

Because TCP/IP software requires much more CPU power than do simple terminal programs, you need a more powerful computer to run it. However, rest assured that every PC and Macintosh made in the past four or five years should run this software and Communicator just fine.

You absolutely need a modem that runs at 9600/14,400 bps or faster to use TCP/IP software. TCP/IP causes many messages to be sent back and forth over the modem, and an old 2400-bps modem just can't keep up. In fact, most Internet providers that offer TCP/IP services specifically disallow you from using anything slower than 14,400 bps.

What's This about Netscape?

Okay, you've gotten through the Introduction and most of Chapter 1, and so far you've encountered only a little discussion of Netscape Communicator, which is listed prominently on the cover of this book. You may be wondering where Netscape actually fits into the Web — and into this book.

Netscape Communicator is a program that you run on your PC or Macintosh to give you access to the Web and other Internet resources. The most popular part of Communicator, *Navigator,* is one of the best Web access programs available for any computer. This book describes all the parts of Communicator but emphasizes Navigator because that's the part that gets you on the Web.

Other parts of Communicator include

- ✔ Netscape Messenger, which used to be just the mail part of Navigator but which now includes the Usenet portion as well.
- ✔ Netscape Composer, which lets you create your own Web pages.
- ✔ Netscape Conference, which lets you talk to and even see other users if your computer is properly equipped.
- ✔ AOL Instant Messenger Service, which lets you send online messages to other folks on the Internet.

Chapter 2 in particular describes where Communicator and similar programs fit into the structure of the Web. Chapters 4 and 5 offer you detailed descriptions of how to use Navigator; Chapters 9 through 12 cover the features of Messenger; and other chapters throughout the book discuss various Communicator features.

In short, if you have Communicator and an Internet connection, you're ready to go! The next two chapters help prep you a bit better for the way things work on the Web, which is a bit like the kind of things you learn in a driver's education course before they give you your license. I promise, however, that it will be much more interesting and that there are no grainy black-and-white films from the 1950s.

Chapter 2

The Web: A Concerto in Three Parts

In This Chapter

▶ Breaking the Web down into its three components

▶ Defining Web content

▶ Glancing over the client programs

▶ Discovering a bit about Web servers

*A*s I mention in the last chapter, describing the Internet is really, really difficult because it consists of so many parts that don't fit together neatly. Some parts of the Internet are simply computers; other parts are the networking software that access the Internet; some parts are what people publish on the Internet . . . and so on. Fortunately, describing the World Wide Web is much easier than describing the Internet as a whole because everything about the Web falls neatly into three categories — *content, client software,* and *servers.*

Granted, three categories aren't as easy to describe as one unified structure. But if you understand the separate parts of the Web and don't try to mash them all together, you'll find what you want much more easily. Imagine trying to describe your local library as a single unified structure; it's probably impossible. However, if you can break it down into a few basic parts (the building, the books and magazines, the reference staff, the other staff), it makes much more sense.

For the moment, stop thinking about the Web as "the Web" and start thinking in terms of the main parts of the Web. By the time you finish this chapter, you should be able to put the three parts back together and talk about the Web as a sort of thing/place/idea combination again — and even help other novices as they start to get their footing on the Web.

The three fundamental parts of the Web — once again, in case you weren't paying attention — are content, client software, and Web servers. *Content* is the stuff you read, see, and hear on the Web. *Client software* is what you run on your computer to access the content you see on the Web (that's where Communicator comes in). *Web servers* are the computers to which you connect (by using your client software); these computers are what store the Web's content.

As you read this chapter, keep repeating "content, client software, servers, content, client software, servers. . . ." The three are separate parts that, obviously, work together, but keeping them separate in your mind should make the rest of your Web experience much more understandable.

This book uses both the terms *Web client* and *Web browser* to mean the same thing. *Web client* is more technically correct because all the popular Web software do more than just browse. On the other hand, *Web browser* has crept into the vocabulary so much that both now mean essentially the same thing.

It Is Written: Content

Multimedia. Hypertext. Interactive entertainment. Buzzword-o-rama. Phooey! The stuff you get on the Web is the *content*. Ignore for a moment *how* you get it and where it comes from. The content is what you see as you move around in the Web. (By the way, in describing the Web, the words *content* and *information* are interchangeable. Unfortunately, *information* has lost its value as a word because many people now think that information is something you find on a superhighway.)

Even in our packaging-happy society, content is the most important part of what you do online. A book can be exquisitely bound, have really beautiful text, and smell just right, but if it's poorly written or covers some obscure, uninteresting topic, you won't find it worth reading. A TV show that offers nothing worth watching can't keep your thumb away from the remote control.

In many ways (such as the following), the Web is much like a well-stocked local library.

  ✔ A library houses materials on an incredibly wide variety of topics. Some of the materials are books about a single topic, and others are collections of information, such as multi-volume encyclopedias.

> ✔ A library contains materials in many forms. Every library keeps books and magazines, and many libraries stock videos, CDs, tapes, pamphlets, computer databases, and other media.

> ✔ All the material in the library is freely available to anyone who can read it.

The content on the Web exhibits these three characteristics as well: a variety of topics, a variety of media, and (mostly) free access.

Topics on the Web

To say with any certainty exactly what topics comprise the Web's content at any given time is impossible because the list grows daily. A few years ago, the Web offered merely lots of topics; now it overflows with an incredible number, rivaling the breadth of a medium-sized college library; now, almost every kind of content that you can find in print is also available on the Web.

Throughout this book, you find examples of the type of content you can expect to see on the Web. (I hope that you also find something of interest in these examples.) Even if you don't see anything that grabs your attention right away (either in this book or your own browsing), rest assured that the Web probably contains something, somewhere that should interest you. (And if it doesn't, well, remember that you can go out and create your own content!)

Yahoo!, shown in Figure 2-1, has become one of the most-visited sites on the Web for a very good reason: It has a lot of good information for all levels of users. The content is organized well and includes plenty of news, and finding your way around is easy if you just want to browse. Find your own way there at `www.yahoo.com/`.

You can find content that covers many topics on the Web — but perhaps not in the depth you want. The Web today is like a library with books and magazines on all the shelves in every category — but not, as yet, very many books in most categories. As time goes by, however, you can look for the Web's almost-empty shelves to fill up considerably — but don't expect the Web to replace your local library or bookstore any time soon.

The content on the Web is, in many ways, just like any content on paper. Nothing is especially magical about what you read on the Web that makes it more likely to be true than what you read anywhere else. Thirty years ago, some people believed that if they "saw it on TV, it must be true." (Some of those people are still around, of course, saying the same thing about what they see on the Web.) Just because the Web is a new medium, don't assume that the people putting content on it are any more progressive or honest than those putting content on TV, in magazines, or anywhere else.

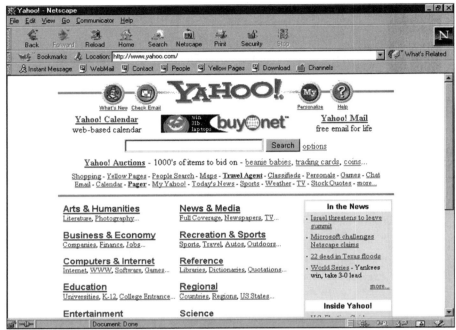

Figure 2-1:
Yahoo! is a
popular
online
destination.

The many media of the Web

The content you can find on the Web comes in many forms, and the number and variety of these forms also are increasing as more companies publish information on the Web. It used to be that the most common form of Web content consisted of just plain text — that is, text with no formatting or adornment of any kind. For the past few years, however, Web content mostly comes with specific formatting, such as headings, character attributes such as **boldface**, tables, pictures, and so on. But converting all the old, plain text takes a long time, so don't be surprised if you find a mix of plain text and formatted text at the same Web sites for the next few years.

If the only form that Web content took was text, the wonder of the Web would never have caught on as well as it has. From the beginning, however, the Web was designed to handle almost any form of content, and people are experimenting more and more with those exotic forms that go way beyond plain, vanilla text. Today, in fact, you can find all types of multimedia content on the Web, including the following categories:

- ✔ Pictures and photographs
- ✔ CD-quality sound
- ✔ Video

✔ Interactive discussions (chat)

✔ Animation

✔ Games

✔ Programs that you can run on your computer

Tomorrow, you're sure to find even more exotic types of content on the Web.

As you can do to the content in a library, you can also divvy up the content on the Web into categories such as "books" and "periodicals." On the Web, you can find plenty of articles — and even many book-length tomes — that people have written on a one-shot basis. You can also find a fair number of Web-based magazines that circulate new issues weekly or monthly. Although other types of multimedia (such as audio and video clips) are still rare because these files are so large, they are definitely available on parts of the Web.

The Web already boasts a particularly impressive collection of reference materials that fall somewhere in that gray area between books and periodicals. Some states, for example, have already put all of their laws on the Web. In printed form, these materials may fill up an entire bookcase and need to be revised in the form of inserts or reprinted in their entirety every year; on the Web, they are handily in reach (and out of sight) just a couple of clicks away.

We interrupt this Web for a commercial announcement

One way in which the Web differs from the standard library is that a huge amount of plain old advertising also exists online. You are probably familiar with the process of looking through a magazine devoted to a particular topic, such as food, and finding yourself just looking at the ads. (A dirty little secret of the magazine world is that, for many topics, the readers care much more about the ads than they do about the articles. In fact, many readers rate magazines not on how good the articles are, but on how the ads make them feel.)

You can find ads upon ads upon ads in plenty of places on the Web. Many companies set up their own Web areas that contain little more than product literature. These kinds of Web sites are wonderful for Web users who want an interactive catalog that they can search through without some salesperson hanging over their shoulders. Depending on how creative the companies are, they can make the Web-based catalog more valuable to you than most print-based catalogs could possibly be.

If you want to check out some Web catalogs, the Publishers' Catalogues Home Page, shown in Figure 2-2, lists many of the hundreds of book publishers' catalogs on the Web. The list is arranged by country, and you can get a feeling for how much commercial penetration has occurred in countries outside the United States. See it for yourself at `www.lights.com/publisher/`.

The commercial Web content can be much more than just a catalog library, however. At some Web sites, you can purchase items immediately after shopping for them. In this way, some areas of the Web act like a shopping mall. Shopping in the stores on the Web may not be as much fun as browsing through a real mall (if you like that sort of thing), but you may find that the convenience of not having to leave your home or office makes up for the lack of ice cream parlors and the fun of searching for your car in the parking lot.

The most common kinds of commercials you see, however, are *banner ads* on the top and bottom of pages at many sites. A few years ago, banner ads were rare; now it's hard to find an interesting site that doesn't have them, unless that site is already selling you something. Most of the free magazine-style Web sites get all of their income from banner ads. Recently, Web site designers have noticed that Web users hate banner ads, and so the prices that a Web site can charge for a banner ad are going down.

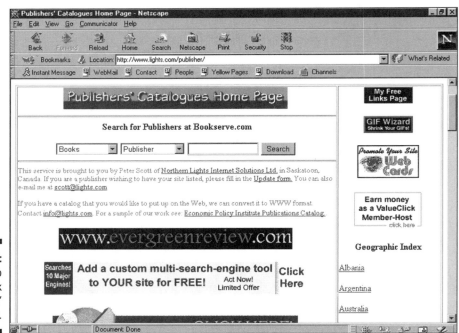

Figure 2-2:
Your link to book publishers' catalogs.

Web content is still mostly free

The comparisons between the Web and a local library are reasonably apt because in both places, reading the content doesn't cost the users anything. Of course, a library needs money to buy books, and people who publish on the Web incur a cost to put the information there as well. To the Web user, however, all that information is mostly just there for the taking.

"Mostly?" Um, yes, mostly. For the first few years, everything on the Web really was free. No one had found a way to charge for the information. In the past couple of years, however, a few sites on the Web have started charging for their content, and a definite trend toward for-fee (as opposed to for-free) materials is growing on the Web. That number is still pretty small, however.

Fortunately, because so much of the content on the Web is still free, any time someone is charging you for anything, you know it right up-front. It wouldn't be right for you to be shown something and then asked for money later; in fact, this practice is illegal in many states.

Netscape gets into the content business

When Netscape started giving Communicator away for free, it needed to find another way to make money in the Web client business. As a result, Netscape hitched its hopes on content. When it released Communicator Version 4.5, Netscape also announced its new content Web site, called *Netcenter*.

Netcenter looks much like many of the other popular places on the Internet, but it has some features that you won't find anywhere else. Netscape added special features into Communicator 4.5 to make it work better with Netcenter, allowing you to take advantage of some added-value options that users of other Web client software can't access. For example, you can get instant updates to your Netscape software at Netcenter. This feature may not be enough of a draw to keep you returning to Netscape's content site, but many people find wandering around Netcenter to be as interesting as other Web sites like Yahoo! and Excite.

As I write this book, people have invented a new term for these content sites that are designed as places from which people will want to start their Web wanderings: *portals*. Most portals are for beginners, but a few business portals are already appearing. I expect portals on other topics to appear soon, seeing as how Wall Street has fallen in love with the current portals.

Netcenter is certainly an important portal because it's so easy to get to from Communicator. In fact, in Communicator 4.5, the Netscape button on the screen now takes you to a part of Netcenter called *My Netscape*. You can customize this page to get news on particular subjects, see local weather reports, check the value of your stocks (if you have any), see sports scores, and so on. This same kind of information is available at many of the other portals as well. Netscape hopes that you like its portal so much that you keep coming back — and look at the ads that it has on those pages.

Your End of the Deal: Client Software

Now that you know that all this content is available out on the Web, the next logical question is "How do I get it?" For that, you need software that can access the Web itself and, therefore, access the Web's content as well. That software is called a *Web client* (or, sometimes, a *Web browser*). For readers of this book, that means Netscape Communicator.

To run a Web client, you need a computer or access to a computer. All the popular Web clients run on PCs or Macintoshes — that is, on the very computer that sits right on your desk. The most popular Web clients for these computers are Microsoft's Internet Explorer and Netscape's Communicator. Figure 2-3 shows a typical screen from Internet Explorer. Other Web clients, such as Lynx, run on UNIX systems that people dial into. Dozens of different Web clients are available, and almost every popular type of computer has at least one Web client available to it.

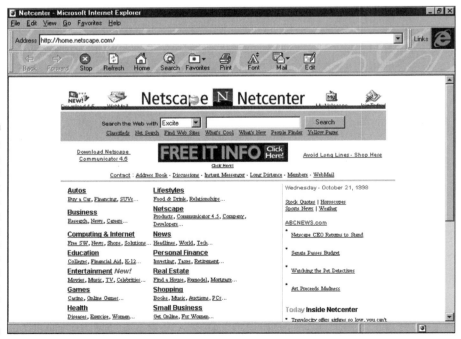

Figure 2-3:
Because the features in Internet Explorer are mostly the same as those in Communicator, the screens look fairly similar.

If servers serve clients, what do clients do?

The word *client* comes from the technical term for the structure of the Web and many other Internet services. A *client-server* information system is one in which you run a program (the client) on your local computer and that program accesses information from a different computer running a different program (the server). The client and the server are programs; however, many people also refer to the computers themselves as clients and servers, which can be a tad confusing to people trying to think of the hardware and software separately. Client-server systems have been all the rage in the computer industry for the past ten years because they allow much faster and smoother changes in information systems.

Understanding a bit about the client-server mentality can help clarify how and why many things happen as they do on the Internet, especially on the World Wide Web. In the old days (up until the mid-1980s), getting information from a database required first getting access to a terminal that was connected to the computer on which the database resided. This style of monolithic computing is still in use in many places today.

The server program speaks in a *protocol* (which is similar to the structure of a human language) that can be spoken by client programs. Server programs speak only one language, but client programs can sometimes speak many languages. As the client starts to talk to the server, both programs verify that they can speak the same language and then start a conversation.

Using the client-server style for getting information from computers offers many advantages. The server program and the client program can run on different computers as long as they can communicate through some sort of network. Users, therefore, don't need a direct connection to the server before getting information from it.

Another wonderful feature of the client-server model for information retrieval is that people can write many different client programs that all speak the language of the server. This is precisely what has happened on the Internet. Instead of being forced to run a single client program to get information, Internet users can choose the program that is best for them from the dozens of different programs available.

In fact, a single client program can speak the language of many different server programs. This diversity, in fact, is what the Web is all about. Before the Web, almost all client programs spoke the language of only one server. Web client programs, however, speak the language of at least four, and often more, server programs, enabling you to get that much more information from the Internet.

The most important aspect of a Web client is how well it enables you to get around on the Web. All Web clients, and certainly Communicator, do certain basic things, as described in the following list (which contains a heap of technical jargon that isn't explained until Chapter 3 — or you can check out the glossary):

✔ Access files on HTTP (hypertext), Gopher, and FTP servers

✔ Show HTML documents from HTTP servers with some formatting

✔ Move between links in hypertext documents

✔ Show pictures in Web pages

✔ Save files that you retrieve on your computer

✔ Let you fill in forms

Some Web clients also enable you to perform the following tasks, which you may find important (Communicator does all of these jobs):

✔ Access content from other Internet services, such as mail and Usenet news

✔ Remember places on the Web where you went recently so that you can return to them quickly

✔ Keep lists of interesting places you find on the Web so that you can easily find them again later

✔ Print Web pages

✔ Mail documents to other Internet users

✔ Look at the HTML source of hypertext documents

The page shown in Figure 2-4 is part of the WWW Virtual Library section on Web development. Located at `www.stars.com/Vlib/Software/Browsers.html`, it contains a list of almost all the clients known. The WWW Virtual Library is discussed in much more detail in Chapter 13.

Some people would have you believe that the most important feature of a Web client is how good it looks. "Ooooh, this one has a *nice* toolbar." "Check out the *cool* background pattern on that one." Ignore the temptation to pick a client based on its visual appeal. The client's speed, its features, and how well it is supported are much more important than whether it exhibits a few extra gizmos on-screen that perform essentially the same functions as the menu commands. Fortunately, Communicator has all of these important features (including many that are just nice fluff).

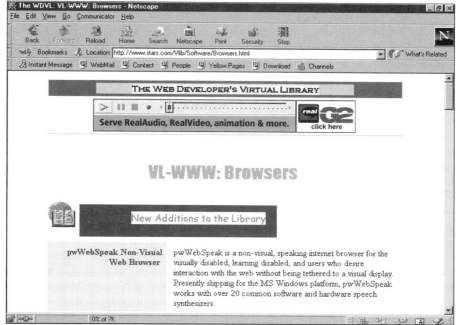

Figure 2-4:
Find a list of just about every Web client at the WWW Virtual Library.

They Give It All to You: Servers

You have by now discovered the content and client software of the Web. The promise of accessing all that free content on your client software is tantalizing, but as you may know (or have guessed), that content doesn't simply appear out of nowhere, full-blown and ready for you to access. Just as in the book world, someone must publish the content — and that's where the third part of the Web comes in. *Servers* are computers where you can go to get the content by using your Web browser.

In relation to the Web, a server is a computer that makes its content available through Internet services. To do that, it must run server software that can speak the same *protocol* (language) as your client software. Figure 2-5 shows a list of software you can use to serve information on the Web. This list is available at the WWW Virtual Library at `www.stars.com/Vlib/Software/Servers.html`.

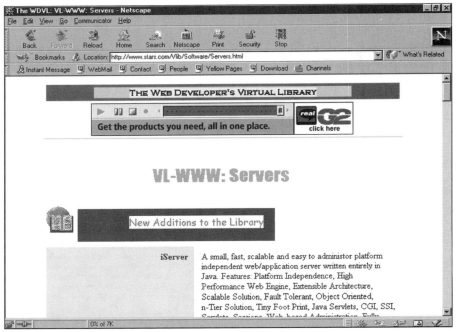

Figure 2-5:
A menu of
server
software
from the
WWW
Virtual
Library.

Server computers are also sometimes called *host computers.* Each Internet service has its own protocol language. Having servers that act as both a computer and the kind of language the computer speaks to make a particular Internet service available to clients can be a tad confusing.

On the Internet, almost all computers have a name, called the *domain name.* Domain names look like the following: `thomas.loc.gov`, `www.kantei.go.jp`, and `www.yahoo.com`. You use a domain name to identify the host computer on the Internet that has the content you want to access.

The case of the letters (whether they are capital or lowercase) in the domain name is unimportant; you can enter them however you want. Thus `www.netscape.com`, `WWW.NETSCAPE.COM`, and `Www.Netscape.Com` are all the same. In this book, domain names are usually shown in all lowercase characters. Be aware, however, that although the case of letters in the *domain names* is unimportant, the case of the letters in the *rest* of what you send to the server may be very important.

As I describe earlier in this chapter, most Web servers do not charge money for access to their content. They need some other reason to offer the content, run the computer, and maintain the server software (which is often not all that easy). Each of the thousands of servers on the Web has a different reason for existing.

For the first few years, most of the Web servers were at educational institutions such as universities. In the long history of the Internet, universities have always been at the forefront of supporting free information. As long as people on the computer-support staff want to run a server, they are usually allowed to do so. Their motivation is often just to make the information free.

In the past three or four years, however, the fastest growth by far on the Web has been in servers at commercial sites. A few years ago, only a handful of brave companies experimented with having Web servers; now, tens of thousands of companies are expected to have their own servers. Some of these commercial servers are just there to promote the company's products, but others are there as bona fide experiments in online publishing.

A third group of people (other than those at universities and commercial companies) serves up content on the Web just because doing so is fun. They have accounts with Internet providers that give free or inexpensive Web service access. At these sites, any user can produce hypertext pages that become part of the site's content. People put all sorts of things at these sites — articles and novels they've written, political tracts, databases they've built, and so on.

Tying It All Together

Okay, you can stop repeating the "content, client software, servers" mantra now. On the other hand, you probably should keep it in mind as you continue your exploration of the Web while you read this book. If you come across an idea that doesn't make as much sense as you'd like, you may find at least a small measure of help by asking yourself in which of the three categories the critter best fits.

Be aware, however, that not everything fits neatly into just one category. Chapter 3, for example, covers the types of Internet services that are part of the Web. Each service relates to two parts of the Web triumvirate — client software and servers — because the client must be able to understand it and display it for you, and servers must be able to serve it to you. Keeping the differences among the three parts of the Web in mind, however, should help you get exactly what you want from the Web more often than not.

Chapter 3
Getting Caught in the Web

. . . .

In This Chapter

▶ Exploring Internet services

▶ Looking into HTTP, HTML, and hypertext

▶ Investigating other Web services

▶ Dissecting URLs

▶ Poking around the non-Web a bit

. . . .

*S*ome folks are interested only in the content on the Web. They simply want to know where the good spots are located to find various types of information or entertainment. That makes sense: Why should anyone care much about what's behind the content on the Web? Similarly, most people turn to television for information and entertainment, but they don't care about the electronics of their sets or of the transmitters that send them the programs.

On the other hand, because the Web industry is still so new (remember, it's only about five years old!), knowing a bit about how the Web works will help you in these early days. For example, you need to understand some of these underpinnings to understand how to select the right settings to make Communicator do what you want. Ten years from now, this kind of information will only be of interest to people in the industry and not to the typical Web user.

Within a country, all television is broadcast in a single manner, and all television sets offer approximately the same set of functions. (You can change the channel, adjust the volume, and so on.) To watch your TV, you don't need to know anything about how electromagnetic signals are broadcast or how your set electronically distinguishes between two channels. Furthermore, few viewers know who owns the various networks they watch, how much profit the networks make each year, and how many people are employed by the companies that create their favorite shows.

If the Web were so unified, you wouldn't need to know much either. But the Web isn't unified. As I mention in the preceding chapter, a great deal of variety exists in all three areas of the Web. Of course, content comes in a variety of flavors in every medium, be it television, books, magazines, or radio. Considerable variety also can be found among the types of Internet services you can access by using those Web clients.

This chapter describes the different kinds of Internet services you find on the Web. As I discuss in Chapter 2, not all Web clients give you access to the same set of Internet services, but Communicator gives you access to all the popular ones. In essence, because Communicator provides access to numerous services, it gives you a bigger Web.

Overview of Internet Services

An Internet *service* is a vehicle through which two computers on the Internet communicate. More than 100 Internet services are currently available, although only a few dozen of these are common. Among the Internet services you may already have heard of are the following:

- ✔ Mail
- ✔ HTTP (hypertext)
- ✔ Usenet news
- ✔ FTP
- ✔ Gopher

(Don't worry, all of these terms are explained later in this chapter.)

Most users on the Internet are connected to computers that use *TCP/IP* for networking. TCP/IP is one kind of networking, and it is the only one that is used between computers on the Internet. It's been around forever (well, okay, for 20 years anyway) and is one of the most-used systems of networking in the world. TCP/IP is a *protocol* — that is, a set of rules for how two computers communicate. Its popularity is not based on the fact that it is the best form of networking, because it isn't. Rather, TCP/IP is popular because most software operating systems work quite easily under TCP/IP. And adding a TCP/IP-based computer to an existing network is also easy.

Not everyone uses TCP/IP, however. Some people are connected to computers with only mail and Usenet connections. These computers do not require full-time TCP/IP connections. A few years ago, the majority of Internet users wasn't on the TCP/IP network; today the majority is.

I don't know anything about how the plumbing in my house works, and I don't want to know about TCP/IP either

When I say that the Internet uses TCP/IP for networking, I'm actually being a bit loose with their language. Networking is a black art that can get incredibly technical in about two minutes of discussion. Part of the problem is rooted in history, back when people thought only computer dweebs would use networks. With so many different ways to network, the second — and more significant — problem is that you must use very precise language to describe just what it is you are doing.

TCP/IP stands for *Transmission Control Protocol/Internet Protocol*. This mouthful (even the abbreviation is hard to say quickly) basically describes how the network works. Some people may have wanted to give it a more colorful name, such as "WonderNet" or "NetAmaze," but the network nerds in the 1970s didn't have that much marketing savvy.

Let me make it all a bit more confusing: TCP/IP isn't just one kind of networking; it's two. Notice that oddly placed "/" in TCP/IP. The slash is dweebspeak for "over." In grade school, you may have learned that 8/4 can be read out loud as "eight over four." Well, TCP/IP can be read as "TCP over IP."

TCP and IP are *network* protocols, or sets of rules, to which every computer on a network must adhere. Different layers of protocols exist in the networking world. The layers are very similar to the ever-popular American system of government. Federal laws take precedence over state laws, and state laws take precedence over city laws.

Everyone in the networking world has agreed to describe network protocols in terms of seven layers. TCP pretty much lives in layer 4, and IP pretty much lives in layer 3. Thus TCP over IP. (Because we're being precise, you may want to know that a bit of TCP slops up into layer 5, and a bit of IP slops down into layer 2 — but then again, who's quibbling?)

Why is this knowledge important to the Web user? If you hang around computer folk, you know that TCP/IP isn't the only network out there. You've probably heard of Novell NetWare, for example. A Novell network runs NetWare, not TCP/IP. Thus, a computer running NetWare isn't, strictly speaking, part of the Internet. The person running the network can buy special software to make his Novell network act nice with the Internet and even be part of the Web, but the network isn't running TCP/IP.

In case you're wondering, yes, you can run something else over IP, but doing so is not nearly as common as TCP over IP. You can even run TCP over something else, but that's also rare.

Internet services are based on TCP, which are sometimes called *TCP services*. The term "TCP services," however, is also a bit of a misnomer because nothing in TCP relates to, say, giving you access to files or hypertext documents. TCP itself, however, is the part of TCP/IP that tells each host computer how to differentiate messages that are coming to it from over the Internet. This process prevents your e-mail message from getting tangled up in an HTTP request or a file that some other user is sending.

Each Internet service has its own rules for communicating. On the Web, you never need to worry about these rules because your Web client and the server do all the communicating for you automatically. You do need to know whether you are using a particular type of service, however, so that you can predict the kind of content you'll get back.

If you send a piece of e-mail to another computer, for example, your computer and the other computer send a few start-up messages back and forth before your computer dumps the whole message out and over the Internet. After the complete message arrives at the other computer, that computer picks and separates out the nonmessage part of the communication that's at the beginning of the message and delivers the rest to the user.

Using HTTP to access hypertext documents is another example of Internet service communication. If your Web client receives a hypertext document from a Web server, it first contacts the host to make sure that the host wants to talk HTTP to you. The host sends back a message that pretty much says, "Yeah, sure." Your client then sends a request for the specific hypertext document you want, and the host sends the document and breaks the connection.

Ports of last resort

Every Internet service is addressed through TCP's *ports*. A port is a number that is significant to TCP but probably insignificant to you as a user. Each service has a standard port number that Web clients use in communicating with servers. The standard port number for HTTP, for example, is 80.

In the best of all possible worlds, users would never need to know about TCP ports. This, however, isn't that world. Sometimes, a particular host puts its Internet services on nonstandard ports. One host, for example, may put its HTTP service on port 8000 instead of on the standard port, which is 80.

The Center of the Web: HTTP

The Web started out with a single Internet service, *HTTP,* which sort of stands for *hypertext transfer protocol.* (The only time you see it written as "HyperText Transfer Protocol" is when computer book authors are trying to force the words to match the letters in the acronym; it really should have been called HTP, but that's another story for another time.) HTTP is the service that enables Web clients to receive hypertext content that can link to other hypertext content — and to nonhypertext content as well.

In and of itself, HTTP isn't anything special. It's just an Internet protocol like so many other protocols. If you look into its technical underpinnings, in fact, you find that HTTP has a few great features, a bunch of mediocre ones, and a couple of dumb ones that can't be eliminated because of their history. (People on the Internet don't like changing things in a way that makes old things not work anymore.) In other words, HTTP is better than some other protocols because it's newer, but the protocol itself is nothing to get incredibly excited about.

What *is* exciting about HTTP is the kind of content it serves up: namely, hypertext documents. These documents can actually be served by a number of different protocols, such as FTP and Gopher. Some servers perform fancy footwork behind the scenes to use other protocols to handle hypertext (such as FTP instead of HTTP). Because Web clients all know how to deal with HTTP-style hypertext documents, however, HTTP has become the de facto standard for serving hypertext.

A bit hyper about hypertext

Long before multimedia, there was *hypertext.* In fact, what people call multimedia today is what old-timers called hypertext back in the 1970s (the Dark Ages before the widespread use of personal computers). If you prefer current buzzwords, feel free to substitute the term *multimedia* everywhere you see *hypertext* in this book.

Hypertext is a type of content that can form links to other content. If you are using a hypertext reader (such as a Web client), you'll notice that some parts of the content are labeled as links to other content. (For example, Communicator normally shows links as underlined text.) The other content may be in the same document, or it may be somewhere else altogether. You can use the hypertext reader to jump instantly to those links, and then to others, or to go back to your original place. This jumping is best described by example.

A user's guide to the Internet

EarthLink has made quite a name for itself as an Internet provider, and its people have created an excellent online guide for novice Internet users. The guide is available to anyone, not just Earthlink's subscribers, and it covers everything that beginning users would want to know. You can find this guide at `www.earthlink.net/book/`.

Imagine that, as you read this chapter, you encounter a sentence that reads: "See Chapter 17 for a list of government resources on the Web." To see that list, you must flip through the book to Chapter 17 and start reading there. After you finish reading Chapter 17 (or at least the parts you find interesting), you flip back to where you left off reading in this chapter and go on.

Now imagine a really nifty book that does things for you instead of forcing you to do them yourself. If you come to the sentence that reads, "See Chapter 17 for a list of government resources on the Web," you simply point to that sentence and click, and the book flips directly to Chapter 17. When you want to go back to your original location, you point to a button labeled "Back," and the book flips back to the page you started from.

Keep your imagination turned on for a while longer. Suppose that Chapter 17 is actually interesting (imagine that!), and you see a sentence that reads: "Congress has made a list available to you of all the bills it is considering." Click that sentence, and the book instantly produces a copy of that list for you to read. You get the list even though it *doesn't actually exist in the book itself.*

As you browse the list, you spy a piece of legislation that concerns you. A sentence in the list reads, "Representative Hornblower is the author of this bill." Point at that sentence and click, and suddenly you are creating an electronic mail message to Representative Hornblower (although you can still see the list in the background). You finish the message, indicate that you want to send it, and — voilà! — it's sent. Next, you decide you'd rather be reading your book about the World Wide Web (or at least this author certainly hopes so). You point to the button labeled "Back" and click it a few times to return to the list of bills, to Chapter 17, and then back to the original chapter you were reading.

Pretty nifty, huh?

The *hyper* in hypertext means that you're not just reading text; you're reading content that knows how to refer to other documents. As long as your hypertext reader — your Web client — knows how to find what the content is linked to, you can wander off and go roaming from link to link to link. (Unfortunately, not every Web client knows how to find every kind of content that you may find in links.) Most people find their first few experiences with hypertext quite engrossing and possibly even addictive. Throughout this book, you're reminded that the nicer Web clients such as Communicator give you extra features to make your wandering even more productive. For example, Communicator can show you which links in a hypertext document you've followed in the past month so that you don't go back to things you've already seen unless you want to.

Why hypertext is popular

Many people like to wander around bookstores even if they don't intend to buy anything. Hypertext on the Web is like a giant bookstore that you can roam around in, jumping from book to book. Many people also like to conduct research by exploration instead of in a linear fashion. This kind of research is easy when using hypertext documents because you can go from the inside of one document to the inside of another with a single click of the mouse and then wend your way back when you feel like you've gone too far.

As mentioned earlier, hypertext is somewhat of a misnomer because the content can encompass much more than just text. Hypertext documents can include pictures, sounds, and movies — and in the future will probably incorporate still other types of content that haven't even been thought of yet. Each type of content can contain links to other hypertext. The most common use for these links is a picture in a hypertext document that offers links based on parts of the picture. Imagine a picture of a baseball team, for example, where you can click each player's image and view his current statistics as well as his history with the team.

Remember that hypertext documents can also be linked to non-hypertext documents. Hypertext documents are commonly used as tables of contents for text documents or pictures. Thus, you can create a hypertext document as an organizer for other documents containing information that you may want to keep track of. Creating hypertext documents is covered in Chapters 18 through 21.

A hypertext document can also have links to parts of itself. This feature is most commonly used as a table of contents for a document. Although not as exciting as links to other documents, such links enable you to skim a document much faster.

What hypertext looks like

Enough text about hypertext. Figure 3-1 shows a hypertext document as seen through the Navigator client. For now, ignore all the menus and buttons; those are covered in Chapters 4 and 5, which describe how Communicator works (as compared to how hypertext works, which is what's important here). The most relevant part of Figure 3-1 is that the hypertext links to other documents are shown as underlined text.

As you can see in Figure 3-1, links to many different documents exist. Notice, however, what is not in Figure 3-1: the names of those documents. The underlined text, the *link,* tells you about what you'll see if you follow the link, but it doesn't tell you where that document is or what kind of document it is.

This fact is one of the most confusing parts of using hypertext. You must look at a different part of the screen (in this case, the bottom) to see where you go if you select the link. Even worse, you don't know what kind of document you're selecting until you select it, although you can learn to look for certain hints on the Web that tell you about the type of content in a link. You learn these hints as you get more experienced with the Web. For example, if you see ".txt" at the end of a filename, you have a good clue that it's a text file, not a hypertext document.

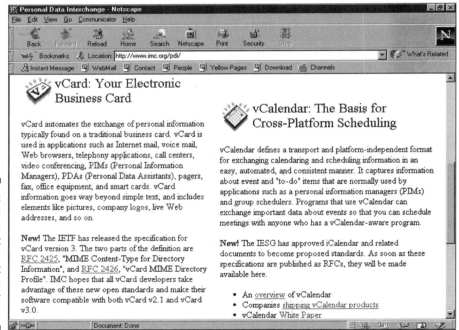

Figure 3-1:
The
underlined
text
sections are
hypertext
links to
other
documents.

Are you an Internet newbie?

We were all new Internet users once. Newbie.net (www.newbie.net/Newbie_Pages/) is a friendly site that emphasizes giving good information and hints to new users. Even not-so-newbies can find some good ideas, such as when to bookmark your favorite sites and how to find people with similar interests.

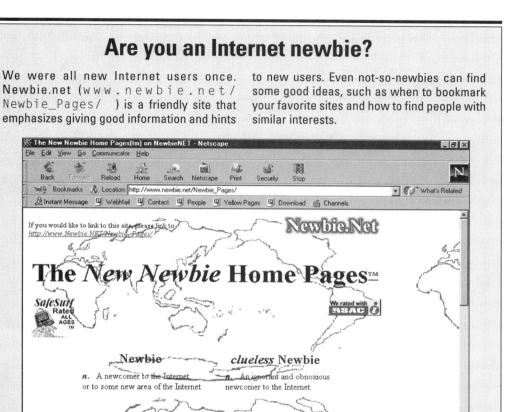

How to hypertext: HTML

Hypertext documents don't magically appear; they must be created by someone. On the Web, these documents are written in a language called *HTML,* which stands for *HyperText Markup Language.* (Yes, there's that silly capital *T* in the middle of *HyperText* again.) HTML has two major features:

> ✔ It enables you to add formatting to plain text.
>
> ✔ It enables you to specify hypertext links.

A *markup language* is a set of special characters that you put in a text document to indicate something other than regular text, such as "make the next characters boldface" or "make a hypertext link to a different document from the following characters." You don't need a special word processor to create HTML documents — any old text editor (like Notepad in Windows or TeachText in MacOS) is sufficient. By the way, using HTML is discussed in detail starting in Part V of this book.

In case you're curious, Figure 3-2 shows a sample of some HTML. In fact, that text is the HTML that created the hypertext you see in Figure 3-1. Even if you don't want to create your own hypertext documents, knowing a bit about HTML is useful because it's the structure that holds the Web together. For now, you don't need to mess with any of that glue; you need only to know that it's there.

A new type of hypertext, XML, has just come on the scene. XML is much more powerful and flexible than HTML, and many people expect that much of the Web will drop HTML for XML in the coming years. For now, you can't find much XML on the Web, but that situation may change within a year or two, at which point you can expect Netscape to have an update to Communicator that can handle XML. The only thing you really need to know about XML is that it makes displaying and finding things on the Web easier, which is something we all want.

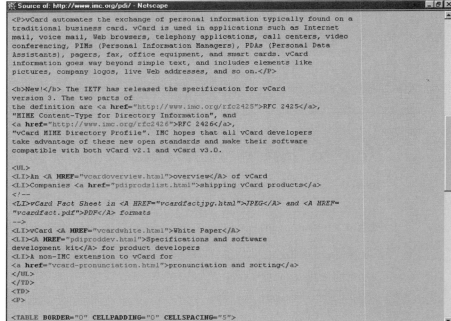

Figure 3-2:
The text inside the "<>" brackets is the HTML; the other text is what appears on-screen.

A Little Farther Out: Other Services on the Internet

Although hypertext documents are the starting point for the Web, they are by no means the only part. One of the great beauties of the Web is that it encompasses so many other Internet services as well.

The Web is generally considered to consist primarily of the following three services:

- ✔ Hypertext (HTTP)
- ✔ FTP
- ✔ Usenet news

As you move around the Web, you frequently run across FTP servers, often on the same server with HTTP. Because many people don't have access to Web clients, the folks who run some servers give other Internet users access to the same information via these different forms. But before discussing other Web services, I want to tell you about e-mail, which is arguably more popular than the Web for many users.

Internet mail

The biggest unrepresented piece of the Internet on the Web is electronic mail. Because your mail is private, the folks who constructed the Web didn't include it in the early design. No one other than you can read your mail, so it made little sense to include it as an Internet resource on the Web.

Let me clarify, however, that the Web doesn't ignore mail altogether. Communicator and other Web clients now contain programs for reading and sending mail. You can also get mail clients that don't do Web browsing, primarily for people who are happy with the Web client they already have but who want more robust mail handling.

The reason e-mail isn't part of the Web is that the users at each end don't have to be connected to the Internet to compose or view messages. You can write a message and then wait to send it until you are connected. Similarly, when a message arrives in your inbox, you don't have to be connected to the Internet; it waits for you until you come and collect it. After sucking the message onto your computer, you can disconnect from the Internet and read the message at your leisure.

Communicator 4.5 now has an *offline mode,* which is a fancy way of saying that you can do some of your work (reading and composing messages) when you aren't connected to the Internet. When you need to be connected, you go into *online mode,* which lets you do the things that need an Internet connection (sending and receiving messages).

FTP

FTP is HTTP's inferior sibling. FTP is little more than a glorified file-retrieval system. Its basic commands are the same as UNIX's directory commands, and all you see are directory names and filenames.

On the other hand, FTP has shown incredible resilience over the years. All the major file repositories and many file-duplication utilities are based on FTP. Still, in the face of HTTP, FTP looks more than a tad arcane. Figure 3-3, for example, shows how an FTP directory looks in Navigator.

Because FTP servers merely show a view of a regular file structure, a server site may easily have both an FTP server and a Web server viewing the same files. Some Web server software, for example, enables a Web administrator to show directories that don't have any real HTML content. The administrator can instruct the Web server software to add some formatting that makes the directories a bit more informative.

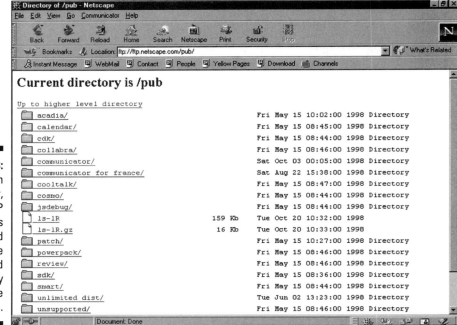

Figure 3-3: In Navigator, FTP directories are pictured as file folders, and files display discernible icons.

The vast majority of FTP sites, however, do not yet use this kind of software, and you're left with the basic view of the files and directories. (Be thankful, therefore, that you are using the Web and not a character-based FTP client software and its myriad of arcane UNIX-like commands.)

Usenet news

Usenet news is often incredibly more interesting than FTP, and this fact should make it a core part of the Web. Unfortunately, most Web clients have meager (if not lame) methods for showing Usenet news. These Web clients may change in the future because Communicator includes quite a nice Usenet viewing mode.

Compared to HTTP and FTP, Usenet news is often more interactive, personal, and fun. It's like a huge party with thousands of topical conversations going on at the same time. You can just sit and listen to a conversation or pipe in at any time. Each conversation has a title that somewhat describes the parameters of the topic, but like in regular conversation, the topic often shifts away from what you're supposed to talk about into what you *want* to talk about.

The content in Usenet news is created by anyone who wants to talk. This fact can be both its blessing and curse. Usenet enables people who would otherwise not communicate in public to finally break out of their shells and say something, even if they're just speaking on a technical subject. On the other hand, it also empowers pushy and overbearing people to be even pushier and more overbearing than usual. To really enjoy Usenet, you must accept a wider range of people than you may normally choose to associate with in your daily life.

Usenet is falling out of favor because of the party crashers who just want to hear themselves talk. You often run into a great deal of advertising that doesn't relate to the topic at hand (called *spam*), and a fair amount of pornography leaks out from the adults-only areas. But some areas of Usenet are still great fun to participate in.

Figure 3-4 shows Communicator's view of one Usenet newsgroup. More than a dozen popular Usenet browsers exist, many of which are difficult to use and burdened by too many commands for most novice Internet users. Netscape, on the other hand, has pared down the range of commands to a manageable number.

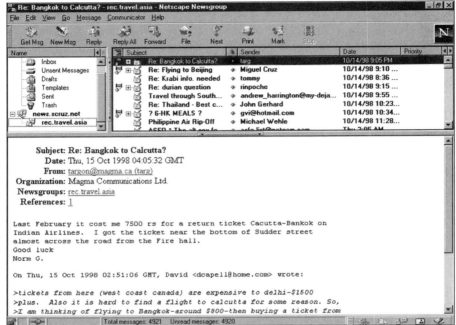

Figure 3-4:
This
newsgroup's
topic
covers, as
you may
imagine,
travel to
and around
Asia.

Gopher

Before the Web, there was Gopher. Gopher is an all-text hierarchical interface that was designed to be easy to set up and maintain. Everything in
Gopher is a simple, line-oriented menu. For a while, it looked like Gopher
would be as popular as HTTP, but now, finding Gopher sites on the Internet
is quite difficult. Figure 3-5 shows Communicator's view of a Gopher site.

In my mind, it's really too bad that Gopher has all but disappeared. For
novice users, Gopher is much easier to understand than hypertext. Of
course, it doesn't look nearly as nice, being only text, but you could easily
figure out where you were when you were using Gopher. And I'm not just
pining for the good old days; I really think that helping new users wherever
you can is important. Gopher did a good job of doing just that, but it got lost
in the "has to look pretty" shuffle.

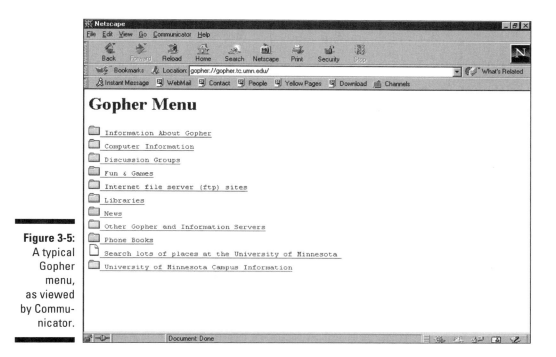

Figure 3-5:
A typical
Gopher
menu,
as viewed
by Commu-
nicator.

WAIS

A few years ago, people noticed that no standard existed for accessing databases on the Internet. That problem was resolved by establishing a standard for access requests that bore the not-so-colorful name Z39.50. This standard is better known, however, as *WAIS* (*W*ide *A*rea *I*nformation *S*erver).

Many people expected that WAIS databases and WAIS servers would sprout up everywhere. They thought that people would access WAIS as much as they do other Internet services, such as FTP. Well, that didn't happen. In fact, WAIS is barely mentioned anymore. Very few Web clients support WAIS directly, and the few WAIS clients available are not terribly interesting.

Telnet

Probably the least used (and least useful) part of the Internet is the telnet service. *Telnet* was one of the very first Internet services, and it shows. If you telnet to another computer, the effect is the same as using a modem to dial up the other computer. The interface you get on the other computer is always character-based.

Today, telnet is generally used only for university library catalogs and computer bulletin board systems (BBSs). The biggest problem with telnet is that after you reach the remote computer, you have no way of knowing how to interact with it. University libraries, for example, use dozens of different programs to access their catalogs. If you telnet to one of these systems, you must first figure out what commands to issue to access its content.

Consequently, few Web clients offer built-in support for telnet. Instead, they start a different program on your computer to run the telnet session. Of course, you must have such a program for this procedure to work, and many people don't because they have little need for telnet.

The Internet outside the Web

As I've mentioned before, the Web is not the Internet. Many Internet services are not yet available to Web clients. That "yet" is there because no real reason exists for these services not to be available on the Web, other than an insufficient demand for them from users.

Another possibility for this lack is insufficient creativity from the folks who write the Web clients, but that's a whole other story.

Other non-Web Internet services

A few other Internet services are not yet represented on the Web. In fact, dozens of other standard Internet services exist that aren't on the Web, but most of them don't make any sense for 99 percent of Internet users. You may, however, have heard of a few of the following services that are still not on the Web:

 ✔ Finger
 ✔ Talk
 ✔ whois
 ✔ X.500 directories

Because these services aren't on the Web, they aren't described in this book. You may want to check out *The Internet For Dummies,* 5th Edition and *MORE Internet For Dummies,* 4th Edition (IDG Books Wordwide, Inc.) to find out more about these services. Nothing currently prevents these services from being added to the Web eventually — maybe even by the time you read this. The Finger service, for example, which is used to describe users on a remote system, is already starting to appear on the Web and in the standards committees that loosely coordinate the Web.

Gateways: On and not on the Web at the same time

Before you start to think that you have it all down when it comes to the Web, a certain gray area exists in the "on or not on" question. Some Internet services that are not on the Web can still be accessed through Web clients by using a Web site called a *gateway*. A gateway is a program that translates between two protocols, somewhat like an automated dictionary for two human languages.

Gateways are very useful for giving users access to a service for which they don't have a client. The University of Michigan, for example, has an experimental X.500-to-Gopher gateway program. If you have a Gopher client (like the one in Communicator), you can send X.500 requests through this gateway. The gateway translates your request into X.500, contacts the X.500 server, gets the response in X.500 format, and translates that back into something Gopher can understand.

Many kinds of gateways are available on the Internet. One of the more interesting (but so far under-used) is the mail-to-HTTP gateway. Such a gateway enables Internet users who have mail-only access to receive hypertext documents in their mailbox. As the Web gets bigger and more popular, this gateway will probably become more popular as well.

You Need URL in That Engine

By now, you should be wondering: "What do the hypertext links to these wonderful Internet services look like?" Well, that subject has been put off until now because, um, well, they aren't very pretty. In fact, they're downright ugly. For example, a typical URL looks like:

```
http://www.arista.com/aristaweb/PattiSmith/
```

Suffice it to say that they were designed by people who didn't put ease of reading or typing first. Seems that if you leave these kinds of designs to dweebs, they often choose, well, fairly *dweeby* designs.

The correct name for these links is *URLs,* which stands for "*U*niform *Re*source *L*ocators. (Some people pronounce these as "earl", but most people spell out the three letters.) A URL tells the Web client the following three things:

- ✔ The type of Internet service that your client uses to get the item.
- ✔ The name of the computer on which the service resides.
- ✔ The request for the item you want (this part may be blank).

The biggest redeeming value of URLs is that you don't often need to type them. Because they mostly exist as links in other hypertext documents, you can simply select them in your Web client if you want to see the documents to which they refer. This section tells you enough about URLs to enable you to recognize them whenever you see them; Chapter 20 gives more detail about how to create your own URLs — if, of course, you create your own Web content.

Note: Throughout this book, URLs are usually shown in lowercase letters. If you need to type a URL, you can type the service name (see the next section) and the computer name in lowercase letters, uppercase letters, or a combination of both. However, you usually must match the case in the request part exactly as it is shown in this book (or wherever you see the URL). In a perfect world, the case of the request part wouldn't matter, but it all too often does.

Service names in URLs

Each Internet service on the Web has its own name for URLs. As you can see in Table 3-1, the URL names match the service names fairly well. The hardest one to remember for beginners is usually *http* for *hypertext.* Also notice that each service name has a colon after it to keep it separate from the host name or request that follows it.

Table 3-1	URL Service Names
Service	*Name in URL*
Hypertext	`http:`
FTP	`ftp:`
Usenet news	`news:` and `nntp:`
Gopher	`gopher:`
WAIS	`wais:`
Telnet	`telnet:`
Outgoing mail	`mailto:`
Local files	`file:`

The last item in Table 3-1 may be new to you. The `file:` name is used if a URL refers to a file on your local computer or on your local network, not on the Internet. PC users may be all too familiar with the file that has a URL of `file://C:/AUTOEXEC.BAT`. (PC users are also probably familiar with the use of all uppercase letters for filenames on their PCs.)

Host names

Almost every computer that serves as an Internet service host has a domain name. (For more on domains, see Chapter 2.) The domain name is the best way to identify the location of the desired computer in a URL. Thus, in a URL such as `www.imc.org/mail-i18n.html`, the `www.imc.org` is the domain name of the host computer, and `mail-i18n.html` is the request. To see a list of the recent distribution of domain names on the Internet, sorted by root domains, go to `www.nw.com/zone/WWW/dist-bynum.html`. The list is also shown in Figure 3-6. The company that keeps this list, Network Wizards, performs other statistical calculations on domain names every few months and publishes the results for free.

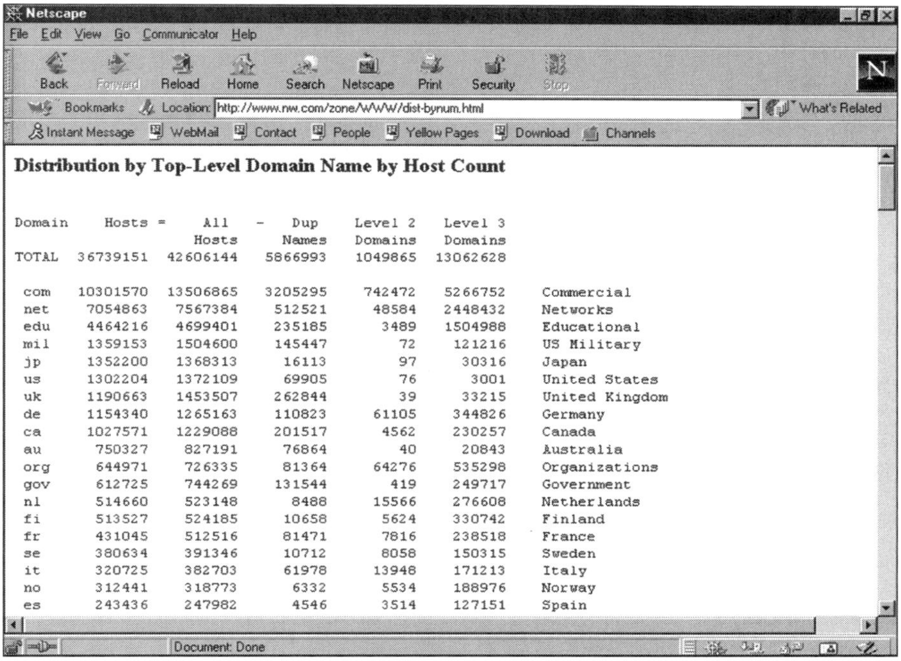

Figure 3-6: A list of domain names on the Internet.

Netscape — http://www.nw.com/zone/WWW/dist-bynum.html

Distribution by Top-Level Domain Name by Host Count

Domain	Hosts =	All Hosts	− Dup Names	Level 2 Domains	Level 3 Domains	
TOTAL	36739151	42606144	5866993	1049865	13062628	
com	10301570	13506865	3205295	742472	5266752	Commercial
net	7054863	7567384	512521	48584	2448432	Networks
edu	4464216	4699401	235185	3489	1504988	Educational
mil	1359153	1504600	145447	72	121216	US Military
jp	1352200	1368313	16113	97	30316	Japan
us	1302204	1372109	69905	76	3001	United States
uk	1190663	1453507	262844	39	33215	United Kingdom
de	1154340	1265163	110823	61105	344826	Germany
ca	1027571	1229088	201517	4562	230257	Canada
au	750327	827191	76864	40	20843	Australia
org	644971	726335	81364	64276	535298	Organizations
gov	612725	744269	131544	419	249717	Government
nl	514660	523148	8488	15566	276608	Netherlands
fi	513527	524185	10658	5624	330742	Finland
fr	431045	512516	81471	7816	238518	France
se	380634	391346	10712	8058	150315	Sweden
it	320725	382703	61978	13948	171213	Italy
no	312441	318773	6332	5534	188976	Norway
es	243436	247982	4546	3514	127151	Spain

What's in a domain name?

Domain names are one of the Internet's greatest features. They enable you to have a nice, usually easy-to-read name for each computer. You don't really need to know much about domain names to use the Web, but you may enjoy some of their fancy tricks.

Every computer on the Internet has an address, called an *IP address*. The address is made up of four numbers; the numbers are always between 0 and 255. The numbers are always shown with periods between each individual number (for example, 152.4.101.50 — in which 152 is one number, 4 is another number, and so on).

If you specify a domain name on the Internet, software converts that name to an IP address by looking up the name in a table of addresses. The method for converting the name to an address is a tad complicated, but it basically boils down to: "If I want to know the address for the name *xxx.yyy.zzz*, I'll ask the computer at *yyy.zzz* because it knows the address of everything that ends with *yyy.zzz*. If I don't know the address of *yyy.zzz*, I'll ask the computer at *zzz* because it knows the address of everything that ends with *zzz*."

On the Internet, the names in *zzz* are predefined by committee, as is the location for finding the computer that knows about the names at *yyy.zzz*. Some of the most common names you see in place of *zzz* are *com*, *edu*, and *net*, although more than a hundred other names are defined. These names, which are always at the right side of a domain name, are called *root domains*.

The great part of this scheme is that, if you control the computer at mycompany.com, you can make up your own domain names such as www.mycompany.com and snorky.mycompany.com without having to ask anyone's permission. If you make up a domain name, you tell the tables what IP address the name is affiliated with (as long as you also control the IP addresses). You can change the table of names and addresses that start with mycompany.com at any time.

Allow me now to make what I consider an interesting point. Don't assume that the computer identified by a particular domain name is always the same. The server whose address is identified by www.mycompany.com today, for example, may be a computer in North Carolina, but that server may change addresses to a computer in New York tomorrow while keeping the same name. The physical location of the computer identified by the name is not important to you — you need to care only whether it is serving the information you want.

Another fun oddment of the Internet: One domain name can point to more than one IP address. If so, the two or more computers with different addresses are, for all intents and purposes, the same computer to someone on the Internet. This feature should see more use in the future as parts of the Internet become so busy that server administrators must create duplicates of their servers to speed up access for Internet users.

You occasionally find URLs that have IP address numbers instead of host names. An example of such a URL with an IP address is `telnet://152.4.101.50`. IP addresses are now rarely used in URLs because domain names are much more flexible for administrators and less prone to typing errors by users.

Some URLs add an additional bit to the host name part: namely, a TCP port number (described earlier in this chapter). If the URL specifies a TCP port number, the number falls after the host name with a colon between them. In the address `cancer.med.upenn.edu:3000`, for example, the TCP port number (3000) is placed at the end of the address.

URL requests

The last part of the URL is the request itself. The request tells the host which of the many pieces of information on the host you want.

Often, the request part of a URL looks like a UNIX filename. Truthfully, it often *is* a UNIX filename. Because of how most servers such as HTTP and FTP work, the URL is really just the name of a file that holds the content you want.

In many URLs, the request part is left off altogether. This absence tells the server that you want the *default* content, which is usually a welcome page or home page of some sort. This page is commonly called a *home page* because it is the starting point for your exploration around a server. One URL minus a request, for example, is `www.info.apple.com`, which is the welcome page of the Apple Computer Web server. If you select a link from that page, you discover that it leads to another page with the full URL `www.info.apple.com/documents/whatsnew.html`, which is a specific page on that same Web server.

Some novices call every page on the Web a "home page," which is really not correct. The term *home* should mean something along the lines of *beginning* or *introduction*. Pages other than a home page should probably be referred to simply as *pages*. (You don't often hear anyone describing content on nonhypertext servers as home pages.)

The request part of a URL may be case-sensitive, meaning that uppercase and lowercase characters in the request are different, even if they are otherwise the same letter.

Note: Some requests end with a slash (/), while others don't. Whether the request should or shouldn't have a trailing slash depends on the server software at the host and the type of information you are requesting. In general, if you request a file by name, the request never has a trailing slash. Also in general, if no actual request is listed (just a service name and a host name), the request doesn't include the trailing slash — but it may. If the request names a directory (such as a request for a directory listing to an FTP server), the request often can have a trailing slash. Not all server software works well with trailing slashes, however, and other server software doesn't work well unless a trailing slash is present. If in doubt, use exactly what you see in the place from which you are copying the URL.

Part II
Knowing Your Navigator

The 5th Wave   By Rich Tennant

"Look, I've already launched a search for 'reanimated babe cadavers' three times and nothing came up!"

In this part . . .

The heart of Communicator is Navigator, which enables you to surf the Web effectively. You can change how Navigator looks and acts and customize its appearance. In this part you receive an introduction to searching for information on the Web, regardless of which Web client you use. You even find in this part an overview of what happens if you encounter any of those nasty error messages during your explorations of the Web.

Chapter 4

Getting into Navigator

- -

In This Chapter

▶ Moving around the Web with one finger

▶ Getting where you want when you want

▶ Saving what you see to disk

▶ Filling in Web forms

▶ Opening files on your computer in Navigator

- -

*E*nough of the "what" and "why" of the Web; it's time to start the "how." The Web is out there, and Communicator is ready to help you get to it. This chapter gets you moving around the Web and understanding what you're doing in Communicator's Web browser (that is, Navigator), while Chapter 5 gets you through all the important Navigator settings. You can probably start without reading Chapter 5, but if you're like me, you probably want to know how to get Navigator set up to work its best. You can zip through these chapters, adjusting the settings to the choices that seem best, and then head out toward all that content.

Where Does It All Begin?

The Introduction to this book describes the many ways available to get your own copy of Netscape Communicator. The most common methods include the following:

- ✔ Receiving it from your Internet service provider (ISP).
- ✔ Downloading it from Netscape's file server.
- ✔ Getting it as part of a software package that comes with other Internet programs.

A system administrator at your company or university may even have installed a copy on your computer already.

All these options mean that you can install Communicator on your PC or Macintosh in many different ways, which makes writing a book that covers every way of installing the program on your computer pretty much impossible. To make matters worse, Netscape changes its installation procedures from time to time.

The preceding statements lead to what you may have guessed by now — this book doesn't cover installation of Communicator. But don't worry. So far, Communicator has been one of the easiest Web browsers to install. Still, to put the exact directions in this book is a bit pointless because they are bound to change by the time you read this.

For most people, setting up Communicator consists of answering a few questions about what name you want to use, where you get your mail, and so on. The answers to these questions usually come from your Internet service provider, and because Communicator is so popular, most ISPs can tell you what to fill in each of the setup dialog boxes.

One hint I will give you, however, is that you should not have two different versions of Communicator on your computer at the same time. It appears that Netscape has tried hard to make it possible for you to run Version 3, Version 4, and Version 4.5 simultaneously, but a few people have had problems with running multiple versions. Because every version of Communicator is really much better than the previous one, I always just overwrite the old ones and go with the new.

Remember that this book covers Version 4.5 of Communicator. If you're running an earlier version, many of the commands are different from what you see here, and the screen is probably different also.

Starting on the Same Page

The fact that you install Communicator differently at different times — or that someone else may have installed Communicator for you — means that what you see as you first run Communicator may be different than what you see in this book. This fact makes writing a book for beginners a bit difficult.

After you first start Communicator, click the little "N" button near the upper-right corner of the screen, next to the words "What's Related." That's the *Navigator logo*. You will see a screen similar to the one shown in Figure 4-1. The screen shown in the figure is the home page for Netscape Communications; Netscape calls its home page *Netcenter*.

You can tell where you're at by looking in the white box next to the word "Location:" near the top of your screen. After you have clicked the Navigator logo button, you see http://home.netscape.com/.

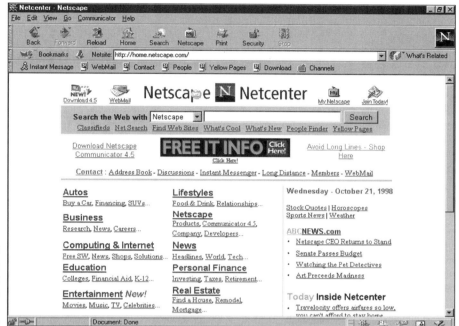

Figure 4-1:
The
Netscape
home page.

The Web weavers at Netscape change the contents of the main Netcenter page quite often, so don't expect your screen to look like the one in Figure 4-1. The main Netcenter page changes because Netscape puts all the latest company news on this page to get you excited about its products. Of course, this variability makes it a tad difficult to show you something in this book that looks like what you see on-screen. Although things aren't arranged the same way each time, don't let the changes confuse you.

Because Netscape makes a fair amount of money from the ads in Netcenter, it has a tendency to force ads on you even when you don't want them. A case in point is the way that they often pop up an ad window on top of Communicator when you go to the main Netcenter page. Personally, I find this quite frustrating, and I hope by the time you read this Netscape will have stopped this practice (but I am not too hopeful).

Figure 4-2 lists the names of the parts of the Navigator window. The navigation toolbar (the top toolbar in the picture, with all the icons), the location toolbar (the second toolbar from the top, with the text area), and the personal toolbar (the third toolbar from the top, just above the content area of the window) may not appear on your screen, depending on the settings in the View menu.

Location toolbar

Navigation toolbar

Personal toolbar — What's Related list

Navigator logo

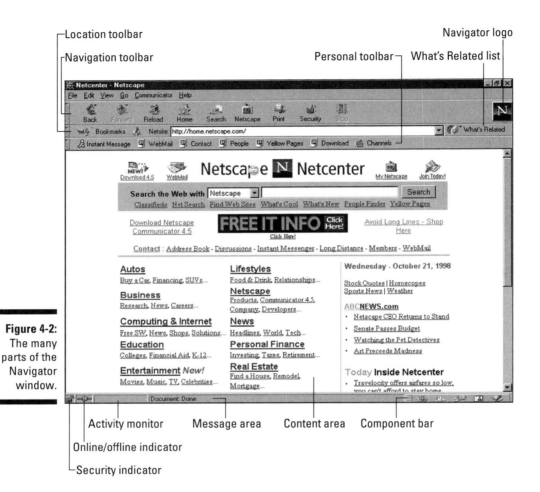

Figure 4-2:
The many parts of the Navigator window.

Activity monitor   Message area   Content area   Component bar

Online/offline indicator

Security indicator

You may notice that many of the screen pictures in other parts of this book don't display the navigation or personal toolbars. Hiding the toolbar and directory buttons enables you to view more text in the content area, which is usually what you want. In general, you don't want to hide the location toolbar, however, because knowing where you are at any given time is valuable. You can hide and unhide the navigation and personal toolbars and directory buttons by using the commands in the View menu.

The component bar is that little area in the lower-right corner of the screen. When you first start up Communicator, the component bar is a big window that is always on top of the main Communicator window. I have no idea why Netscape made this big window the default, because it is annoying and always in the way. Fortunately, you can easily make the component bar small and push it into the lower-right corner by choosing View➪Show➪ Floating Component Bar (or View➪Show➪Dock Component Bar, for you Mac users).

Windows 3.1? Windows 95? Windows 98? Macintosh? Who Cares!

You've probably noticed that all of this book's screen pictures come from a PC running Windows 95. If you're using Communicator on a PC running Microsoft Windows 3.1 or on a Macintosh, you may be thinking, "Oh, great, the instructions in these chapters won't work for me." Fret not, dear reader! Fortunately, the good folks at Netscape Communications made the software for Windows 95 work almost exactly like the software for Windows 3.1 and for the Macintosh. Of course, the program looks the same under Windows 98 as it does under Windows 95.

A couple of small differences exist, but they are pretty much unimportant to most Communicator users. (I cover them anyway, just to keep the people who don't run Windows 95 happy.) A few folks use Communicator on UNIX systems running under XWindows. They, too, can follow along with the directions in these chapters, although they'll probably find a bit more divergence than will the Windows 3.1 and Macintosh users.

Click-O-Rama: Following Links

As I describe in Chapter 2, hypertext is based on *links*. A hypertext document can have links (sometimes called *pointers*) to many other documents or to certain spots within the same document. To jump to the link's destination, click the link, which indicates to the browser that that's where you want to go.

In Navigator, links are shown by default as underlines. For example, look at the text on your screen. Some of the text is underlined, and each set of underlined text is a link. Jumping to linked text is as easy as can be: Just click any of the text in the link. (If you're using a PC, always click with the left mouse button; on the Mac, you don't have any choice because you have only one mouse button to click.)

For example, click any link from the Netscape main page. After a moment, the link takes you to a different document on the Web — for example, the one shown in Figure 4-3. Congratulations, you've just started your Web journey!

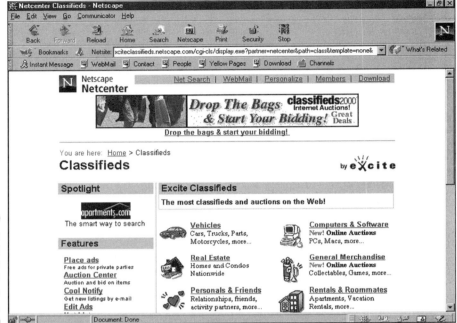

Figure 4-3:
Discovering
what's new
on the
Classifieds
page.

You can tell where you are by looking in the *location toolbar* near the top of the Navigator window (it's the middle toolbar). This area tells you the URL (the address) of the Web page you are viewing, which is often useful to know in case you jump someplace without first looking where you are going.

Look before you link. Just because a link looks interesting doesn't mean that you actually want to follow it. It may, for example, be a link to a system that you recognize as one that is very slow or often unavailable. Or it may be a link to a Web site that contains content you would find offensive and prefer not to link to.

Looking at a link in the main part of the Navigator window tells you what the person who wrote that content thinks is a good description of the link. It doesn't tell you where the link takes you. Fortunately, Netscape gives you an easy way to figure out where you will go if you click a link.

Just look at the bottom of the Communicator window: See the large blank area that takes up most of the bottom of the window? Move your cursor over a link on-screen but don't click it. Notice that the blank area (the *message area*) now contains a URL. That URL is the URL for the link underneath the cursor.

Backward and forward

Okay, say that you followed a link and now you want to get back to where you were. After you jump to a different Web page, that page doesn't know or remember where you came from. Navigator does remember, however, and you can return to your starting location in any of the following ways:

✔ Click the Back icon in the navigation toolbar.

✔ Choose Go⇨Back.

✔ Press Alt+← (PC users) or ⌘+[(Mac users).

All three of these options do the same thing, so you want to use only one.

Navigator usually remembers at least a dozen backup steps. So if you start at Web site A, click a link to go to Web site B, and then travel to Web site C, you can go back twice from C to get to A. Going backward in Navigator is a bit like undoing changes in a word processor.

Going forward with Navigator is just as easy. The three possible actions that take you forward are just what you would guess if you remember the Back command:

✔ Click the Forward icon in the navigation toolbar.

✔ Choose Go⇨Forward.

✔ Press Alt+→ (PC users) or ⌘+] (Mac users).

By using these methods, you can go back and forth in a chain of links to check where you've been and where you're going. (Of course, you can't go forward unless you've already gone backward, because Communicator wouldn't know where you wanted to go!)

Knowing where you've been

If you choose to use the Go menu's Back and Forward commands, you may notice something after you choose your first link: The Go menu changes. Each time you go somewhere new, that location is added to the list near the bottom of the Go menu. The name in the menu is the title of the page you went to. (This may be a tad confusing, but the new places are added to the top of the list that's at the bottom of the menu.)

Instead of using the Back command, you can choose the location you want by selecting its name from the Go menu. This method is much faster than repeatedly using the Back command to navigate. Figure 4-4 shows a typical Go menu after you've been meandering around the Web for a while.

Figure 4-4:
A history of
where
you've been
appears in
the Go
menu.

Who says you can't go home again?

Sometimes you can get lost in all of your wanderings around the Web. You may want to get back to the place from which you started. Getting to home, the page you see when you start Navigator, is quite easy. (Actually, Netscape had to make this process easy because people often use it to bail out of a fruitless search. Even advanced Web users regularly go home.)

To go home, you can either click the Home icon on the navigation toolbar or choose Go⇨Home. If you haven't roamed too far, your home page is the last item on the Go menu; you can also just pick it up from there.

What you call "home" isn't what everyone else calls "home." If you haven't changed it yet (or the person who set up Communicator for you hasn't changed it), home is Netcenter. But for many of you, home is the home page for your Internet service provider, or the company you work for, or something similar. You see in the next chapter how to set the URL that is used for home.

Stop right there

As you link from one Web page to another, you never know how big a new page may be. If you're accessing a file by FTP, the page could be megabytes long. Depending on how fast your modem is and how fast the Internet seems to be running at the moment, you may realize that getting all the text or images on a page is going to take much longer than you anticipated.

No problem! Simply click the Stop icon on the toolbar, or choose View⇨Stop (sounds a bit weird, I know), or press the Escape key (PC users) or ⌘+Period (Mac users). Navigator immediately stops downloading whatever it was getting and lets you go on with your life. If you were downloading an HTML document or image, you can still see what you received before you stopped.

In fact, you don't really need to stop downloading to move on while Navigator is downloading more HTML or images. If you see a link on-screen that you want to explore, simply click that link, even if Navigator is still downloading. Navigator stops what it's doing and takes you to that link, similar to the way that you can skip the rest of a song on a CD by pressing the skip button.

Stopping the downloading process is more common than you may at first think. Because some Web sites are incredibly busy, many pages are horribly slow to access. You click a link and then wait, wait, wait. If you get tired of waiting, or are just plain bored, stop the process and go somewhere else.

Get it again

The opposite of "stop right there" is "give it to me again" — something you want to do occasionally when you're using Navigator. For example, some Web pages are frequently updated (such as current weather reports and stock market quotations).

You can make sure that you are looking at the most recent version of a Web page by *reloading* (getting it again; users of Internet Explorer know this as "refreshing" the page). To reload the current page, click the Reload icon in the toolbar or choose the View⇨Reload command.

Entering Links Instead of Clicking Them

The Web isn't all click-click-click. You find URLs that you want to investigate in other places. I hope, in fact, that you find some URLs that interest you in the later chapters in this book. To get to those places, you need to tell Navigator where to go. (You are, of course, already discovering how to tell Navigator what to do.)

The easiest way to enter links is to choose File⇨Open Page (or if you're a Mac user, File⇨Open⇨Location) in Navigator. The Open Page dialog box that appears asks for the URL or file you want. Type the new URL in the text box, click the Open button, and away you go. You can also achieve the same results by selecting the text in the location toolbar, erasing that URL, typing in your new URL, and pressing Enter.

Communicator gives your fingers a break on typing in URLs if they begin with http://. You can skip that part and just type in the host name and the rest of the URL. For example, if you want to go to http://www.dummies.com, you can just type www.dummies.com in the Open Page dialog box or in the location toolbar. That's a savings of seven characters for every Web URL!

You may notice that URLs are often long and complicated. Typing them can be tedious, and mistyping them is all too easy. If the URL appears in a document that you already have in another program on your computer (such as in a word processor or a mail program), Navigator gives you a great, no-typing-needed option. Just follow these easy steps:

1. **Copy the URL listed in that program to the Clipboard.**

2. **Switch to Navigator by using the Alt+Tab keyboard shortcut (Windows users) or whatever other method you use to switch between programs.**

3. **Choose File⇨Open Page (Mac users: File⇨Open⇨Location) in Navigator.**

4. **Paste the URL in the text box in the Open Page dialog box by pressing Ctrl+V. (And yes, Mac folks use ⌘+V.)**

Filling In Forms

One of the great features of the Web — one that differentiates it from other popular Internet services such as Gopher and FTP — is forms. A form is pretty much like a standard dialog box. Web forms are basically Web pages that contain dialog boxes.

Web forms can have most of the features you've gotten used to in Windows and Mac dialog boxes. Figure 4-5 shows a typical form. If you know how to use dialog boxes, you don't need to stress out about using Web forms.

Every Web form has at least one button, usually labeled Submit or OK or Send, that sends the data you fill in to the host computer for processing. Many forms also have a button labeled Cancel that causes all the information you've entered in the form to be removed.

After you submit a form, it goes to a program, usually located at the same site from which you got the form, which takes the information you fill in and processes it. The program can do just about anything with the information. If the form is an order form, for example, the program can record all of your information and start processing your order. If it is a survey form, the program may just write your responses into a file to be tabulated later.

After you submit a form on the Web, the information you have entered is usually sent over the Internet as plain text; encryption of forms (making their contents secret) is still quite new to the Web. Any information you put in the form, therefore, could possibly be read by someone who is watching information move around the Web. Although this type of snooping isn't

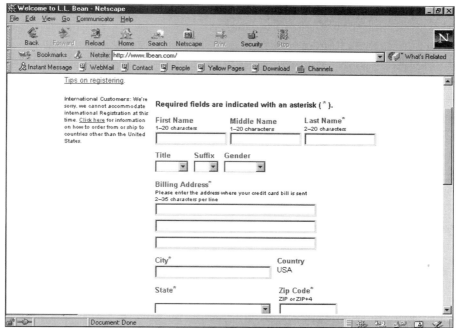

Figure 4-5:
A sample
Web form.

supposed to happen, it does. These nasty folks are usually looking for credit card numbers, but they may also be collecting other personal information that you would rather they didn't have. Think twice before saying something in a form that you may not want someone other than the recipient to read.

And while I'm at it, you should probably think hard about what you enter in a form with a company you don't know. As of this writing, no cases have been reported of companies using information from forms in a malicious fashion, but it's only a matter of time. When you submit a form, you don't know where it's going. (For example, a form on one Web site can point to a program on a different Web site.)

Save That Web Page!

The Web is for more than just looking. You can save the text you're reading (or the pictures you're viewing) to your hard drive. By doing so, you can read them again later without having to go back out on the Web. Another way to save a file is to print it: You can think of this method as "saving to paper."

Saving pages on disk

Saving HTML documents and text files takes a single command: the File menu's Save As command. The Save As dialog box in Navigator looks the same as it does in most programs, but with a single addition. In Windows, the option located directly below the file list is labeled *Save File as Type;* on the Mac, it's *Format.* For Windows, the choices are *HTML Files* and *Plain Text;* for the Macintosh, the choices are *Source* and *Text.*

If you are saving an HTML file (known on the Mac as a Source file), name the file with an HTM extension. (Mac users can use HTML or html if they want.) For example, if you are looking at a Web site that is having a contest and you want to save the list of prizes, you might call the file Prizes.htm. If you're saving a text file, choose Text and name the file whatever you want.

If you save an HTML file by using the Plain Text option, you lose all the formatting. In fact, HTML files converted to text usually come out looking pretty awful — lots of extraneous spaces, odd line breaks, and so on. Generally, you should always save HTML files by using the Source option to retain the HTML codes.

The Save As command also works for images. If the Web page is a single image, such as a GIF or a JPEG file, choose the File➪Save As command, and Navigator tells you the file type. (This only works if the Web page is a single image, however.)

You don't need to save the file as Source if you just want to look at the HTML in the file. Instead, choose View➪Page Source. This command opens the source document as a text file that you can scroll through and, if you want, save to disk. This document appears as a new text window in Navigator.

Printing Web pages

Plenty of people are not on the Web. Heck, plenty of people still don't have a computer. If you want to show them some information from a Web page, the easiest way is to print it out — the good old "save to dead tree" method. Of course, Navigator makes printing easy: the File➪Print command, just like every other program. Navigator also has a Print button in the navigation toolbar. Also available is a File➪Page Setup command that lets you adjust the options for your printer. The dialog boxes for these commands are the same as you find in almost every other program on your computer, which makes them easy to use.

Downloading files that you can't see

Plenty of things on the Web aren't Web pages. Some links are to files that are not displayable but that are meant to be saved on your computer and used with programs other than Navigator. For example, someone may make a Microsoft Word file available to you. Chapter 5 tells you how Navigator knows what kinds of files it needs to download and what kinds of files it knows how to handle in some other way.

When you select a link to a file that Navigator can't display, Navigator tells you so with a dialog box like that in Figure 4-6. Choose Save File, and Navigator asks you where you want to save the file, just like in the File➪Save As command. Pick a place and a name, and the file is saved there for you to use later with a different program.

Figure 4-6:
The
Unknown
File Type
dialog box.

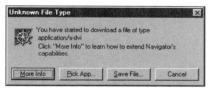

Use What You Have: Opening Local Files

Navigator can do more than open links off the Web. It can open files (such as the files you save by using the File➪Save As command) off your computer's hard disk as well. The same Open Page command (File➪Open Page) can open an HTML file, a text file, or a graphics file. (Yep, this command is different for Mac users: It's File➪Open➪Page.)

In fact, Navigator can read these files no matter what program created them. For example, if someone mails you an HTML file, Navigator opens this file just fine. The same is true for the JPEG and GIF files you may have on your system.

Many Windows to the Web

So far, everything you've done in Navigator has been in a single window. If you click a link, the old page disappears and the new page replaces it. What do you do if you want to view more than one Web page at a time?

Easy! Choose Communicator⇨Navigator; the same thing happens with File⇨New⇨Navigator Window. A second window appears. You can use it to roam around the Web while the first window stays the same.

In fact, Navigator keeps separate history lists for each window you open. This feature means that you can easily keep track of your wanderings in different windows. You can also change the windows' appearances separately. For example, you can have a particular toolbar showing in one window but not in the other.

So Go Out and Have Fun

You now know 80 percent of what you need to use Navigator well and 100 percent of what you need to really start exploring. Follow links. Click here and then click there. Get lost. Get found. Get lost again. Go home and start over. Enjoy.

Chapter 5, by the way, fills you in on the various Navigator commands and options not covered here. You really should read it at some point, but you don't need to read it now. Go ahead and play. Hey, you can even feel free to experiment with the commands that aren't covered for you. Come back if you want to find out about the other 20 percent.

Chapter 5
Making Navigator Work for You

In This Chapter
▶ Changing how Navigator looks and acts
▶ Finding text on Web pages
▶ Plugging in plug-ins and helper applications
▶ Understanding security

Chapter 4 describes everything you need to know to traverse the Web. You can do more with Navigator, however, than just wander around the Web. This chapter discusses how to set up Navigator so that you can use it more efficiently and it looks the way you want. You also find out how to do some advanced tricks such as find text on a Web page, deal with plug-ins and helper applications, and become familiar with Navigator's security.

What More Could You Prefer?

The first topic in this description of how to use Navigator is a big one: how to use the various commands accessed through Edit⇨Preferences.

Fortunately, most (but not all) of the preferences that Navigator comes with are preset to work just fine. A few settings, however, you need to change before you can use certain Navigator features. Figure 5-1 shows the main window of the Edit⇨Preferences dialog box. Note that many of the categories have "+" signs next to them (on the Macintosh, they're little triangles); this sign indicates that subcategories exist. To see the subcategories, click on the "+" sign or the triangle.

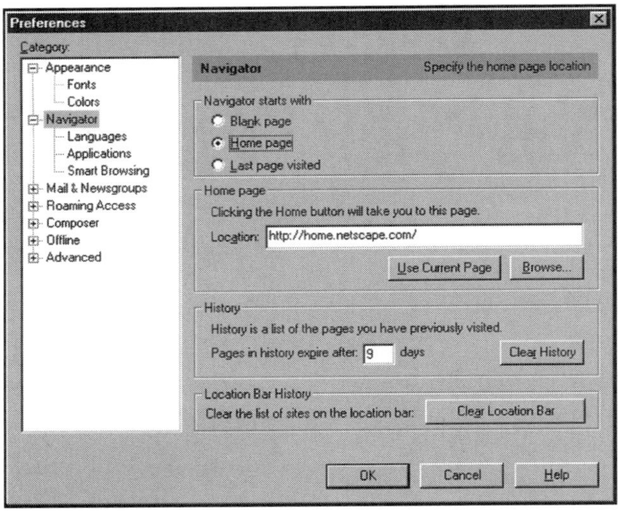

Figure 5-1:
One place
to make all
of your
settings.

Because you can change so many settings in Navigator, the Preferences dialog box consists of many pages. At the left side of the dialog box is a set of tabs from which you can choose which of its pages you want to work in. The names of these tabs describe the settings you can alter on the pages. The tabs for each command are as follows:

✔ Appearance

- Fonts
- Colors

✔ Navigator

- Languages
- Applications
- Smart Browsing

✔ Mail & Newsgroups

- Identity
- Mail Servers
- Newsgroup Servers
- Addressing
- Messages
- Window Settings

- • Copies and Folders
- • Formatting
- • Return Receipts
- • Disk Space
- ✔ Roaming Access
  - • Server Information
  - • Item Selection
- ✔ Composer
  - • Publishing
- ✔ Offline
  - • Download
- ✔ Advanced
  - • Cache
  - • Proxies
  - • SmartUpdate

Appearance

Well, many people say that the Web is more about looks than content, so it's appropriate that Navigator's first preference category is "Appearance." The choices in this category let you tell Navigator what you want to see and how it should look.

The first set of choices let you specify which of the many parts of Communicator you see when you first launch the program. The default, Navigator, makes the most sense unless you mostly use Navigator for mail, in which case you may want to choose Messenger.

You can also specify how you want your toolbar to appear: as pictures and text, pictures only, or text only. In the screen pictures in this book, I've mostly chosen the text-only toolbars so that you can see more of the content area of the screen, but you are free to choose any of the three that best suits your visual tastes.

Fonts

Navigator has a small number of choices for applying fonts. These are clearly stylistic choices meant to make Navigator easier on the eyes as you use it. The choices available to you depend on the kind of computer you own, which fonts you installed, and so on.

The choices for fonts are shown in Figure 5-2. The first choice, "For the Encoding," affects the next two choices, the fonts to use. An *encoding* is a type character set, such as "Western characters," "Japanese characters," "Greek characters," and so on. Most readers of this book use the Western encoding.

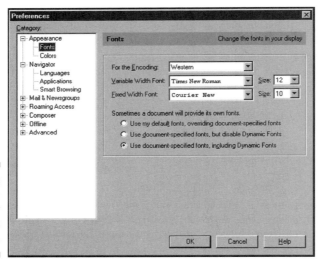

Figure 5-2:
Choosing
fonts for
various
encodings.

For the Western encoding, you have two font choices: variable-width fonts (most of the text that you see), and fixed-width font (the typewriter-looking font you see in some lists). You can also choose the size. For example, I've made the font sizes 9 instead of the default of 12 and 10 so that I can see more text on the screen at one time.

For cases in which a document supplies its own fonts, such as on some newer Web sites, you should choose the third option: Use Document-Specified Fonts, Including Dynamic Fonts. This choice almost always gives you the best-looking page you can get, at least as far as the text on the page goes.

Colors

Playing with the Colors subcategory is more fun than playing with fonts. Many modern Web sites come with their own sets of colors and backgrounds. If you select the Always Use My Colors, Overriding Document option, you prevent these colors from being loaded. By clicking one of the color buttons, you can choose the color of the following elements:

- Text
- Background
- Links you have not clicked on yet
- Links you have already visited

The defaults for these elements are usually okay, but you may, for example, want to change the text color to something other than black. If you choose not to underline links, you should certainly keep the link color something different from the text color; otherwise, you can't tell what is and isn't a link. Make sure, too, that you don't choose a background pattern that makes your text unreadable.

Navigator

With a name like "Navigator," you would think that the preferences in this category apply only to Navigator, not the other components of Communicator. But you would be wrong. I have no idea why Netscape named these choices this way.

In these choices, you can specify what you see when you first launch Navigator: a blank page, a home page (that is, a starting page) that you specify, or the last page you saw before quitting Navigator the last time. If you want to always start with a particular Web page, you can enter that page's URL in the Location text box. You can also go to that Web page and then click the Use Current Page button to set that page as the home page. If you want to always start with a particular file from your hard disk, you can specify that file by using the Browse button, which then lets you specify the exact file you want to use as your home page.

Navigator keeps track of where you have visited, in the History option so that it can change the color on links that you have already visited. You can tell Navigator how many days to remember these locations. The location toolbar also keeps track of where you have been so that you can go back there easily. You can clear this list with the Clear Location Bar button.

Languages

Slowly but surely, some Web content is appearing in languages other than English. Navigator can tell Web servers what languages you are willing to accept for documents. That way, if a Web server has a document in a language you don't understand, it can tell you that instead of showing you the document.

You can add other languages to the list with the Add button. Navigator brings up a list of all the popular (and not-so-popular) languages, or you can even add your own.

Applications

The Applications part of the dialog box is still one of the weakest parts of Navigator. Netscape could have made this page much easier to understand, but instead it's just a mess. Instead of putting a few sentences here about how to use the dialog box, I go into much more detail later in this chapter about what applications and plug-ins actually do for you.

Smart Browsing

The Smart Browsing features, new in Communicator 4.5, allow you to find out what is related to the Web site you are currently looking at and to find keywords through Netscape's keyword index. (This is covered in more detail in Chapter 6.) You may or may not want these features enabled, however, so Netscape gives you an easy way to turn them off. You can also specify particular domains where you don't want What's Related information loaded.

You can also specify whether or not you want to enable Communicator's *Internet keywords* feature. This feature enables you to type words into the location toolbar or the File⇨Open command and have Netscape look up pages that may relate to those words. Some people prefer not to select this option because they don't use the feature, and not selecting it prevents Netscape from doing a keyword search when you mistype a domain name in either location.

Mail and Newsgroups

See Chapter 9 for the description of the many submenus in the Mail and Newsgroups section.

Roaming Access

Some companies and ISPs allow their users to keep their profile information on a *roaming server* instead of on their personal computers. This kind of roaming access is handy if you move from computer to computer a fair amount and don't want to have to keep putting in your settings at each computer you are at. For example, you may want to use Communicator 4.5 from a "kiosk" computer in an airport, and you don't want to have to put in all your personal information. In fact, using a roaming server helps increase security for roaming users, because most users forget to erase their settings after they are done with a borrowed computer.

If your company or ISP is set up to allow roaming access, your system administrator can tell you what to enter in the fields for this part of the dialog box. Because these features are new in Communicator 4.5, it may take a while for companies to start implementing roaming access. So don't be surprised if your network administrator has no idea what you're talking about when you ask about Communicator's roaming features or how to set up this part of the dialog box.

Composer

The preferences in this category are for the Web page creator called Composer, which is covered in Chapters 19 through 21.

Offline

The choices in the Offline page affect how Navigator tells your computer to interact with the Internet. Some people are connected to the Internet all the time, such as on an office network, but most people are only connected to the Internet when they dial in to their ISP. This setting is important because you may want to read your old mail or look at pages on your hard drive without causing Navigator to start up your network connection. Figure 5-3 shows the dialog box for these options.

Communicator can't easily tell whether you are offline or online when you start up. That's why the first option in the dialog box tells Communicator what to assume: to use the state you were in the last time you signed off or to ask you each time you start Communicator. When you go from offline mode to online mode and you have unsent messages in Messenger, you can have Communicator send them automatically or wait for you to tell it to send them (I prefer to wait, in case I've changed my mind about sending any particular messages).

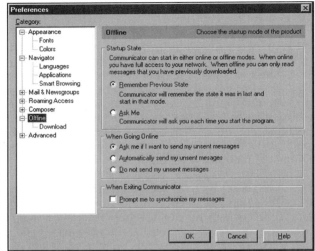

Figure 5-3:
Telling
Communicator
about your
offline
preferences.

The Download options tell Communicator what to download when you go online. Generally, you want to get all of your unread messages unless you have not been online in a long time, in which case you can specify how long back Communicator should look.

Advanced

It's dweeb time. Feel free to skip over this "Advanced" category. It's really mostly for advanced folk, and even then, you don't find much of importance here. On the other hand, if you want to know something about how Navigator is more flexible than other Web browsers, feel free to read along.

The first set of choices are things that you may want Navigator to do, or not do, automatically. The items you can turn on and off are

- ✔ **Automatically load images:** If you are on a slow connection, you may not want to automatically load the images on Web pages. If you unselect this option, you will see your Web pages faster, but you won't see any of the graphics. For some Web pages, this prevents you from seeing important information that is only in the graphics, unfortunately.

- ✔ **Enable Java:** This item allows Java applications that you download to run automatically. Some people worry about how secure Java is, and therefore they don't want to run Java programs automatically from sites they don't know.

✔ **Enable JavaScript:** JavaScript is a language that can be used in HTML pages to perform certain tasks on a Web page. Like Java, it may not be as secure as you want, so you may not want to run JavaScript programs without being asked. You can also specify whether or not to enable JavaScript programs that arrive in e-mail or Usenet news articles.

✔ **Enable style sheets:** The latest version of HTML has an experimental extension called *style sheets* that lets Web designers make better-looking pages.

✔ **Send e-mail address as anonymous FTP password:** Most FTP servers force you to give an e-mail address when you log into them, but you may not want to give your real address, so Navigator gives you the choice.

The second set of choices tell Navigator whether or not to put up a dialog box before you get a cookie from a server. *Cookies* (cute name, huh?) are items used to store information about you when you visit a site. For example, cookies are often used to create shopping baskets, telling the server what you have ordered so far. More and more sites are using cookies, so getting an alert each time may be pretty annoying. On the other hand, if you're concerned about your privacy and the kind of information that is kept on you, you may want to disable cookies altogether or at least get a warning before accepting a cookie.

Cache

A *cache* is an area to which Web pages and images that you have read are copied. Using a cache can increase the speed of access if you read the same page off the Web a second time, and it can also reduce traffic on the Internet (because you don't need to actually access the page from the Web a second time). Navigator includes two kinds of caches: memory caches and disk caches. The memory cache is kept in RAM memory, while the disk cache is kept on your hard disk.

The content of Web pages sometimes changes, so you don't want to always assume that the version of a page you have in one of the caches is the most recent. On the other hand, if you never trust the cache, you force Navigator to go out to a remote (and possibly slow) Web site every time you revisit a page. Navigator checks whether the page still exists, and whether it has been changed since you last looked at it.

The default sizes for the two caches are usually fine, but you can increase or decrease them if you think that may help. Decreasing the cache size means that fewer copies of pages are kept in memory or on disk, but it also means that Navigator is using fewer of your computer's resources.

You can tell Navigator whether to check the Web site if the document you are requesting is already in one of Navigator's two caches. These buttons function as described in the following list:

- ✔ Once Per Session means that the first time during a Navigator session you choose a particular document that is in the cache, Navigator always obtains it from the remote server; after that, Navigator gets it from the cache (if it is still there).

- ✔ Every Time means that Navigator always gets the page from the remote server, even if the document is in the cache.

- ✔ Never means that Navigator does not ever bother to go to the remote server if the document is in the cache. Using this option may be a bit risky because the document may have changed since it got in the cache. On the other hand, this option gives you the best performance.

Proxies

Oh, my. I would love to skip this topic altogether. Describing proxies well in a book on this level is impossible. For that matter, few advanced Internet books do even a halfway decent job of describing proxies. They're a very dweeby, very confusing issue that you do best to avoid if you can; fortunately, most Web users can. Proxies don't relate to the Web per se; they relate to security and the Internet. Basically, proxies intervene between you and the Internet for the greater good of the people at your site.

Most people do not use proxies and therefore choose the Direct Connection to the Internet option. If your ISP uses a proxy, you can hope that it lets you do automatic proxy configuration, in which case you only need to enter the URL of the configuration system. You may, however, have to configure the various proxies manually, at which point you need some very detailed instructions in how to set up Navigator for your proxy system. In any case, your system administrator or ISP should tell you if you have to change this setting, and if you do, what to put in for the values.

SmartUpdate

Communicator's SmartUpdate feature lets Netscape update your copy of Communicator automatically if any updates are released, such as security patches or new features. This feature is very convenient because you don't have to keep going to the Netscape site to find out whether a new version of the software is available. The updating process is fairly painless, and it can help keep your copy of Communicator working as well as possible.

Customizing Your Toolbars

The toolbars at the top of the Navigator screen are pretty handy, but you may not always want to see them, or you may want them to be smaller at times. For example, you may notice that I've hidden them at times in the pictures of the screens in this book. That's so you can see more of the content window. To hide or show toolbars, use the first three commands in the View menu.

You don't have to hide the toolbars if you just want to make them smaller, however. Notice the little gray area at the far left of the toolbar that looks like a small handle. If you click on this handle, the toolbar becomes just a few pixels tall but doesn't disappear altogether. You can then click on it again to make the toolbar reappear.

You may have wondered about the name of the personal toolbar. What's so personal about it? When you start Navigator, the items in the personal toolbar are what Netscape put there, not what you want. Fortunately, changing what's in the personal toolbar is an easy task.

At the top of the Bookmarks window, you see an item called Personal Toolbar Folder. As you may imagine, the items in the folder are the things that appear in your personal toolbar. You can change the items here just like the items in the rest of the bookmarks. You can add folders, get rid of the folders that Netscape started you with, and so on. (There's much more about bookmarks in Chapter 7.)

In other words, the items in your personal toolbar are treated like the items in your bookmarks list. The only reason why you'd want them in your personal toolbar is that they are a bit easier to get to than if they were in your bookmarks list. For my part, I don't use the personal toolbar and instead rely on the bookmark list. Consequently, I always hide the personal toolbar to give myself a bit more space on the screen for Web content.

The Best Commands at Your Fingertips

After you've seen a slew of useful commands in Navigator, how do you remember where to find them all? Well, for many of them, you don't need to remember. If you press the right mouse button, Navigator displays a pop-up menu of the most common commands you need (depending on the location of the cursor as you right-click the mouse). Figure 5-4, for example, shows the list of commands that appears on the pop-up menu if the cursor is over a link. (Other commands appear on the menu if the cursor is elsewhere in a page.)

Figure 5-4:
The pop-up
menu for
links.

(Yes, yes, I hear the Macintosh users complaining that they have no right mouse button on their systems. The good folks at Netscape haven't forgotten you, nor do they require that you press some odd combination of keys; simply press and hold down the usual mouse button for about a second or so without moving the mouse and the same menu appears.)

To choose a command from this pop-up menu, keep holding the mouse button down and then slide the pointer up or down the list. When you highlight the command you want to execute, release the mouse button. If you realize that you don't want to use any of the commands, left-click in a clear area to make the menu disappear. (On the Mac, slide all the way off the menu and release the mouse button.)

Finding Text

Okay, here's a command that's not too thrilling but is useful in certain situations. The Edit menu's Find in Page command enables you to search for text on the current Web page. It works just like the Find commands in most word processors. You can specify the text that you want to find, case sensitivity, and the direction to search in the Find dialog box.

Simple as it may be in function, the Find in Page command can be handy if you are looking through a long document for some specific information. It's particularly useful if you want to find where on a page an e-mail address appears (you simply search for the @ character).

Plug-ins and Helper Applications

Even though Navigator is pretty versatile, it can't handle every kind of information on the Web. If you access data in a format that Navigator doesn't understand (for example, a movie), Navigator can launch another program or just save the data to disk for you to deal with later. The options in the Applications section of the Edit⇨Preferences dialog box specify which programs Navigator launches in such cases.

Generally, you never need to change any of the settings in this subcategory because they come preconfigured for the best values. You may, however, want to change them if you consistently download a certain type of data and want Navigator to always launch a program that it doesn't currently know about. You may also want to change the values if you want Navigator to always save certain kinds of files to disk without asking you what to do first.

Each kind of data on the Web has a file type, more accurately called a *MIME* type. These data descriptions consist of two words separated by a slash (/) character. Movies in the MPEG format, for example, have a file type description of video/mpeg. These types are defined in Internet standards committees, although some of them are temporary names until the committees get around to approving them.

For each file type, Navigator can take the following actions:

✔ For many formats, you can display the data in Navigator using the "Navigator" choice. This option works only for elements that Navigator knows about, such as simple text, HTML, GIF, and JPEG images, and for formats for which you have a plug-in.

✔ Navigator can just store some types of data on disk with the "Save to Disk" option. You can open the file later with some other program.

✔ Navigator can start another program and give that program the data. For this, choose the "Application" option and enter the name of the program to run.

For each MIME type, you can tell Navigator what to do. Select the description of the type and click the Edit button. You can also add new MIME types with the New Type button.

Security Preferences

Security is a hot topic on the Internet. Because so few people understand how to keep themselves safe from snooping and tampering on the Internet, malicious people can do plenty of damage without much risk of getting caught. Navigator gives you a few opportunities to avoid security problems, but you must assume most of the responsibility yourself.

To access the security preferences, choose Communicator➪Tools➪Security Info or click the Security button on the navigation toolbar. The Security dialog box looks somewhat like the Preferences dialog box and is shown in Figure 5-5.

The first category, Security Info, tells you what kind of security the Web page that you're currently viewing in Navigator has. Most pages on the Web do not use any form of security, so this information isn't all that useful. The Passwords category is useful if many people use the same computer. Each person can have her own Navigator setup, and you can make sure that no one uses your setup without knowing your password.

The Navigator category lets you tell Navigator how you want to handle security when you're surfing the Web. The first set of choices in the Navigator category tell Navigator when to warn you about changes in security.

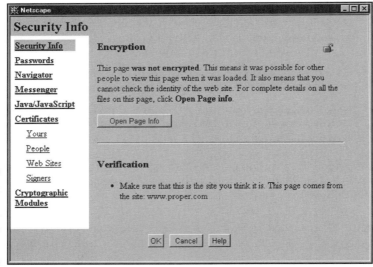

Figure 5-5: The Navigator security settings.

Security warnings may sound great, but they are often just a nuisance. These options open a dialog box whenever you enter or leave a secure or insecure area of the Web. Well, if you don't know by now, only a handful of areas on the Web are secure; you can tell whether you are in one by looking for the little lock icon at the lower-left corner of the screen. If it's a closed lock, you're in a secure area; if it's an open lock, you're not. I doubt that you want to respond to a dialog box every time you go from secure to insecure area and vice versa, but if you do, you can turn on that feature here.

The Navigator category also lets you specify which version of SSL to use (SSL is a method for keeping conversations over the Web private). Two versions of the SSL security protocol are now on the Web. You can choose whether to use one or both of them; you're fine to leave both of these selected because both versions are quite good. You need to use the Configure buttons only if a particular site tells you to.

The Messenger category lets you specify how your Internet mail is encrypted and signed. These topics are covered in Chapter 12. Before you can use this kind of security, you need to get an S/MIME certificate (which is described in the next section and is also covered in depth in Chapter 12). After you have such a certificate, it appears in the "Yours" subcategory under the Certificates category.

The Java/JavaScript category specifies who can access your computer (as compared to just the Communicator screen) with a Java or JavaScript program. Under no circumstances should you add any certificates to this area unless you are very, very sure that you trust the company who wants to have this access. You are, in effect, letting them have free access to your computer, which I think is a pretty dangerous thing to allow.

The Certificates category lets you view all the certificates you know about. You can view, edit, and remove your own certificates, the certificates that other people may have sent you (such as in signed e-mail), the certificates of secure Web sites that you've visited, and the certificates of the companies that sign certificates.

The Cryptographic Modules category lets you add different methods for implementing security. However, no additional modules are available now, so you can safely skip this section unless your system administrator tells you that you need to add some new modules here.

Personal certificates

As more and more people use the Web to perform financial transactions and to communicate about business, asking the question, "How do I know that you are who you say you are?" becomes important. Conversely, the people communicating with you want to know the same thing about you.

A *personal certificate* is somewhat akin to a driver's license: It is a form of identification from someone whom everyone trusts (well, most everyone trusts) stating that you are who you say you are. If you trust the company that issued the certificate, you can trust the certificate holder.

If you don't already have a personal certificate, click the Get a Certificate button in the Yours subcategory and follow the directions. You can have more than one certificate, and you may get them from different certificate-issuing authorities. If you do get more than one certificate, you can specify the default certificate that Navigator presents to sites you visit.

Personal certificates are just starting to be widely used. Because you need a personal certificate in order to secure your e-mail, many people are getting their first certificates as you read this. Within a year or two, personal certificates will probably be much more popular.

Site certificates

A *site certificate* is like a personal certificate, but you use it to be sure that a Web site is who it says it is. In order for a Web site to be trusted, a Web site has to have a certificate from someone you trust. Who do you trust? Well . . .

Certificate authorities

A *certificate authority,* or "CA" for short, is someone who vouches for the authenticity of someone else by giving him a signed certificate. You can find several public CAs in the world, and some companies act as their own CAs for certificates issued by the companies.

Navigator comes with a bunch of certificates for CAs that Netscape Communications trusts. If you trust Netscape, you can probably trust its list of CAs and the certificates that those CAs issue. It's too early in the Internet security game to know which CAs are better than others, so I generally advise people to trust all the Netscape-trusted CAs until you hear otherwise.

Onward to the Web!

Whew! You made it through all the preferences. I hope that you find many of them useful in your day-to-day use of Navigator. The next time someone tells you that "using a Web browser is so easy," you may want to direct him to all the choices you had to make here.

Chapter 6

Searching High and/or Low

In This Chapter

▶ Knowing where to look for resources

▶ Getting smarter browsing with Navigator

▶ Snooping around on your own

*Y*ou can find what you want on the Web in more than one way. Because the Web is a collection of places and content at those places, you need to know where something is located on the Web before you can access that something. As I discuss in Chapter 3, URLs specify the content's location.

For example, `www.bigstate.edu/people/index` is a URL that points to some content; you know that this content resides on the computer that has the domain name `www.bigstate.edu`. You may find it helpful to think of URLs as book identifiers that include indicators of the library name and the shelf location.

If you know the URL for the specific content you want to examine, you can type the URL into Navigator and zip to it in a jiffy. But what if you don't know the location of the content you want? If you were in a standard library with real books, you would probably look in a card catalog. In most libraries, the card catalog (which rarely contains cards these days) enables you to search for books in the library by title, author, or subject. The subjects are all categorized in a standard manner, and searching is pretty easy.

Nothing even remotely like a card catalog exists for the Web. You won't find a complete listing anywhere of what's on the Web; some partial listings are available, but even they are not searched for information the same way a library card catalog is perused, usually for the following reasons:

- ✔ Pages on the Web often don't have terribly descriptive titles.

- ✔ The exact author of a Web page is often unclear.

- ✔ No standardized subject classification system exists.

Even worse, because it's impossible to know where everything is on the Web, you have no way to make sure that the search listing you're using is anywhere near complete.

All is not lost, however. A few places do enable you to search parts of the Web; if you're looking for a fairly common topic, you can at least get a good start. Furthermore, some attempts are made to categorize topics on the Web, and I describe those attempts in Chapter 13. This chapter describes some of the ways you can search for content for which you have no URLs.

Don't be surprised if your search for particular information comes up empty. Finding nothing (or finding information that isn't relevant) isn't necessarily a sign that what you want isn't on the Web. It's merely a sign that the Web search systems are still in their infancy. Five years from now, much better ways to look in one place on the Web and stand a good chance of finding a list of valuable pointers probably will exist; right now, however, searching is all very hit and miss.

Web Catalogs

You may be wondering what good any sort of directory is if cataloging the entire Web is impossible. The answer is that you don't need to catalog the whole Web (or an entire library) for a directory to be useful. Many partial Web catalogs (like catalogs of just part of a library's collection) offer easy-to-use search features that, although incomplete, can often get you going on your searches.

You may find the way these catalogs work interesting. The person creating the catalog starts with a list of major and/or interesting sites on the Web and then launches a program that reads the home pages at those starting sites. The program starts following the links from those home pages to other sites, keeping track of where it has been. The program keeps looking around the Web by following these links, grabbing copies of whatever it finds, and using the links it finds as fodder for the giant index.

These programs are generally called *spiders,* an excessively cute term based on Web imagery. A better term for them is *robots* because they perform their tasks much like classical mechanical robots would; fortunately, people have pretty much stopped using "spiders" and have shifted to "robots" even though they are the same software.

Robots have many problems, but given the imperfection forced on those trying to catalog the Web, they also have many nice features. The problems include the following:

✔ New Web sites are added slowly to the catalogs because few links to them exist.

✔ Updates usually aren't reflected in the catalog because pages are not checked regularly.

✔ The kind of material that appears in the catalog is heavily based on the pages it started from.

Some of the big advantages of using robots instead of catalogs are as follows:

✔ Pages near the top of a site hierarchy are favored. Those pages usually contain more general information than the ones farther down the hierarchy.

✔ The robot can be modified to emphasize certain link chains. This capability makes the catalog better for certain kinds of information that interests the person putting the catalog together.

Very few Web robots do anything other than index HTTP content. Almost all of them completely ignore the other important parts of the Web, such as FTP sites. So if you're searching the Web for something and you don't really care whether it comes to you in HTML or some other form, you are kind of out of luck.

The page at info.webcrawler.com/mak/projects/robots/robots.html (see Figure 6-1) is an excellent resource if you want to create your own Web catalog service. It tells you how to construct a robot, describes important things not to do, and mentions the other catalog services already on the Web.

Many places offer lists of Web catalogs. Experienced Web users have their favorite catalogs, but their preferences are usually not based on quantitative criteria such as biggest or fastest. Instead, they generally choose their preferred searcher based on the user interface, the perceived quality of results they got the day they needed to find something fast, and so on.

Figure 6-2 shows the list of Web search spots maintained at Netscape Communications. You can find this list at home.netscape.com/escapes/search/ntsrchrnd-3.html. It contains links to the most popular search sites and a brief description of each.

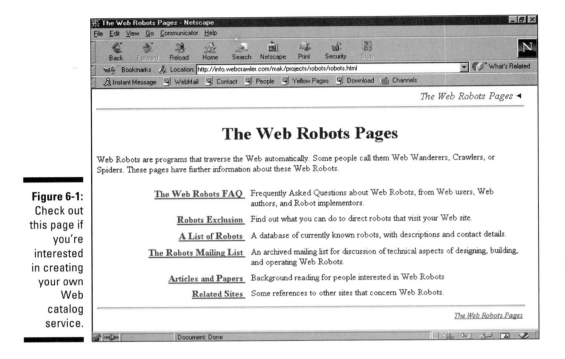

Figure 6-1:
Check out
this page if
you're
interested
in creating
your own
Web
catalog
service.

Figure 6-2:
Netscape
maintains a
list of Web
search
spots.

Get Smart with Smart Browsing

One of the snazziest new features of Communicator 4.5 is Netscape's "Smart Browsing," a set of technologies that Netscape bundles into Communicator so that you don't have to work so hard to find what you want on the Web. Smart Browsing consists of two parts: Netscape's own keyword search and a list of what is related to the Web page you're on. Netscape plans to add even more features to Smart Browsing, probably in Communicator Version 5.

Internet keywords

All the Web search sites let you search for subjects based on keywords that you know. For example, if you want to find a Web site about bird watching, you can go to any of the search sites and enter "bird watching" in its search engine. But that method takes two steps: Go to the search site and then enter the term.

With Smart Browsing, you can start your search without going to a search site. Simply enter your search term in the location box — the white box to the right of "Go to" or "Netsite" — in the location toolbar. You can type in whatever word or phrase you want.

What happens next depends on what you typed in and what the computers at Netscape can find out about it. If you type in a domain name, Navigator takes you to that Web site, if it exists. If you type in a word or a phrase, Navigator takes you to a page of search results, much like a Web search site would. In this way, the Internet keywords feature is like a combination of two dialog boxes in one: Look up the domain name, or look up this phrase in a Web search.

Figure 6-3 shows a typical result of an Internet keyword search. Note that the folks at Netscape fed this search through the Excite search services. In the future, it may choose different search services or even offer multiple search services at once. You don't have to change anything in Communicator when Netscape chooses these options: The folks at Netscape change things back in Netcenter so that the choice happens automatically for you.

Like all Web searches, the Internet keyword search is inherently incomplete. In addition, many people find it a bit disingenuous of Netscape because the company gets paid when you use the feature. For every page it returns, you'll encounter at least one ad (and possibly a bunch of them). You'd better believe that Netscape is getting paid for showing you those ads. More significant, the position of who gets mentioned first may also have to do with who paid the people at Netscape or at the search service. Don't assume that first means best; it could easily mean richest, which may not be what you had in mind.

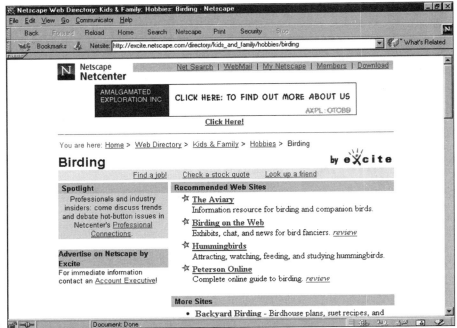

Figure 6-3:
Results of
an Internet
keyword
search.

What's related

So, you're at a Web site you like, but you want something more. (Isn't life always like that?) The What's Related button at the right side of the location toolbar may give you some advice. Simply click the button and down drops a list of sites that may be related to what you're looking at. Figure 6-4 shows how this drop-down list looks for a typical site. If you see a site on the list that you want to go to, just drag down the list and let go at the desired site. You're automatically taken there.

Figure 6-4:
Seeing
what's
related to a
Web page

The operative word here is *may*. Netscape's computers use a very sophisti-cated database to determine what is related to a particular Web page. It includes questions like "What Web pages have links to this one?" and "What Web pages have the same words and phrases as this one?" Many of the Web search engines have similar features, but I have found Communicator's What's Related button to be more accurate than the search engines.

Guessing How to Get What You Want

Sometimes searching by using indexes is not enough. If the search sites in this chapter don't help you find what you need, check through the many resources that I discuss in Chapters 13 through 17. Many of the sites in those chapters offer lists of links to other sites on the Web. Some of the larger sites can even be searched.

If you can't find what you're looking for directly, however, you may find help in some indirect methods that advanced Web users wield. Many of these methods lead nowhere, but they take only a few minutes at most to try and sometimes yield results.

One of the most common site-searching methods is creative name-guessing in a URL. Suppose that you're looking at the Web page for a department at a university, and you want to see the page for a particular professor. The department's page lists some professors, but not the one you want. You notice that all the URLs from that page look like www.bigstate.edu/polisci/smith and www.bigstate.edu/polisci/yu. If the name of the professor you want is Sugarman, you can enter the URL www.bigstate.edu/polisci/sugarman as a guess.

More often than not, this tactic yields only an error. If you do get where you want, however, you may find the result worth the effort. Remember that generating errors doesn't have a significant effect on Web sites or on your browser. Sometimes the error itself is helpful in your guessing. (You may, for example, receive a message saying that the URL you gave is too busy, which at least means that the server you asked for exists.) Errors are described in much more detail in the next chapter.

Chapter 7
Playing Favorites

· ·

In This Chapter

▶ Keeping track of where you have been

▶ Organizing your collection of bookmarks

▶ Editing your bookmarks

▶ Collecting other people's bookmarks

· ·

*A*s you meander around the Web, you often find places that you think are particularly interesting. You can keep a list of those places by using Navigator's bookmark feature. *Bookmarks* are pointers to Web pages, and they include the title of the pointer as well as other notes you may want to keep. Bookmarks are a great way to keep track of your favorite places so that you can go back to them quickly.

Bookmarks appear in two places: in the Bookmarks list in the location toolbar and in a separate Bookmarks window. I use the Bookmarks list in the location toolbar when I want to go to a bookmark I remember, but I use the Bookmarks window for when I don't remember the name of a desired bookmark or when I want to use one of the more advanced bookmark features like searching. I've got a zillion bookmarks (well, about 500), and it's easy to forget where in the Bookmarks list I keep each one, so the Bookmark window is very handy.

Getting Acquainted with Your Bookmarks

The good folks at Netscape didn't want you to feel like you had nothing to start with, so they loaded Communicator with dozens of bookmarks. Figure 7-1 shows the Bookmark list that comes with Communicator 4.5. Note that it's all folders; when you select a folder, you see the bookmarks (and other folders) inside the selected folder. In this figure, the News and Sports folder is selected, showing the bookmarks that Netscape supplies on this topic.

You can also view your set of bookmarks in the Bookmarks window. Open the Bookmarks list in the location toolbar and choose the Edit Bookmarks command (even though you're not quite ready to edit) or choose Communicator⇨Bookmarks⇨Edit Bookmarks. You use this command to open the window even if you aren't going to edit any bookmarks. In the Bookmarks window (shown in Figure 7-2), double-clicking a bookmark acts just the same as choosing a bookmark from the Bookmark menu: Navigator takes you to that Web page.

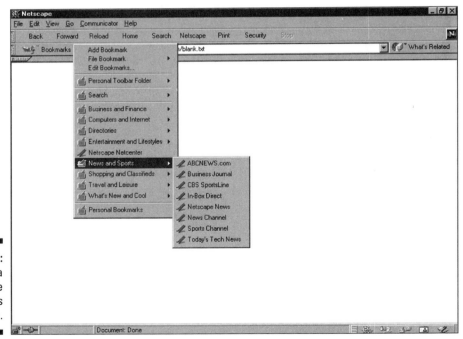

Figure 7-1:
Inside a
folder in the
Bookmarks
menu.

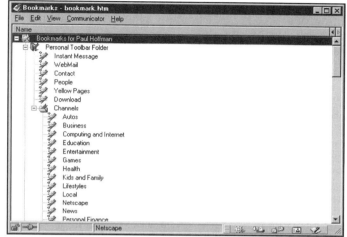

Figure 7-2:
The
Bookmarks
window
gives a
different
view of your
bookmarks.

Adding a Web Page to Your List

Okay, so you're at a great Web page and you want to be able to get back to it directly later. Or you're at a not-so-great Web page, but you need to remember it later for work. To add the current page to your bookmarks, open the Bookmarks list in the location toolbar and choose the Add Bookmark command. You can also choose Communicator⇨Bookmarks⇨ Add Bookmark to do the same thing. Done!

This command puts the bookmark in the main Bookmarks menu. The name for a bookmark that you add this way is the title of the Web page you are viewing. You can keep adding bookmarks this way for as long as you want, even after the Bookmarks menu gets longer than your screen: Navigator is still able to show them all by scrolling. To go to the location referenced by one of your bookmarks, you just select it from this menu.

Organizing Your Life — Or At Least Your Bookmarks

If you have dozens (or hundreds, or thousands!) of bookmarks, you don't want them in a single list. Navigator lets you organize your bookmarks in folders, and each folder can have more layers of folders inside it. Of course, you probably want to rearrange your bookmarks at some point, such as by grouping related bookmarks together in folders.

You use the Bookmarks window (not the Bookmarks menu) for all of your organization. The Bookmarks window acts very much like the Windows Explorer program in Windows 95 or the Finder on the Macintosh. If you are comfortable with either of those operating systems, you'll find organizing your bookmarks a breeze.

Folders are your friends

My many hundreds of bookmarks came without any help from Netscape. The only way I can find any of them is by organizing them into folders. Of course, my folder titles are very different from the ones Netscape gives you, mostly because most of my bookmarks have nothing to do with the topics Netscape starts you off with.

To create a new folder, use the File⇨New Folder command (remember that all these commands are in the Bookmarks window, not in the main Communicator window; you can get there with the Communicator⇨Bookmarks⇨ Edit Bookmarks command). A dialog box appears, in which you enter a folder name. When you click OK, the folder is created at the top of your folder hierarchy. Deleting folders is just as easy: Select the folder and use the Edit⇨Delete command or just press the Delete key.

Double-click a folder to open it and see its contents. You can also click the "+" to the left of a closed folder to open it. To close a folder, double-click it again or click the "−" to its left.

Moving things around

After you add your own folders, you probably want to move some of your bookmarks into them. No problem: just click and drag. Select the bookmark you want to move into a folder and drag its icon over the icon for the folder in which you want to put the bookmark. When you have the icon positioned over the folder icon, the whole line on which the folder resides highlights. Let go of the mouse button, and the bookmark goes into the folder.

Moving folders into other folders is just the same. Select the icon of the folder you want to move, drag it on top of the folder you want it to go into, and let go.

You can also rearrange the order of the bookmarks. Just select the bookmark and drag it up or down. As you drag, you see a horizontal line indicating where the bookmark will go when you stop. Just let go, and the bookmark drops right there. Moving folders takes exactly the same steps.

And yes, you can also use the Clipboard for moving things if you want. The Bookmark window's Edit menu has the familiar Cut, Copy, and Paste commands that work just like they do in your other favorite programs.

Another handy feature makes your Bookmarks list even more usable. You can add *separators* (a fancy term for a horizontal line) between your folders or bookmarks as a way to group them visually. Select the folder or bookmark that is just before where you want the separator and then choose File⇨New Separator. Separators can be treated like bookmarks, in case you want to move them around or delete them.

Changing Your Bookmarks

To change the name or URL of a bookmark, select the bookmark and give the Edit⇨Bookmark Properties command. Figure 7-3 shows the dialog box for the properties of a typical bookmark. As you can see, you can edit the name and URL for the selected bookmark just by changing those fields in the dialog box. The bottom of the dialog box tells you when you last visited that URL and when you first created the bookmark.

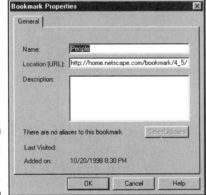

Figure 7-3:
Editing a
bookmark.

The Description field is quite useful if you have many bookmarks. You can put whatever text you want into this field for all of your bookmarks. When you want to find a bookmark later, you can search for it by looking for keywords that you put in the description. The Edit⇨Find in Bookmarks command lets you search for text in the bookmark name, the URL, or the description.

Getting Bookmarks from Other Places

You don't have to rely on Netscape's "starter" bookmarks or your own collecting to fill your Bookmarks menu. Two additional commands either add new bookmarks to your current list or completely replace your list with a new one.

The File⇨Import command copies bookmarks from a file you have on your hard drive into your current bookmarks list. This command is useful if, for example, someone has mailed you a list of bookmarks and you want to include them in yours.

You can also just switch bookmark files. The File⇨Open Bookmarks File command closes the current bookmark file and opens another one that you select. This option is handy if you have a different set of bookmarks for personal and work use (although I would just keep them in different folders in one list).

Chapter 8
It May Be Broken

In This Chapter

▶ Figuring out error messages

▶ Staring at a blank screen

▶ Avoiding problems

*B*rowsing the Web isn't always fun and flowers. You're bound to encounter some problems in your travels, and you may find it difficult to figure out what is wrong. But then, what would a computer be without aggravating error messages and weird results?

The kinds of errors you see and the amount of help you get in figuring out the problem depend, to a large extent, on your Web browser software. Some browsers send you cryptic error messages that don't give you much help; others, such as Communicator, give you as much help as possible. In fact, better error messages is one of the best improvements in Communicator 4.5. Even the best programs, however, can't always give good advice on what went wrong and how to prevent it from happening again. This chapter describes the most common problems you may come across on the Web as you use Communicator.

Whenever your Web browser gives you an error message that you don't understand, or something really weird happens while viewing the Web, the first thing to do is remember to breathe. Yes, that sounds like simple advice, but you'd be surprised how many people stop breathing or breathe very shallowly if something goes wrong on their computer. If you see an error message or if you realize that something's not working, remember to breathe. Breathe again, slowly. Think, "It's just a piece of software; it's just a computer network. It's not worth not breathing."

The Errors of Your Ways

In a chapter about errors, starting with the easy ones — the ones that come with reasonable error messages — is best. These errors also happen to be the most common ones you see as you wander around the Web.

The URL doesn't exist

The number-one, most-common, happens-all-the-darn-time error is the *404 error*, which is a dumb name for a simple problem: You have tried to access a Web page that doesn't exist. This kind of error is reported by the Web server at the site you are trying to reach, and the message you get back is created by that Web server. Therefore, the message is different from Web site to Web site. A typical 404 error is shown in Figure 8-1. You see this message if the server exists and is accepting requests, but the requested page doesn't exist on the server.

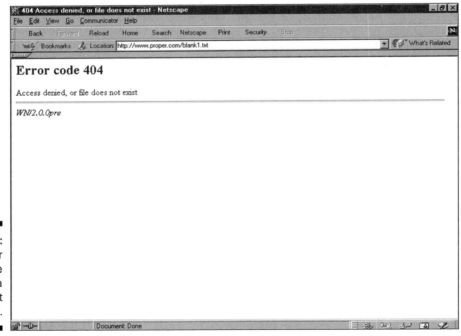

Figure 8-1:
The error message for a nonexistent Web page.

This error is most commonly caused by following a link that used to exist but no longer does. If you link from a page you found on a not-too-busy Web site, for example, the page maintainer may no longer be keeping that page up to date. The link may have been fine months ago, but it has since moved or changed names.

The kinds of responses you get for these kinds of errors come in a wide variety. Some servers give you polite explanations, and some even suggest what you may want to do next, but many give you terse messages with very little helpful information.

Typing the URL incorrectly is another common reason for getting the 404 message. If you see a link in a book such as this one, for example, and you enter it into Navigator, you may miss a letter or transpose a pair of letters, resulting in a URL that doesn't exist.

If the URL you are giving is for a directory, not a document, some Web servers require a / at the end of the URL. Assume, for example, that you are entering the following URL:

```
www.bigstate.edu/candle-making
```

If you receive a 404 error, you may next want to try the following URL instead:

```
www.bigstate.edu/candle-making/
```

Notice the added / at the end of the URL. This change works only if the URL is for a directory, not a file. So you wouldn't try this trick on a URL that ends in .html or .txt or other endings that indicate that the URL is that of a file.

Errors such as the 404 error come from the server software and are sent back to your browser. Many such errors can come from servers that follow the HTTP standard correctly. If you really want to know, the list of all error messages is in the full specification for HTTP, which can be found at ftp:// ftp.isi.edu/in-notes/rfc2068.txt on the Web. You certainly don't need to know about the other HTTP error codes to use the Web. Errors other than 404 are very uncommon, and even if you do get other error messages, a bit of explanatory text usually comes with them.

The server name is wrong

You may see an error similar to the one shown in Figure 8-2. This error indicates that your URL is bad for a very basic reason: The domain name of the host is wrong. You may have typed the domain name wrong, or the domain name may no longer exist, or your computer may be having a problem looking up domain names.

Figure 8-2:
The Communicator 4.5 error message for a bad host name.

Note that this page is new in Communicator 4.5; in older versions of Communicator, you see a small, not-terribly-informative dialog box. Netscape provides this service because it may be able to help you even more. That is, if Netscape knows some relevant information about the domain name you entered, it can tell you that information on this page.

Sometimes very busy and very dead look the same

Another error you get while roaming the Web is a server that is too busy to accept your request. This error can happen because you are trying to access a very popular site, such as a server that has downloadable software or pictures, or because the server at the site is set up to handle only a few users at a time. A few years ago, you got this error frequently, but most Web sites have gotten better Web servers, so this problem has become much less common.

Figure 8-3 shows the error message that Communicator displays after you try to access a server that is too busy. The wording in the dialog box is a tad vague for a good reason. The first sentence explains all that Communicator knows is definitely true: The connection was refused by the server. This problem, however, can exist for a number of reasons. The following are some of the causes of this message:

Figure 8-3:
The
dreaded
"too busy"
error
message.

✔ The server may really be too busy. Your browser sends the query to the server, but the server takes too long to respond.

✔ The server may not be accepting requests on the port to which you sent the message. If, for example, the URL you sent has a port number indicated by a colon and number after the site name (such as www.acompany.com:8012), the server may not be accepting messages on that port.

✔ The server may be temporarily or permanently off the Internet because of technical problems.

✔ The path on the Internet from your computer to the server may be so clogged that the message or the return is delayed for longer than your browser permits.

As you can see, many different symptoms can lead to the same diagnosis — nothing came back from the server, so who knows what's wrong? You can sometimes get a clue, however, if the message comes back immediately. An immediate return indicates that the server is up, but it really is too busy, or you may have tried to access an incorrect port. On the other hand, if it takes a long time (like more than 15 seconds) to even get the error message back, you can probably assume that something on the Internet connection between you and the Web server is badly messed up.

Hmmmm, Nothing Happened

The worst errors are those that you can't tell are happening. Something's wrong, but you receive no error message, no problem indicator, nothing. All you can do is wait to see whether something happens after a while. These errors are all too common on the Web.

The "nothing happened" errors occur mainly due to the slowness of the Internet. Of course, the entire Internet isn't slow at the moment, just the connection between your computer and the Web site you are trying to access. As more and more people start using the Internet, the pathways for messages get more and more crowded. Conveniently, the Internet is well equipped to handle slowness, so crowded message pathways aren't usually a serious problem.

Sometimes, however, a pathway becomes more than slow — it gets completely clogged. Actually, any one part of the pathway between your computer and the Web site can cause you to get nothing on your system. This situation is much like traveling across town on surface streets to attend a meeting: One congested block can make you miss the meeting entirely. That you eventually get to your destination doesn't matter if the meeting is over by the time you arrive.

Clogging isn't the only problem you can encounter: The link can actually be completely dead, forcing all the information to go some other route to get around the broken part of the Internet. Web clients don't enable you to follow the path of the messages on the Internet, so you can't tell where a dead link occurs. That's actually okay because you can't change the path of your message anyway. You just have to sit and wait for the network folks to fix the broken link or start rerouting messages around the broken link more quickly.

Fortunately, programs such as Communicator can give you clues in cases such as these. Watch the bottom line of the Communicator window, in which the status messages appear. The messages you see after you connect to a system appear in the following order:

- ✔ **Looking up host.** Communicator translates the domain name in the URL to the IP address of the host. It must perform this translation before it can communicate with the host computer. This translation usually goes fairly quickly, but it can sometimes take a long time if the host is in a different country or if traffic problems occur on the Internet.

- ✔ **Contacting host.** Communicator has sent the request to the host computer but hasn't heard anything back yet. This step is usually where you get stuck the longest because the Web host must accept the request before you can proceed. If the host computer is very busy, this process can sometimes take a while.

- ✔ **Host contacted. Waiting for reply.** This message is a good sign. It means that the host computer has accepted the message and is thinking about it. Web hosts usually process the requests reasonably quickly after they get in, so you rarely get hung up in this stage for very long.

- ✔ **Transferring data.** You're almost home free. You are receiving the information from the host, and you can watch Communicator as it renders the information you are receiving on your computer's screen.

- ✔ **Done.** Communicator has all the data for the page and is finished with its tasks.

You can still lose the connection during the last step. Communicator is merrily getting data and then — nothing. It stops dead. Many problems can cause this failure but, unfortunately, you can't do anything about them. If you're sure that nothing is coming from the server anymore and want to abort the connection, you can click the Stop icon on the toolbar.

Surviving Netstorms

In the past few years, as more and more servers were added to the Internet, some other major problems started to appear. These problems aren't caused by the increased number of Internet users. Instead, they are caused by the Internet's system software having to manage so many host addresses and routes between systems. The term *netstorm* means bad weather on the Internet, and the symptoms of these storms usually manifest as mysterious errors.

One all-too-common type of netstorm is caused by bad routing tables. Large intersections on the Internet use *routing tables* to determine how to pass information around. Say that you sent a Web request to the site www.bigstate.edu. After your browser determines the address of www.bigstate.edu, it sends the request out on the Internet with that address. Remember that addresses tell only the address of the destination, not how to get messages from your computer to their destinations.

Each stop holds your message while it looks up the destination address in its routing table to determine the next hop on the route. Most of the time — like 99.999 percent — the routing tables are fine. If a routing table is bad, however, all hell breaks loose. Messages going from one computer to a nearby computer can actually go all the way across the country and back. Worse yet, some messages can go bouncing around the Internet indefinitely, never arriving at the destination computer. (After a while, however, the Internet's system software kills these messages.)

Sometimes major nodes on the Internet go down for a while, which is another cause of netstorms. If minor nodes experience breakdowns, the data flows around them without much difficulty. If a major node goes offline, however, the redirection of traffic can be incredibly disruptive because significant amounts of data suddenly must be rerouted.

The symptoms of netstorms are hard to pin down, but the following are some typical ones to watch out for:

- ✔ Requests that have been taking about two seconds suddenly start taking 20 seconds.
- ✔ Sites that you know exist on the Internet disappear, and your Web browser tells you that no such domain exists.

✔ You are receiving a 50K file and, after 30K has arrived with no problems, it just stops.

In all these cases, the best you can do is just accept that this sort of thing happens on the Internet, realize that it will probably continue to happen for the next year or more, and hope that the problem gets fixed within an hour or so.

Fixing Broken Pictures

One last all-too-common problem you may find on the Web is that of broken pictures. *Broken pictures* are inline images that are unreadable because they contain bad or missing data or because the link to the picture is incorrect. Communicator illustrates these images by a broken picture icon, as shown in Figure 8-4.

Fortunately, broken pictures are fairly easy to fix. Simply click the icon, and Communicator downloads the picture again. Unless the picture is broken on the host system, it probably downloads fine the second time you try it. If the host does have a messed-up graphics file or a bad link, the only thing you can do about it is to send a message to the Web site maintainer and point out the problem.

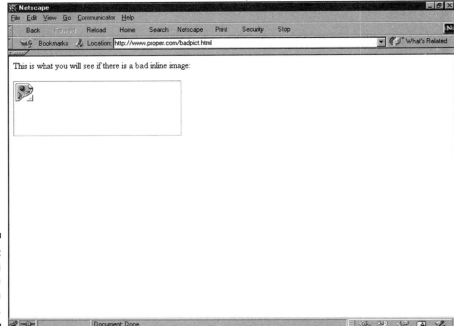

Figure 8-4:
The broken
picture
icon in
Communicator.

Part III
Your E-Mail Messenger

The 5th Wave   By Rich Tennant

In this part . . .

Messenger is the e-mail component of Communi-cator. With Messenger you can send and receive Internet mail and explore Usenet newsgroups. In this part you discover how to format e-mail messages, add con-tacts to your address book, add and send attachments in e-mail messages, post messages and replies to Usenet newsgroups, and much more. Securing your e-mail messages so that only your intended recipients read your messages is also covered in this part.

Chapter 9

Starting Up Your Messenger

· ·

In This Chapter

▶ Exploring mail and Usenet news

▶ Setting up Netscape to send and receive mail

▶ Creating an address book

· ·

*T*he Web is wonderful and all that, but it isn't the only thing on the Internet. To many people, Internet mail (better known as *e-mail*) is more useful and more interesting than the Web. The Web and e-mail are not an either/or choice: Most people use both quite happily. The Web is good for what it does, and e-mail is good for what it does.

Fortunately, Communicator is good at both. The earlier chapters of this book cover how to use the Navigator part of Communicator to work with the Web; this chapter and the next three chapters tell you how to use the Messenger part of Communicator to work with e-mail. Netscape does a good job of making the two parts look fairly similar, so if you've already set up Navigator, setting up Communicator is a snap.

Messenger actually does more than just e-mail. It is also your gateway to Usenet news. Netscape jammed these two different pieces into Messenger for a good reason: They both look similar to the user. Even though e-mail and Usenet news are very different in many ways, you do the same kinds of things with them, namely reading messages and sending messages. Even if you don't use Usenet news much at all, setting it up is easy, and you can do it at the same time you set up your e-mail.

As you read these chapters, remember that e-mail and Usenet news are quite different. Most Internet users only use e-mail and don't use Usenet news at all, or use Usenet news only occasionally. Because of this imbalance, I cover Internet mail in much more detail than I do Usenet news, but Netscape has made them similar enough for you to explore both at the same time.

The Marvelous World of Mail

E-mail is the modern way to communicate. Many businesses now rely more on e-mail for business-to-business communication than they do on the telephone because the people getting the mail can read it when they want and reply to it when they can.

E-mail comes in two flavors: Internet mail and non-Internet mail. As the name implies, *Internet mail* is what you get on the Internet. *Non-Internet mail* is e-mail that goes over local area networks (LANs) that do not use Internet protocols. A fair amount of non-Internet mail is still used, making life tough for those of us who want to communicate using the same methods so that we can all get each other's messages. Fortunately, the amount of non-Internet mail is going down as LAN administrators switch to Internet mail because of its ubiquity.

Communicator's mail component, Messenger, is Internet mail all the way, and it always has been. Netscape is known for having always been very interested in Internet protocols, both for the Web and e-mail. If you are on a local area network that uses non-Internet mail, you can't use Messenger with your e-mail system.

Internet mail works remarkably well. You may hear stories about mail getting lost or taking hours or days to get to the recipient, but those stories usually relate to non-Internet mail, because connecting non-Internet mail and Internet mail is pretty complicated. These connections, called *gateways,* are usually okay at getting the messages through, but sometimes they are flat-out awful. Bad gateways do things like lose parts of messages, lose whole messages, send them to the wrong person, and so forth. On the other hand, it's rare to find Internet mail systems that have any problems with sending mail on the Internet.

In and out are different

One of the most confusing aspects of Internet mail is that software like Messenger uses different systems to send mail and receive mail. That is, how you send mail to someone else is quite different from how you receive it. You can think of this difference as if you always had to go to the post office to send a letter, but you could only receive letters at your home or office. The post office becomes the "sending place" and your mailbox is your "receiving place."

POP for many, IMAP for some

You may be wondering why there are two ways to get your mail off the message store. After all, the store is just a hard disk — why do you need more than one way to access it? The quick answer is that POP came first and was fairly primitive, and IMAP is a more robust (but complicated) protocol than POP.

POP does a couple of useful tasks with the message store, and IMAP does all of what POP does and then some. The basic things POP does are:

✔ Logs you in so that only you (or anyone who knows your password) can look at your mail

✔ Tells you how many messages you have and how big each message is

✔ Copies the messages from the message store onto your computer

✔ Lets you delete the messages out of the message store

Notice that the last item says *lets you delete:* You are not forced to delete the messages from the message store after they get to your computer. Not deleting your messages is called *offline mode:* You connect to the POP server, get your mail, and then disconnect.

For example, assume that you are borrowing your friend's PC at her desk at work. You may want to just zip through your messages to check them but keep them in the message store, waiting to download and then delete them until you are at your own PC. Or you may want to delete some your messages if you're sure you don't care about them.

IMAP makes these decisions to delete easier and handles offline mode just fine. Many IMAP users leave all their messages on the IMAP server, copying only a few of them to their computer. In this case, Messenger remembers which of the messages you've already seen and which are new. You read your mail while still connected to the IMAP server, which is called *online mode*.

A third method, called *disconnected mode*, is a combination of offline and online mode. If you copy some of your messages to your PC (so that you can read them on the road, for example) but leave many on the IMAP server, Messenger has to not only keep track of what messages are new but also which messages you have moved from the server to your PC. This tracking is pretty complicated, but it's very useful if you travel with your PC a lot.

IMAP has many more features than just two additional modes. Because IMAP's designers saw how people were using POP over the years, they threw in a bunch of new capabilities that POP users wished they had, like allowing a single user to have multiple mailboxes that they can access as a group and letting groups of people share a single mailbox.

Today, most companies and ISPs still run POP. Even though IMAP has been around for years and has many great new features, only a small percentage of companies have switched to IMAP. However, that number is starting to rise quickly, and in a few years, IMAP servers are likely to outnumber POP servers.

In Internet mail parlance, you send using an *SMTP server,* and you receive from a *POP server* or an *IMAP server.* You probably don't need to know much about these servers other than their names, but it is handy to understand a bit so that you can see why Messenger has the settings it does.

 ✔ SMTP (Simple Mail Transport Protocol) is the method that moves mail over the Internet. Most messages only go between two servers: the originating server, where the message is posted, and the terminating server, where the message is received and then stored on the hard disk until the recipient comes to get it. Some messages bounce between three or four SMTP servers before getting to the terminating server. All servers that move the mail this way run SMTP.

 By the way, the *hard disk* in this case is called the *message store.* Actually, *message store* is a good term for what it is. Some SMTP servers write out messages as simple text objects, and others store them in complex databases. In fact, at big sites, the message store may be spread over many disks and even over many computers. Given the many ways that messages can be stored, calling it a message store is a good way to view it, like a giant file cabinet.

 ✔ POP and IMAP are methods used to get mail from the message store. You can think of the terminating server as the mailbox in front of your house; POP and IMAP are the ways you get the mail out of the mailbox. You don't need to know much about either of these protocols, other than to know that your Internet service provider (ISP) probably only uses one of the two, and you have to set up Messenger to use which- ever one your ISP uses.

Messages are amazingly flexible

If you started using e-mail five years ago, before the first version of Netscape had even come out, you would have found that you were often limited in the kind of messages you could send and receive. At that time, almost all e-mail programs could only send mail that was plain text and that didn't use any international characters, didn't have any formatting, and didn't include any pictures or other files. Life today is very different.

Mail messages can now contain all those features, and Communicator makes it easy to create messages with all of them in a single message, if you want. If you talk to someone who says, "But Internet mail messages can't have more than one attachment" (attachments are files that include a message) or "You can't make your messages look like a word-processing document," tell them to update their thinking. Better yet, use Communicator to send them a message so that they can see how much Internet mail really can do.

Usenet Isn't Really News

As I say in the early chapters of this book, Internet mail is a way to send a message from one person to another, whereas Usenet news distributes messages to millions of potential readers. The format of Internet mail and Usenet news messages is essentially the same, but there's a big difference in who sees what you write.

Netscape revolutionized Web browsers by having a really useful Usenet client built into it. In fact, Netscape's interface to Usenet is better than the ones on many of the dedicated Usenet news readers available for the PC and Macintosh. The only thing you need to be careful of when using Messenger's Usenet news features is to be sure that you know the difference between Usenet news and Internet mail; they look very similar in Communicator, and you can get confused as to which you are using.

Setting It All Up in Messenger

In order to use Netscape's e-mail or news features, you must first tell Netscape a bit about the servers you are using, and you should set some of your other preferences. All preferences are set in the Mail & Newsgroups category of the dialog box that you access with the Edit⇨Preferences command. This category has a bunch of different subcategories that affect the way that Messenger works.

Your Internet service provider probably can help you fill in many of the fields in this section, particularly the ones that relate to the servers you are using and your e-mail address. Check with your ISP before making these settings, because the folks there can help prevent mistakes that may cause you embarrassment or, even worse, lost mail.

General

The first subcategory, General, describes overall setup of Internet mail and Usenet news. The choices for this subcategory appear when you select the Mail & Newsgroups name in the Preferences dialog box (accessed with the Edit⇨Preferences command), as shown in Figure 9-1.

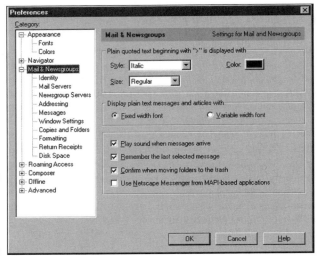

Figure 9-1:
Overall
settings for
Messenger.

As you see in Chapter 10, replying to messages you receive is a common practice. If someone replies to your message, their reply typically includes parts of your message, and each line of the part they have copied usually has a ">" symbol added to the beginning of each line. Messenger can detect this symbol in messages that you are reading and add different formatting to these sections.

When you get a message that has no formatting in it, Messenger displays it as plain text. In this case, you can choose whether to see the message with a *fixed-width font* (where each letter takes up the same amount of space on the screen, like the fonts on a typewriter) or a *proportional font* (where different letters have different widths, such as the font used in this book). The actual fonts used are the ones you select in the Fonts subcategory in the Appearance category of this dialog box, which I describe in Chapter 5.

The next set of four options is a hodge-podge of settings:

✔ **Play sound when messages arrive.** When you get a message, you can have Messenger play a sound. If you have Messenger retrieving your messages automatically, you may find this option useful, so that you know when something new arrives.

✔ **Remember the last selected message.** Each time you open Messenger, you can have it begin by showing you the last message you selected. This feature is useful when you don't remember what you were doing the last time you quit the program.

✔ **Confirm when moving folders to the trash.** As you see in Chapter 10, you can arrange your work area by creating folders that hold the messages you've received. You may also want to get rid of some of the folders you create, and this option lets you specify that you want to be warned when you toss out a folder.

✔ **Use Netscape Messenger from MAPI-based applications.** The last option tells Messenger that it can be used with programs that use MAPI, which is a non-Internet e-mail protocol. You can safely ignore this option.

Identity

Yes, you get to give yourself a real name, not just an Internet address, in the Identity subcategory. You can type whatever you want in the Your Name field, but remember that this name will be seen by anyone to whom you send mail or anyone who sees your Usenet postings. The Email Address field is for the address to which people will send you e-mail. You must also fill in your Reply To address if it is different than your mail address (it rarely is).

If you want, fill in an organization name, although this feature is not widely used. If you want to sign each outgoing mail message from Netscape with a standard signature, create a text file with the signature and specify that file with the Choose button. Some people create elaborate text signatures, but that has become less popular over the past few years, and many people now choose simple signatures, such as just their name or just their name and company name.

You can also choose to always attach your vCard (which Netscape still calls an *address book card*) to each message you send. A *vCard* is a specially-formatted attachment that contains the kind of information that appears on a business card, such as your name, phone number, and so on. Most modern e-mail clients, including Messenger, can read and write vCards. *Reading* a vCard means automatically creating entries for your address book (a task that is described later in this chapter).

Mail Servers

The Mail Servers subcategory gives all the information that Netscape needs in order to get your mail for you. If you used Netscape's standard installation, the choices here are already filled in for you; otherwise, you need to get this information from your ISP or from the mail administrator at your company.

Incoming servers

Messenger lets you collect your mail from more than one incoming mail server. Each mail server listed in the Incoming Mail Servers section has settings associated with it. You can create a new entry by clicking the Add button, and you can edit an entry you have already created with the Edit button. Figure 9-2 shows the dialog box that you see when you add or edit an incoming mail server.

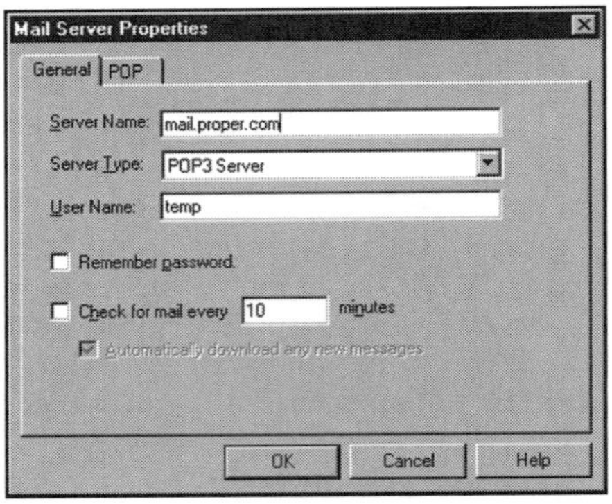

Figure 9-2:
Specifying an incoming mail server.

For each incoming mail server, you specify the server name (that is, the domain name of the server), the type of server (POP or IMAP), and your user name on that server. Note that your user name may be different than the name at which you receive your mail. This possibility is the primary reason I suggest that you talk to your ISP or mail administrator before you fill in this section.

You also can tell Messenger whether or not you want it to remember your password after you log in the first time. If you select this option, Messenger remembers your password and doesn't prompt you each time. The advantage of this option is that you don't have to type your password each time; the disadvantage is that if someone else gets access to your computer, they can read your new mail. I don't worry about someone else reading my mail too much, and I have the option selected. On the other hand, if you have a desktop PC at work and you worry about your co-workers reading your incoming mail, you should not select this option.

Messenger has a handy option that automatically checks for new mail every so often. If you have a constant connection to the Internet, this option can be really useful because you don't have to remember to check your mail yourself. On the other hand, I prefer to check my mail only when I feel like it, so that I feel a bit more in control of what's happening on my computer; therefore, I don't select this option. Also, if you are in a sea of cubicles, your neighbors may not appreciate hearing the announcement that you have new mail every time Messenger checks.

If you have said that you are using a POP server, the POP tab of this dialog box lets you specify whether to leave your mail on the POP server after you download it to your computer. Generally, you should not choose this option; if you do, your mailbox on the POP server will get very large. However, your server administrator may tell you to select this option in particular cases.

If you have said that you are using an IMAP server, you have many more options, because IMAP has many more options. Consult your mail administrator about how to set these options. When you talk to the administrator, be sure to tell him or her which version of Communicator you are using, because Netscape changes the options in this section relatively often.

Outgoing server

The Outgoing Mail (SMTP) Server is the domain name of the server you use for sending out e-mail. Occasionally, you may have a user name that you must use to send mail, although this arrangement is still rare. Some systems also protect your connection to your SMTP server with a security protocol called SSL (Secure Sockets Layer) or TLS (Transport Layer Security). Again, ask your ISP for the values that you should fill in here.

Newsgroup Servers

The Newsgroup Servers subcategory lets you set up your Usenet news servers. Messenger lets you have more than one server — for example, if you have a corporate news server and a separate server from your ISP. When you add a newsgroup server, you need to know the domain name of the server and whether that server requires you to log in with a name and password. Again, ask your ISP or news administrator about these settings.

Addressing

When you want to send a message to someone, you need to know her e-mail address. If you don't know her address off the top of your head, Messenger can look it up in your address book or in a directory on the Internet (Netscape calls this automatic looking up *pinpoint addressing*). Netscape runs such a directory through its Netcenter service. In the Addressing subcategory, you can tell Messenger where to look if you enter a name that is not an e-mail address.

Note that the information in any Internet-based directory can be wrong or out of date. If a directory has an address for someone and that person changes his address, the directory may not get updated. Don't assume that a person's listing in a directory means that it is safe to send a message to the address listed there. For example, if you are sending a private message, sending it to the wrong address would allow someone else to see the message. Similarly, sending a time-urgent message to an address that is years out of date could mean that the intended recipient would never see the message.

Messages

When you reply to a message, you often want to copy some or all of that message in your reply. For example, if someone asks you whether you want to have lunch on Thursday and you reply with a single word "Yes," that person may not remember to what you are replying. Instead, it's better to copy the question you were asked into your reply. Similarly, when someone sends you a message that you want to forward to another person, you often want to add a note saying something like, "I got this message from Chris and I agree with her thinking," instead of just sending the message with no note.

The first option of the Messages subcategory lets you describe how to forward a message. The most common choice is Quoted, meaning that the original message is part of the message you are sending and Messenger makes it clear that the quoted material is a reply. The Inline option tells Messenger to put the original message into the forwarded one but not to make it clear that you are creating a reply. As Attachment indicates that the forwarded message comes as an attached file, an option that is rarely used.

Most people also choose to add their replies below the quoted text, not above it.

No one has perfect spelling. If you're like me, you should probably check your spelling before sending mail messages so you can avoid embarrassing mistakes. Messenger lets you check your spelling quickly and easily, and the option in this subcategory tells Messenger to do so every time you're about to send a message.

Different Internet mail clients create text messages differently. Some wrap each line at about 75 characters per line, and others create long lines of text and expect the recipient's mail client to wrap the text correctly when it is being displayed. Because of this variance, you may need to select the Wrap Incoming, Plain Text Messages to Window Width option, although most users don't need this setting. You always want Messenger to wrap your outgoing plain text messages, and the default value of 72 characters is a good value.

If you create a message that has 8-bit characters, such as international characters, Netscape has to choose whether or not to send them directly. Your two choices are to send them As-Is, which doesn't work with a few older mail servers, or to send them as Quoted Printable, which doesn't work with many mail clients. My suggestion is to use the first choice (send them As-Is) because most mail systems are able to handle these characters now.

Window Settings

Messenger has two basic layouts for its main window, as you can see at the top of Figure 9-3. If you have many folders or are subscribed to numerous Usenet newsgroups, you probably want to choose the first layout choice (the one on the left) so that your list can go all the way down the length of the screen. However, the layout on the right gives you a wider screen for your messages.

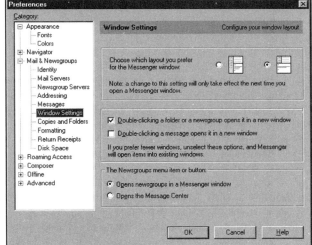

Figure 9-3:
Window
layout
settings.

Because you can get too much information on a single screen, Netscape lets you choose whether to open separate windows for each message you read or to use only the main mail or news windows to see the messages. I normally choose not to use just the main window; this decision means that I have to switch back and forth between the main window and the message window, but I get to see more in each window. You should try both reusing and not reusing and see which choice best suits you.

The last option in this category lets you choose what happens when you say you want to look at newsgroups. The first choice opens a window just for newsgroups, and the second option opens the Message Center, from which you can also read your mail.

Copies and Folders

In the Copies and Folders subcategory, you can choose where to send copies of outgoing mail and Usenet messages. These options let you always send copies of the messages you create to yourself so that you can keep them for future reference. You can store a copy of the outgoing messages in a mail folder, or you can have Messenger send a blind carbon copy (that is, a copy that no one who gets the message sees) of each message to a particular e-mail address (usually your own address). It is generally best to just store the copies in the default mail folders listed.

Formatting

Netscape lets you specify how outgoing messages are formatted. This feature is important because some mail users have different capabilities than others, and you want to be sure to send messages that your recipients can read. For example, the first choice is whether to send HTML-formatted messages by default. I suggest that you *not* select this option because many people still don't have HTML-enhanced mail clients. You particularly don't want to send HTML-formatted messages to a mailing list, because probably many people on the mailing list don't have HTML-enabled mail clients. You can still choose to use HTML formatting when you send individual messages, as you see in Chapter 10.

Because many people can't receive HTML-formatted messages, Messenger lets you specify in your address book whether or not a particular person can receive HTML. When you're about to send an HTML-formatted message, Messenger checks your address book. If the recipient is listed as being able to accept HTML, that's fine, but if not, Messenger needs to know what to do. The four choices in this subcategory tell Messenger what to do if it doesn't know whether a recipient can accept HTML in e-mail:

- Ask you what to do each time this situation occurs
- Automatically convert the message to plain text
- Always send the message with HTML
- Send the message as both plain text and HTML

The last option should never be chosen, in my opinion. Sending the message as both plain text and HTML causes your messages to be twice as long, and people who can't read HTML see the HTML at the bottom of your message every time anyway.

Return Receipts

Modern Internet mail clients can request and generate receipts so that the sender knows what happens to the message after he or she sends it. Return receipts come in two flavors: *MDNs* (Message Delivery Notifications) and *DSNs* (Delivery Status Notifications). MDNs come from the recipient's mail client, and DSNs come from the recipient's mail host. Thus, an MDN tells you whether the person you sent the message to got the message; a DSN tells you whether the recipient's mail host got the message.

You can tell Messenger that you want receipts on the messages you send. You can chose to request an MDN, a DSN, or both. Because you can get many receipts, it is common to have all the receipts you get automatically moved to your Sent Mail folder so that you don't see them in your Inbox, but you can still find them if you want to determine whether the recipient got your message.

Messenger can take different actions when someone asks for a receipt from you. Your two choices are to always refuse or to return receipts based on some criteria. You can specify whether you should always return a receipt, never return a receipt, or have Messenger prompt you when someone sends a receipt request to you.

Disk Space

If you have a slow Internet connection, you may not want to download large messages until your connection is faster. The first choice in the Disk Space subcategory lets you tell Messenger not to download large messages and to specify what you consider large.

If you have a limited amount of space on your hard disk, you can tell Messenger to compact the folders it stores your messages in if space is being wasted. This compacting takes a bit of time, so you don't want to do it often, but it can save a great amount of space if you move messages from one folder to another often.

You can also tell Messenger what to do with old Usenet news articles. Generally, you should leave these settings alone because changing them may cause Messenger to delete Usenet news articles that you may be interested in.

It's Not Little, and It's Not Black, but It's Your Address Book

Enough of mail settings. When you think of sending a postal letter, you don't need to set a whole bunch of user options for your pen, your paper, or even your stamps. But you often need an important piece of hardware: an address book. Unless you remember everyone's postal address, you're not going to be able to send mail without a list of the names and addresses of your potential recipients.

Sending e-mail is no different. Fortunately, Messenger comes with a great address book that lets you store everyone's names and e-mail addresses in one easy-to-use program. In fact, you can store plenty of non-e-mail information about them as well, such as their postal address, phone number, and so on. It's an all-in-one address book that has special properties for sending e-mail.

Communicator's address book keeps its entries in what it calls *address book cards.* These cards use a format called *vCard,* which is a standard way to keep information that may appear on a printed business card. The advantage of this feature is that you can mail out your own vCard, and when someone sends you her vCard, you can easily add it to your address book.

No more crossed-out entries!

In typical paper-based address books, you have a limited amount of space for each letter. Worse yet, because of the properties of paper, if you change someone's address too many times, the new address becomes unreadable due to imperfect erasures. Messenger's address book has none of these problems.

Because of all these features, you can use the address book for all your personal contact needs, not just for keeping track of e-mail addresses. Instead of keeping some of your contacts in a word processing program, some in a database, and some in Messenger, you can put them all in one place.

You access the address book with the Communicator⇨Address Book command. Figure 9-4 shows the Address Book window. The left column is a list of address books, as well as some directory servers from which you can get addresses. The right column shows the contents of the selected address book.

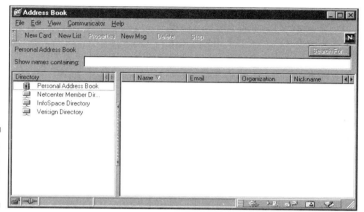

Figure 9-4:
The address book.

Careful readers note that I said "address books" in the previous paragraph. Messenger lets you keep more than one address book, such as if you have a personal address book and a company address book. You can add address books to the address book window with the File⇨New Address Book command. However, I generally recommend that you keep everything in one address book in order to make searching easier.

Entering a card in the address book is easy: Give the File⇨New Card command, or select the New Card button near the top of the window. You see the dialog box shown in Figure 9-5. Note that this dialog box has four tabs: Name, Contact, Notes, and Conferencing. The Name tab and the Contact tab have the fields into which you will enter information.

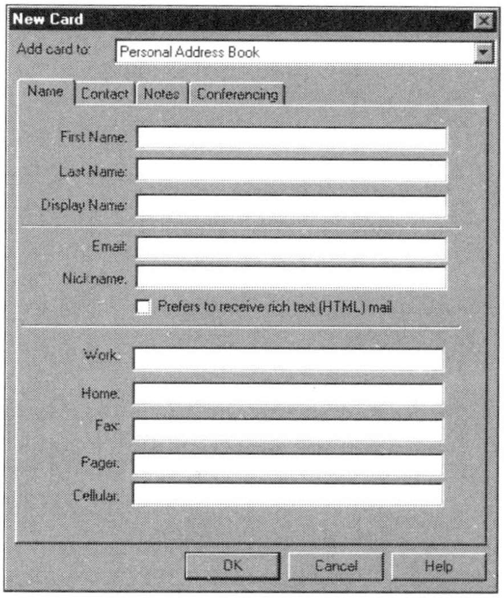

Figure 9-5:
Entering a new card.

Editing an existing card is similar to adding one. There are three different ways to start editing a card: Double-click on the card in the right panel of the address book, select the card and choose Edit⊳Properties, or select the card and click the Properties button near the top of the window.

Automating entries with vCard

When you create a message, you can attach your vCard to it (see Chapter 10), which is a handy way to let someone know your contact information.

On the other hand, when someone sends you a message with his vCard attached, Communicator asks you whether you want to add the vCard to your address book. You don't have to accept it, of course, because you may not ever want to communicate with that person again, but if you may, let Communicator fill in your address book with that person's information. Letting Communicator do so is, of course, much easier than you typing in the information yourself.

Accessing an LDAP directory for addresses

Yet another way to get information for filling in your address book is by downloading it from a directory on the Internet. Netscape keeps a directory of its Netcenter users, and many other services and companies make their directories available as well. For example, many large companies keep their corporate directories on directory servers.

The protocol most commonly used for these directories is called *LDAP*, which is an abbreviation for Lightweight Directory Access Protocol. Some companies make their LDAP servers accessible by anyone, and others restrict access only to people who work for their company.

Netscape provides access to many Internet directories from the address book window. If you want to search one of the directories, select the directory's name from the left column, enter the name you want to search for, and click the Search button.

Making mailing lists

Sometimes you want to send mail to more than one person at a time. If you frequently send messages to a particular group of people, you can make a mailing list of those folks in the address book. To create a mail list, choose File⊳New⊳List or click the New List button. You see the dialog box in Figure 9-6.

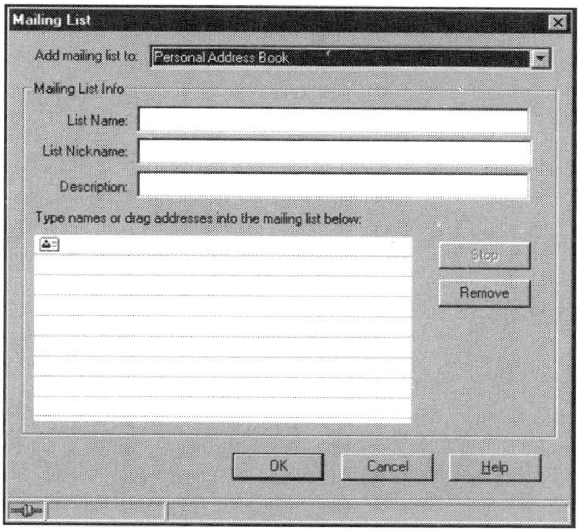

Figure 9-6:
Entering a
new mailing
list.

Each list can have a name and a nickname, just like people in your address book. You can also give the list a short description. Enter each e-mail address for the list on a separate line in the main part of the dialog box. If some of the members of your list are already in your address book, you can drag their card entries from the address book to the dialog box instead of typing their e-mail addresses.

Chapter 10
There's Something in Your Mailbox

In This Chapter

▶ Getting mail into Messenger

▶ Receiving messages and files

▶ Organizing all your messages

▶ Reading Usenet news

*I*t may be better to give than to receive, but it sure is fun to receive e-mail. Many new Internet users are much more comfortable with getting e-mail than they are with sending mail because they worry that they'll make mistakes when they create messages. Becoming comfortable with getting mail makes you much more comfortable with sending mail, so I've put this chapter on using Messenger to receive mail before the chapter on sending mail.

Of course, in order for you to use the information in this chapter, you have to have received some mail. Fortunately, getting some mail sent to you is pretty easy. These days, you probably have plenty of friends, coworkers, or relatives who can send and receive Internet mail. Ask a couple of them to send you a message or two. Just be sure to tell them that you may not respond to their first messages immediately because you're "still getting used to this Internet stuff."

Getting to Know the Messenger Window

Before you read your mail, you first have to have Messenger open. If you haven't done so already, choose the <u>C</u>ommunicator⇨<u>M</u>essenger command to display Messenger's window. Or you can click on the second icon from the left (the one that looks like a letter sitting in an inbox) in the component bar instead. The main Messenger window opens.

Messenger has three main panels, as shown in Figure 10-1. The top-left panel is called the *folder list,* and it shows your mail folders. Mail messages are stored in mail folders. You always have a main folder, called Local Mail, which has other folders in it (these are sometimes called *subfolders*). The folders that you start with (such as Inbox, Unsent Messages, and Trash) have special properties, and you see later in this chapter how to create other folders to help you organize the mail that you receive.

You can change the size and shape of the three panes in Messenger. Drag the borders of the panes to make them wider or taller, depending on the location of the panes. You can also click the gray dotted bars near the middle of the panes to quickly make one of the panes disappear without having to drag it. If you never want to see a particular pane, you can make it go away with the View⇨Show command.

Messenger has a different toolbar than Navigator. Some of the buttons in the Messenger toolbar are specific to Internet mail (just as the buttons in the Communicator toolbar are specific to the Web). For example, the first two buttons in the toolbar, Get Msg and New Msg, are for retrieving your messages and for creating new outgoing messages, respectively. Other buttons, like Print and Stop, act the same in Messenger as they do in Communicator.

Folder list   Message pane   Message list

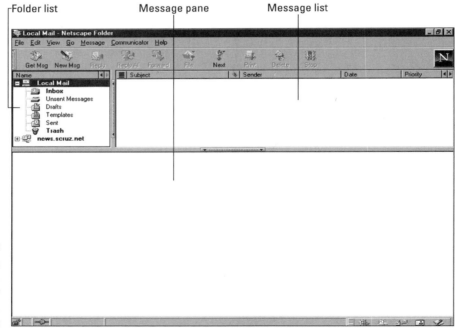

Figure 10-1:
The main
Messenger
window.

Getting Your Mail

Your mail is held for you at your incoming mail server until you retrieve it in Messenger. At that point, it may reside on your computer, or it may still reside on the incoming mail server. Why the ambiguity here? It depends on whether your incoming mail server uses the POP or IMAP protocols, and whether your system administrator has you leaving the mail on the server or on your computer. These concepts are covered in Chapter 9 and are quite important, so you may want to review that chapter before reading on.

Most people take their mail off the incoming mail server each time they check their mail. That means that, after you get your mail, it is kept on your computer until you choose to delete it. If you leave your mail on the incoming mail server, it is kept there until you tell the server to delete it. Deleting mail that you've already read is covered later in this chapter.

To get your new mail, click on the Get Msg button in the Messenger window or choose the File⇨Get New Messages command. Either method causes Messenger to go to the incoming mail server that you specified with the Edit⇨Preferences command (refer to Chapter 9) and log in. If you are not connected to the Internet when you give this command, Messenger asks whether you want to connect. If you have new mail, Messenger retrieves it and puts it in the Inbox subfolder of your Local Mail folder.

Looking through a folder

Getting mail isn't interesting unless you can read it. To read messages in a folder, simply select the name of the folder in the folder list. The top-right panel, called the *message list*, then lists the messages in that folder. For example, Figure 10-2 shows the contents of a typical Inbox (of course, your Inbox is different because you have received different mail than I have). Each row in the message list indicates an individual message. To see the contents of a message, simply select it in the message list; the contents appear in the bottom pane of the window.

The message list has many columns. Initially, the columns you can see are

- **Subject** of the message
- Whether the message has been read
- The message's **Sender**
- **Date** the message was sent
- **Priority** of the message

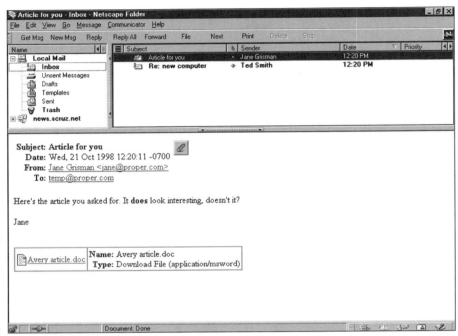

Figure 10-2:
Looking at
your Inbox
with
Messenger.

The subject, sender, date, and priority are set by the sender of the message. The read or unread flag (the light green diamond or dot in the second column) is set by Messenger. When you first receive a message, it is set as a diamond, meaning that you haven't read it. After you look at the message, the diamond turns to a dot, indicating that you have read the message at least once. After you read a message, the text for that message's row changes from bold to plain.

The column headers at the top of the message list are not just decorative. If you click on one of the column headers, Messenger sorts the messages based on that column. For example, clicking on the Date column header arranges the messages by date, clicking on the Subject column header alphabetizes the column by subject, and so on. If you click on a column header a second time, the order of the column reverses, from last to first. You can also choose the sorting of the messages from the View⇨Sort command.

Each message line also has other columns that are not initially visible. Notice the tiny left-pointing and right-pointing triangles at the right of the column headers. If you click on the left-pointing button, you see additional columns, including a personal flag that you can use for making your own notations of groups of files (you set the flag by clicking on the dot), an "extended" **Status** indicator, and message **Size**.

You can change the width of the columns and rearrange the order of the columns. To make a column wider or narrower, put the pointer on the right border of the column header and drag the border in either direction. To rearrange the columns, click on a column header and drag it to a new position.

Following threads through the cloth

When you have just a few messages, it's easy to keep track of them by looking at the subject line. However, imagine that a friend sends you a message, you reply to it, she replies to you, and so on. The subjects for all the replies are the same, making it harder to follow who said what when as you look in the message list.

Messenger helps make viewing these kinds of lists easier with threads. A *thread* is a chain of messages. If you sort your message list by thread instead of by subject, all the messages that are from the same back-and-forth discussion are grouped together. You can sort by thread by clicking on the far-left header in the message list (the one with four horizontal lines).

Using threads is particularly useful when reading Usenet news because Usenet conversations often include a great deal of banter back and forth, which is exactly what threads are good for tracking. For example, in Figure 10-3, notice the hierarchy of the threads in the Subject column.

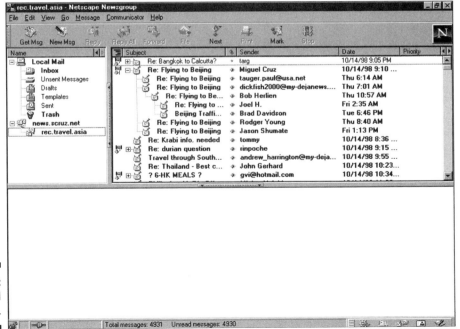

Figure 10-3:
Threaded
messages.

Using this threaded view, you can quickly hide all the messages of a thread that you aren't interested in by clicking on the minus sign at the left of the hierarchy. Similarly, a collapsed thread has a plus sign (+) at its left, and clicking on that plus sign exposes all the messages in the thread.

Reading the message

Of course, you don't just want to look at the messages as a group; you want to read individual messages. Reading messages is easy: Select the message from the message list, and it appears in the *message pane* in the lower half of the window. To read another message, just select a different one in the folder list.

Because the message pane is fairly small, reading the message in the message pane may be, well, a pain. You can easily create a new window that contains just the message (no folder list or message list) by double-clicking on a message in the message list. Messenger opens another window with just that message. If you keep this window open and double-click on another message in the message list, Messenger uses the already-opened window for displaying the new message. The Next button shows you the message after this one in the message list, and the Delete button (no surprise) deletes the message you are reading.

Mail messages have headers that may or may not be useful as you read a message. Standard headers include Subject, Date sent, the name of the Sender, and so on. Many less-useful headers may also come on a message. Messenger usually shows you only a useful subset of headers on a message. To see all the headers, give the View➪Headers➪All command. The View➪Headers➪Brief command shows you only the most important headers (Subject, From, and To).

Reading mail offline

After you receive your mail, you can read your messages at your leisure because they now reside on your computer. You don't have to be connected to the Internet to read your mail, so if you connect to the Internet through a modem, you can hang up and still read your mail after downloading it from the mail server.

Reading your mail when not connected to the Internet is called working in *offline mode*. If you have a full-time connection to the Internet, such as an Ethernet connection at your work, you never need to go into offline mode because it doesn't cost anything extra to stay connected. However, if you or your company has a part-time connection through a modem, disconnecting when you are not getting your mail or using the Web can save money.

To switch between the two modes, choose the File➪Offline➪Work Online or File➪Offline➪Work Offline commands. You can tell whether you are in online or offline mode by looking in the lower right of the Messenger window. The icon that looks like a plug (it's in the third box from the left) is the online indicator. If the plug is connected, you are in online mode; if it looks un-plugged, you are in offline mode. You can also switch between the two modes by clicking on this icon.

One disadvantage of reading mail in offline mode is that some messages have links to the Web embedded in the message, and those links are not readable if you are offline. A message that contains pictures, for example, may have come with the pictures as part of the message, but more likely came with links to a Web site that has the pictures. When you read that message in offline mode, you can't see the pictures. Figure 10-4 shows how such a message may look.

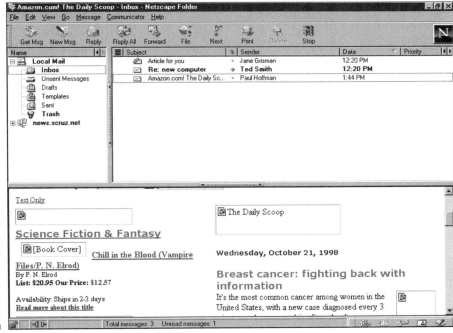

Figure 10-4:
A message with pictures being read in offline mode.

Organizing Your Messages in Folders

I tend to collect everything and only throw things away under duress. Of course, this propensity leads to my having to organize an awful lot of old material. All my old papers go into folders organized by topic. All my old e-mail messages go into mail folders, also organized by topic.

Moving messages

You can move a message from one folder to another by opening the folder that the message is in, selecting the message in the message list, and dragging the message to the name of the folder that you want to move it to in the folder list. You can also select one or more messages, choose the Message⇨Move Message command, and then select the folder to which you want to move the message.

Creating folders

Of course, moving a message doesn't do you much good unless you have a good place to move it. Thus, you need to create new folders and subfolders for your messages; otherwise, you'll probably leave them all in the Inbox folder. Use the File⇨New⇨Folder command to create a new folder. The dialog box for that command lets you enter the name of the folder you are creating. The dialog box also lets you specify the folder under which the new folder will be a subfolder.

Copying messages to other folders

The Message⇨Copy Message command is very useful for organizing your mail. This command makes a copy of the message in the different folder. I can hear some of you saying, "Great, now I'll have twice as much mail!" But you may find a good reason to keep copies in different folders. Imagine that you have one set of folders relating to the different projects you work on and another set of folders for people you work with. What if you get a message that relates to a specific project from one of your coworkers? Do you file that message under the project or the person? My suggestion: Put it in the project folder and then copy it from that folder to the person folder.

Searching through your old mail

If you're like me, you have a wonderful organization for all your folders, but your organization doesn't always work. Sometimes, you want to find a message that you got a long time ago, but you don't remember what folder you put it in. Fortunately, Messenger makes it easy to find messages regardless of what folder they're in.

The Edit⇨Search Messages command is a powerful and flexible way to find the needle in the haystack. You can specify text to look for in the message and the part of the message that the text appeared in, such as a specific header or the body of the message. This trick is handy if you remember that the message has a particular set of words in the subject or that it is from a particular person.

You can also specify which folders to search in. If you have no idea where the message is, you can search the Local Mail folder, but if you have an idea which folder or subfolder the message is in, you can make the search go faster by limiting it to that folder. The command also has options to tell Messenger whether to look in subfolders.

Deleting folders

You can move your folders around like you move messages: Select the folder and drag it to the desired new location. To delete a folder that you no longer want, select the folder and click the Delete button in the toolbar or choose Edit⇨Delete Folder.

Be careful when you delete folders; deleting a folder that has messages in it deletes all the messages as well. If you accidentally delete a folder, find it in the Trash folder and drag it out to the Local Mail folder.

Unless you get an awful lot of messages, keeping all your old messages is perfectly reasonable. Many people think, "Oh, that would fill up my hard disk," but very few people get more than a megabyte a week of e-mail. Even at that rate, it would take you nearly two years to fill 100 megabytes with your old mail, and most people have way more than 100 megabytes free on their hard drives. Of course, keeping all the old messages doesn't serve much purpose unless you have them organized in a way that allows you to find the ones you need when you need them.

Handling Attachments

Mail messages are often more than just text. When you receive a message, it can have one or more *attachments,* or files, that come with it. In fact, anything that you can store as a file on disk can be an attachment to a message.

Attachments are a very useful way to pass information over the Internet. For example, if someone has a word processing document that he wants you to review, he can easily attach the file to a message and send it to you. A message can have many attachments, and the attachments can be of any size.

Well, almost any size. When someone sends you a message with one or more large files attached, downloading the message from your incoming mail server to your computer takes a long time if you're using a modem. Modems only go so fast, and a typical 28.8 Kbps modem takes about a minute to download a file that is 125K. A file that is a megabyte can take nearly ten minutes.

After you download your messages, the attached file is indicated in the message with a button that has a paper clip on it near the top of the message. Figure 10-5 shows an example of a message that has one attachment. If you want to view the attachment, you click on the button in the message, just as you would click on a link in a Web page. Messenger then prompts you to save the attachment on your hard drive.

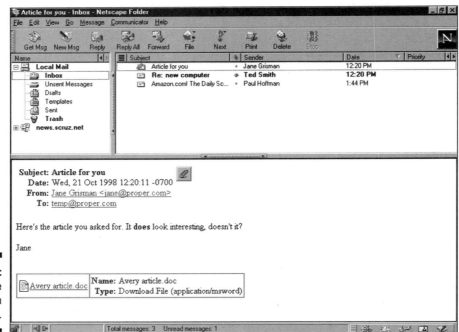

Figure 10-5:
A message with an attachment.

Starting Up with Usenet News

Usenet news is arranged in newsgroups, with each newsgroup having messages in it. Messenger arranges the newsgroups you want to read like e-mail folders, so reading Usenet messages is almost identical to reading mail messages. (The basics of Usenet are covered in Chapter 9.) The main difference between reading Usenet news and e-mail is that your Usenet news is arranged under a folder with the name of your mail server instead of under the Local Mail folder. If you specified more than one Usenet news server through the Edit⇨Preferences command, each of those servers is listed in the folder list of the Messenger window.

Finding your groups

The other important difference between reading your mail and reading Usenet news is that you do not create new folders in the news server when you want to specify a newsgroup to read from. Instead, you *subscribe* to a newsgroup with the File⇨Subscribe command. This command shows you the dialog box in Figure 10-6.

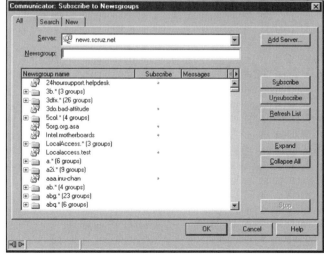

Figure 10-6:
List of
all the
newsgroups
you can
subscribe
to.

The first tab of this dialog box lists all the newsgroups that are known by your news server. The groups are shown in *hierarchies,* which is the method used to organize the thousands of newsgroups. For example, the alt. hierarchy is shown in a single level until you click on the plus sign (+) to the left of the name to expose the next level of the hierarchy, and so on. You can also use the Expand and Collapse buttons in the dialog box to show and hide parts of the hierarchy.

To subscribe to one of the listed newsgroups, select it in the list and click the Subscribe button. When you do so, Messenger changes the small dot to the right of the newsgroup name into a check mark so that you can tell which newsgroups you are subscribed to. You can unsubscribe from a newsgroup by selecting the newsgroup and then clicking the Unsubscribe button.

The Search tab is useful when you want to subscribe to a group but you are not sure of its name. Instead of searching through the hierarchies in the All tab, you can enter a part of the name in the Search tab, and Messenger lists all the groups that have that name in them.

Reading Usenet messages

After you subscribe to the groups you want to read, Usenet is fairly easy to navigate. You can select a newsgroup to view from the folder list, and the current messages are shown in the message list. To look at a particular message, click on it in the message list, or double-click it to open a window with just the message in it.

Chapter 11

Getting the Word Out with Messenger

In This Chapter

▶ Sending messages and replying to messages that you've received

▶ Formatting the text in your messages

▶ Attaching files to your messages

▶ Posting to Usenet news groups

*A*lmost everyone loves to read e-mail, but some people don't like to send it. As you see in Chapter 10, reading mail in Messenger is easy. Sending mail is easy, too. Of course, it's only easy if you like doing it, and I hope that I can convince you that sending mail is nothing to be afraid of. Sending Internet mail opens up a great communication medium to you.

Creating an E-Mail Message

When you compose a message, you do three simple things:

✔ Say where the message is going

✔ Indicate what it is about

✔ Put in the content of the message

You can do these tasks in any order. When you finish creating your message, you tell Messenger to send the message over the Internet.

To start creating a message from Communicator or from Messenger, choose File⇨New⇨Message. If you already have the Messenger window open, you can instead choose Message⇨New Message or click on the New Msg button. All these commands do the same thing: They bring up an empty New Message window, as shown in Figure 11-1.

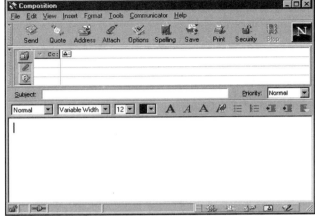

Figure 11-1:
Creating a
new e-mail
message.

The message creation window has a few areas that control what goes into your message. Under the message toolbar is the *addressing area,* which has three tabs along the left side and a large area to the right to enter information about where the message is going. Beneath that area is the *subject line,* where you enter the subject of your letter. Beneath that is the formatting toolbar, which you use if you want to add formatting to the text of your message, and the bottom of the window is the *message area* that you use to enter and edit your message.

Where is it going?

You specify the address or addresses of the people to whom you want to send the message in the addressing area. Messenger gives you many ways to add e-mail addresses to your message:

✔ You can type in an address by clicking to the right of the To button in the addressing area.

✔ You can open the address book (described in Chapter 9) and drag entries from the address book to the addressing area.

✔ If you have copied an address to the Clipboard (for example, you select it in a document and use the Copy command), you can paste it in the addressing area.

To remove someone that you have added to the addresses, click on the icon to the left of that person's name and press the Delete key or choose Edit⇨Delete.

Messenger has a feature called *pinpoint addressing* that lets it help you complete an address that you're typing as you type it. For pinpoint addressing to work, you have to turn it on in the Addressing subsection of the Mail and Newsgroups section of the dialog box that you open with the Edit⇔Preferences command. In that dialog box, you can tell Messenger whether to compare what you are typing to just your address book or to an address server on the Internet.

If you have pinpoint addressing turned on, type in part of the name you want to address the message to and then press Enter. Messenger looks up what you typed in your address book and the Internet service you specified and lets you choose which of the addresses it finds you want to use. You can then click on one of those addresses, and Messenger fills in the whole address in the addressing area for you.

You do not need to put everyone you are sending the message to in the To header of the message. If you click on the To button for an address, you see other choices for the header. Cc is another header that appears in messages, so if you put someone in the Cc header, it's like announcing to everyone who got the message, "I sent this person a copy of the message." The Bcc header is different: The message goes to the person you list in the Bcc header, but no one else who gets the message knows that you sent it to the person in the Bcc header (Bcc stands for *blind carbon copy*).

Adding the subject and body of the message

Of course, a message is more than just its address. You want to add a subject to the message and the body of the message. The subject, which can be only one line long, goes in the subject line, next to the Subject label. Most mail programs (including Messenger) show the subject to the recipient before he opens the message, so you want to put something in the subject that makes him want to open the message.

The body of the message is where you put the main content. You can type text into the body, or you can paste text that you have in the Clipboard into the message area.

You can also format the text in the message area with the buttons on the formatting toolbar or the commands in the Format menu. If you add formatting to your message, Messenger changes the message type from *plain text* to *HTML*. HTML is the method of formatting used by most modern mail programs, but not all recipients can read messages that are formatted with HTML. Unless you know that the people you are sending the message to can read HTML, you should not use formatting, because adding HTML makes it much harder for people with older or more limited mail programs to read your message.

HTML is covered in much more detail in Part V of this book. In those chapters, you see how to use Composer's HTML formatting commands to create Web pages. The same commands are available to you in Messenger for creating HTML mail messages. Instead of covering the commands twice in the book, I refer you to those chapters.

You've written it: Now send it!

The last step, sending the message, is the easiest. After you compose your message and say where it is going, and you're sure you want to send it, simply click on the Send button or choose File⇨Send Now. Messenger contacts your outgoing mail server, passes it the message, and closes the message window. You're done! The message is on its way. If you instead choose the File⇨Send Later command, Messenger puts the message in your Unsent Mail folder and sends it later when you choose to send other messages.

Going Back and Forth: Replying to and Forwarding Messages

If someone has sent you a message and you want to respond to that person, you do not need to start a new, empty message for your response. When reading your mail, you can *reply* to the message, which causes Messenger to start a new message that already contains a copy of the message you are responding to and that is already addressed to the person who sent you the original message.

To reply to a message you are reading in Messenger, simply click the Reply button or choose Message⇨Reply. (If the message had more than one addressee, the Reply All button or the Message⇨Reply to All command addresses the reply to all the original recipients, not just the person who sent the original message.) For example, Figure 11-2 shows the message window immediately after clicking the Reply button. Notice how the To header already has the address; the subject has been prefaced with "Re:"; and the message is filled in. The vertical bar down the left side of some of the text in the message area indicates that the marked text is from the original message to you.

You can edit a message that you are replying to; in fact, this is probably the reason you are replying. For example, you may want to say, "Yes, I agree with that" after one of the paragraphs in the message. You use the same editing techniques to edit the message you are sending back to the original sender as you do when you are creating a new message.

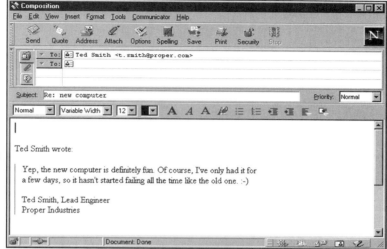

Figure 11-2:
A reply,
already
filled in by
Messenger.

Often, you want to take a message that someone has sent to you and send it to someone else. For example, if your boss sends you a message and you want a coworker to see the message, you may want to send that coworker a copy of the message without bothering your boss. In this case, you *forward* the message you got to your coworker.

Forwarding works just like replying, except that Messenger does not pre-address the message. That is, when you're reading a message and click the Forward button or choose Message⇨Forward, Messenger creates a new message with the content of the original message, but the To field is empty. You can then add one or more addresses to this message and send it.

Attaching Files to a Message

In the early days of the Internet, mail could only be used for sending messages (and not even messages with formatting). Since around 1995, however, almost every Internet mail client has allowed you to also send files with your messages. When you create a message with Messenger, you can attach one or more files to your message; that's why the files that come with a message are commonly called *attachments*.

Sending Web pages

Not all message attachments come from your hard disk. Messenger allows you to send pages directly from the Web in your messages. Sending Web pages is very convenient because it gives you a quick way to send some information you find on the Web to someone who you think is interested in the content of the Web page.

You can send Web pages while you are browsing the Web in Communicator or directly from Messenger.

- ✔ In Communicator, choose File⇨Send Page to send the page you are currently looking at.

- ✔ In Messenger, start a new message and choose File⇨Attach⇨Web Page command or click the Attach button. Messenger then opens up a dialog box, asking you for the URL of the Web page you want to send.

You can send more than one Web page in a message, although some mail programs have a hard time displaying multiple Web pages in a single message (Messenger does this chore just fine, however).

To attach a file to a message, click on the Attach button or choose File⇨Attach⇨File. Messenger prompts you for the name of the file you want to attach. You can type in the full path to the file, but most people find it easier to get the name of the file by using the Browse button. After you attach a file, you can see the list of files that you have attached to your message by clicking on the paperclip icon in the addressing area or choosing View⇨Attachments.

You may think that sending huge files through Internet mail is convenient, but the receiver of the message may not. For example, she may have a much slower Internet connection than you do, and if she has to spend an hour downloading the file you sent her, she may not be too happy with you. Some people might think that a 50K file is large, while other people wouldn't mind getting messages that are a megabyte or more. Before sending a large file, check with the recipient and warn her about the size.

Checking Your Spelling

If you have perfect spelling, feel free to skip over this part. If you're like the majority of people, however, you probably need help with catching spelling mistakes in what you write. Some people (like me!) are pretty hopeless when it comes to spelling and can never remember things like whether *surprise* has an "s" or a "z" in it.

To help avoid embarrassing yourself when you write e-mails, run Messenger's spelling checker before you send off a message. You can do this any time you're writing a message. Simply click the Spelling button or choose Tools⇨Check Spelling.

Messenger's spelling checker has a similar interface to the spelling checkers you may be familiar with in word processing programs. It finds words that it does not recognize, suggests possible alternatives, and lets you add new words to its dictionary.

If your spelling is really atrocious, you may need more than just Messenger's spelling checker. For example, you may have spelled a word so badly that Messenger can't guess what word you mean. At that point, you probably have to resort to a paper-based dictionary. Because my spelling is so bad, I use the "three-foot rule" when I write e-mail: I never write e-mail if I'm more than three feet from a dictionary.

Creating Usenet Messages

As you can see in Chapter 10, reading your mail and reading Usenet news is almost identical. When you create a new Usenet message (which is also called *posting* to Usenet) or when you reply to a Usenet message, Messenger uses the same dialog box it uses when you create mail. Figure 11-3 shows the window when replying to a posting. Notice that the address area has the header listed as "Group" instead of "To." That's the only difference you see when creating Usenet messages.

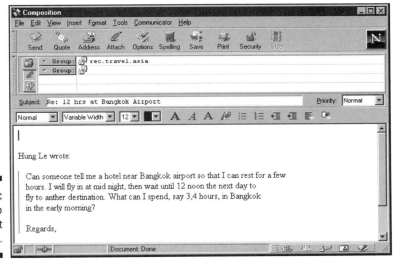

Figure 11-3: Replying to a Usenet posting.

Be careful about how you post to Usenet, however. Many Usenet readers cannot deal with HTML postings. Thus, the warning that I gave for sending e-mail formatted with HTML is even more relevant here. On the other hand, more and more users are getting HTML-aware Usenet readers (like Messenger), and many people do include attachments, pictures, and formatted text in their Usenet postings today.

Chapter 12
Making Mail Even Better

- -

In This Chapter
▶ Having Messenger help you organize your mail
▶ Exploring digital signatures and encrypted e-mail
▶ Getting and sending receipts
▶ Sending instant messages

- -

*A*s you probably have discovered already, Messenger has a plethora of features that you use when you receive and send e-mail. Many of those features mimic things that you do when you send and receive regular paper mail, but others are unique to electronic messages. This chapter covers a few more advanced ways to use Messenger that are a little like paper mail but have a very different feel to them.

Getting Organized by Filtering Messages

Most homes and businesses get their mail once a day. On heavy mail days, I can spend quite a bit of time just sorting through all the letters, magazines, and catalogs before I even get to read them. With e-mail, the problems are similar: You get a slew of messages, and you want to separate them into piles such as "I need to read this now," "This can wait a while," "Throw this away immediately," and "I can't tell what to do with this until I open it."

Fortunately, Messenger's filtering feature makes this kind of decision-making easier. Messenger can open each message that you get and, depending on what is in the message, move it to a different folder before you even have seen it. Chapter 10 describes how to move messages to folders by yourself. With filtering, you can teach Messenger to move messages for you automatically.

For example, you may want to have all mail that comes from a particular person automatically moved to a folder with that person's name. Or if you're on a mailing list, you may want all the messages from that mailing list put in their own folder. You may even have Messenger look through messages for particular words and move all the messages that contain those words to a different folder. Messenger can also filter Usenet news articles as you receive them.

Defining filters

To create or edit your filters, use the dialog box that you get when you choose Edit⇨Message Filters. In that dialog box (shown in Figure 12-1), you first specify the folder you want to filter on; normally, you filter on your Inbox, because that's where Messenger puts your new mail. Each folder can have many filters, and they are acted on in the order that you specify in the large box in the middle of the dialog box.

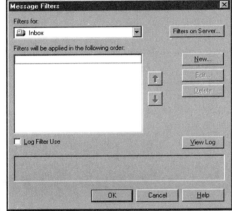

Figure 12-1:
The
Message
Filters
dialog box.

Each filter tells Messenger where to look in the message, what to look for, and what to do when it finds what it's looking for. When you add a filter or edit an existing filter, you see the dialog box in Figure 12-2. The first field is the name of the filter, which is any name you want to give it. The last field is a description, which is also anything you want to enter, such as a note to yourself about why you created the filter.

The "guts" of the filter are the two sections in the middle of the dialog box. The top section tells Messenger what to look for in the message; the bottom section tells Messenger what to do if the selection criteria in the top section are matched.

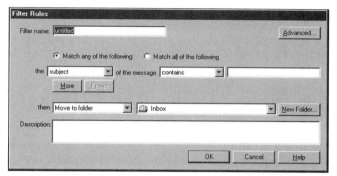

Figure 12-2:
Anatomy of
a mail filter.

When telling Messenger what to look for, you can have it look in different parts of the message, including the subject, the name of the sender, text in the body of the message, and so on. For any of these parts of the message, you also specify the text that Messenger is looking for. You can say that the text can be anywhere in the field, just at the beginning of the field, and so on. For example, you can create a filter that triggers when the sender of the message is the name of a mailing list you are on.

You can have more than one selection rule in a filter. For example, suppose that you want to move all mail from a friend of yours to a particular folder, but that friend sends you mail from two different addresses. To filter on more than one criteria, click the More button, and you see a second line of selection criteria that can be filled in just like the first. You must also choose whether this filter triggers when *any* of the criteria are met or only if *all* the criteria are met. In the scenario of your friend with two addresses, you would select Match Any of the Following, for example.

Messenger gives you plenty of choices of what to do when a message matches on a filter. The most common choices are to move the message to a different folder, delete the message, or mark the message as if you have already read it. For example, I usually move all the messages from a particular mailing list to a folder that is just for that mailing list.

Think twice when you are creating filters that look for text in the subject or body of a message if you are trying to filter for key words. You will probably find that many messages about the subject you are filtering for do not use the keywords, or the sender spells those words incorrectly and therefore the messages go unfiltered. Similarly, someone writing a message that has nothing to do with the topic may use one of the keywords, such as a friend of yours asking you what you know about that topic.

If you have more than one filter for a particular mailbox, you can change the order in which the filters get tested with the up and down arrow buttons in the Message Filters dialog box. Changing the order lets you list your more important filters first.

Filtering incoming mail and Usenet news

After you define your filters, Messenger automatically uses them as it collects your new mail and Usenet messages. Unfortunately, there is no way to tell Messenger to filter messages that you have already received.

If you specify that you want a log of what the filters did, you can look through that log to see what Messenger did. I recommend that you check out the log after you create new filters to see whether Messenger is moving messages in ways that you didn't expect because you were not narrow enough in your filtering rules or because two filters conflict in an unexpected way.

Securing Your Mail

Most of us don't think twice about the fact that someone might be able to read the e-mail messages we send. However, some Messenger users need to be absolutely sure that no one other than the recipient of a message can read that message. For example, the message may contain sensitive corporate data, a contract negotiation, or other such corporate secrets. This kind of privacy is needed in many business situations, and you get it through *encryption* (the scrambling of messages so that only people who know a particular secret can unscramble them).

Similarly, most of us don't worry about whether the messages we receive are really, truly from the person whose name is in the From header. We kind of assume that the message is from the named person, even though it is very easy for a malicious person to send you mail with a forged From header. Of course, if you receive something that promises to give you money if you do something, you may want to be really sure that the person sending you the message is really who he claims to be. You would want to have some assurance that the message is authentic (that is, that it was really sent by the person who is identified in the message) before you act on it. That assurance is called a *digital signature,* which is like a handwritten signature but much harder to forge. A digital signature is a method for assuring the recipient of a message that a particular person wrote that message and that the message was not changed after the sender wrote it.

These two topics, privacy and authentication, are related to each other, and the solution for the two problems involves the same process. The method that Messenger uses for sending private e-mail or e-mail that assures the recipient that you are who you say you are is with the *S/MIME* e-mail protocol. S/MIME (which stands for Secure MIME) is a particular way of using *public key cryptography* to secure e-mail, and it's becoming the most popular method for this type of security. *Cryptography* is the study of how to keep information secret when it passes from one person to another; public key cryptography is a modern form of cryptography that allows two people who haven't met to be able to send private mail (that is, encrypted mail) without having to first share a secret key.

An *encrypted* message is one that has been made unreadable to anyone other than the recipient. That is, you use the recipient's *public key* to make the message unreadable to anyone who doesn't have the *private key* that goes with the public key. As long as the recipient hasn't revealed his or her private key to anyone, that message can only be read by the recipient.

A digital signature assures the recipient of two things: that it was you who sent the message, and that the body of the message was not altered before the recipient verified your signature. An S/MIME message that was signed for you by Messenger can be read by anyone, even if that someone doesn't have S/MIME. If that person isn't using S/MIME, however, she can't read your signature and can't verify that you were the person who sent the message. In order to sign a message with Messenger, you need to have a *digital certificate,* which I describe in the next section.

Security is an incredibly complex topic, and I don't go into detail about it here. The governments of every country in the world rely on cryptography to keep national secrets, and all the banks in the world rely on cryptography to secure their accounts. Rest assured that cryptography is very heavily studied by some of the best minds in the computer industry.

Getting your key pair and certificate

S/MIME uses public key cryptography for both privacy and authentication. In order to use S/MIME, you need to have a *key pair,* which is a set of two keys. You must keep the first key, your *private key,* secret at all times; otherwise, someone can read private messages sent to you (making those messages not at all private any more). Interestingly, you must let anyone who wants to use S/MIME with you know your other key, your *public key;* if that person doesn't know your public key, he can't create private messages for you and can't verify that you were the person who sent a digitally signed message.

A key pair is not that useful without a *digital certificate*. The certificate is used to let a recipient know that your public key is really yours; likewise, you want to look at the digital certificate of someone who sends you secure mail to be sure that the public key really belongs to them. Digital certificates are signed by companies called *certificate authorities,* or *CAs,* whose job it is to assure others that people are who they say they are. (Certificates and CAs are introduced in Chapter 5.)

The odd thing about digital certificates is that in order for them to work, you and the person with whom you are communicating must both trust the CA to be honest about who each of you are. None of the common CAs in the United States are well-known companies, so this trust is based more on faith than long-term relationships. In other countries, the postal service or major banks act as CAs. CAs and digital certificates are quite new, so expect to see many changes in who is a CA, and which CAs you trust, in the coming years.

In some companies, a system administrator gives the key pairs and certificates to people using Messenger. Those administrators probably also install the key pairs and certificates for you to be sure that it is done correctly. In most situations, however, you have to create your own key pair and certificate. Earlier versions of Communicator were set up to use one particular CA, a company called VeriSign, as the CA that signs your key pair. Communicator 4.5 supports many CAs for personal certificates.

What does a certificate certify?

When a CA gives you a certificate, it is assuring anyone who trusts that CA that the public key that you have said is yours is really yours. But who are you? This is a philosophical question that has been asked for thousands of years before the Web came into existence.

In the case of an S/MIME certificate, "you" are your e-mail address. Sounds kind of depressing, doesn't it? But it makes sense when you think about it. The CA who gives you the certificate has never met you, has never talked to you on the phone, and doesn't know that you really exist. Thus, a CA can't verify that "you" are any of the things that people normally associate with themselves, such as their names, what they look like, and so on.

However, the CA can send you mail and verify that you got it by telling you to send mail back to them in reply. Thus, the only thing that most of today's CAs associate you with is your e-mail address. Note, however, that some certificates associate a public key with more than just an e-mail address. For example, in some countries, CAs issue public certificates that associate a public key with someone's driver's license. Expect to see more kinds of certificates in the United States in the coming years.

The steps to get a new certificate from a public CA are as follows:

1. **Choose Communicator⇨Tools⇨Security Info.**

   This command brings up the Security Info dialog box.

2. **Click on the Yours link under the Certificates option in the left column of the dialog box.**

   This step brings you to the list of certificates that you have, as shown in Figure 12-3. Notice that the list is empty, because you haven't gotten a certificate yet.

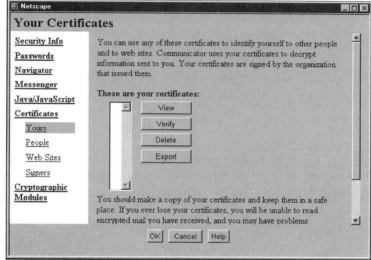

Figure 12-3:
The Security
Info dialog
box
showing
your
certificates.

3. **Click the Get a Certificate button.**

   You may need to scroll in this window to see all your certificates or to see the Get a Certificate button.

   This button leads you to a list of CAs that Netscape likes (probably because thse CAs had to prove to Netscape that they were reliable and had to pay Netscape to be on this list). The links on the list take you to the Web sites for the various CAs.

4. **Register for a certificate.**

   From here, the procedure for how to get a certificate is different for each CA. You have to look at the CA's Web site and determine whether they are offering *end-user certificates* (be sure not to get a *server certificate,* which is used for something completely different). Some CAs give you a free certificate, some give you a certificate for free but it's good for only a short time, and others charge you for the certificate you get from them.

At one point in the process, you see a Communicator dialog box that says you are generating a private key. This process can take only a second or a long time, depending on the speed of your computer. After you generate your private key, you have to choose a password to protect the key. Do not forget the password you choose, or you will be unable to use the key in the future.

5. Verify your e-mail address to the CA.

CAs who issue S/MIME certificates should verify that the e-mail address that you give them is valid. They usually do so by sending a message to that address and having you respond to the message. This procedure means that they can be sure that your identity (that is, your e-mail address) is really associated with your certificate. However, it is up to the CA to decide how to verify your e-mail address, so there is no set procedure that I can describe here about how it is done in your case.

6. Install your certificate.

At some point in the process, the CA has you go to a particular place on the Web site that has your certificate. When you go there, you see a dialog box similar to the one in Figure 12-4. Be sure you read everything in the dialog box, because it is telling you that you are about to associate a new certificate with your mail address. If you are sure that this is what you want to do, click OK.

Figure 12-4:
Communicator prompting you to install a certificate.

7. **Save your certificate on a diskette.**

After installing the certificate, Communicator prompts you to save it on a diskette. This dialog box gives you a stern warning that if you lose your certificate, it cannot be recovered. They mean it. For example, if you have a problem with the hard disk on your computer or the certificate accidentally gets erased, you can no longer send signed messages with that certificate, and you have to get a new one. (Some CAs will give you a new copy of the certificate, but most won't). Insert a disk in your disk drive and make a copy of the certificate on it.

8. **Verify that your certificate was installed.**

Choose Communicator⇨Tools⇨Security Info again, click on the Yours link under the Certificates option in the left column of the dialog box, and make sure that the certificate you just downloaded is there. If it isn't, you need to go back to your CA's site and retrieve that certificate again.

Using your digital signature

To sign a message before you send it, click on the Options button in the New Message window. The message sending area now looks like Figure 12-5. Select the Signed option. When you mail the message, Messenger prompts you for the password that you put on the certificate. Enter that password, and Messenger signs the message and attaches your certificate.

Figure 12-5: The message sending options for signing a message.

When you receive a piece of signed mail, Messenger shows you an icon in the upper-right corner of the message, as shown in Figure 12-6. If the message was signed but Messenger can't verify the signature, such as if the message was somehow changed before it got to you, the icon is different and clearly indicates that the signature could not be validated.

Sending and receiving private e-mail

When you send an encrypted message, the actions are similar to sending a signed message, but the effects are very different. If the person to whom you send the encrypted mail does not have S/MIME running on her computer, she can't read the message you sent her. In fact, no one can without a large (or impossibly large) amount of effort.

In order to send an encrypted message, you have to have the certificate of the recipient. This stipulation may make you think that the recipient is, therefore, always able to read encrypted messages, but that's not always the case. Remember that some people read their e-mail on different systems, and the system that the recipient is on when he gets your message may not have S/MIME capabilities, or he may not have installed his certificate on that system.

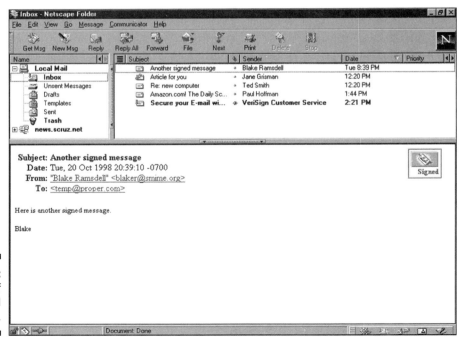

Figure 12-6:
Indicator of
a signed
message.

To encrypt a message before you send it, click on the Options button in the New Message window. Select the Encrypted option. When you mail the message, Messenger encrypts the message and sends it.

When you receive an encrypted message, Messenger prompts you for the password for your certificate. Actually, Messenger is not accessing your certificate but your private key, which it needs to decrypt the message. Type in your password, and Messenger decrypts the message and displays the message with an icon indicating that it was encrypted. You can click on the icon to see some technical information about the method used to encrypt that message.

Incidentally, you can both sign and encrypt a message. Simply be sure that both the Signed and Encrypted options are selected in the Message Options window.

Receiving and Sending Mail Receipts

When you send a letter using the U.S. Postal Service, you can request a return receipt (which you have to pay for, of course). When the letter is delivered to the recipient, the delivery person has the recipient sign a post card, which is then mailed back to you. When you get the card, you know that the recipient actually got the message.

Receipts in Internet mail are similar. Before you send a message, you can tell Messenger to request a receipt for the message. After you send the message, the recipient has the opportunity to return the receipt, or to ignore your request but to read the message anyway.

To request a receipt before you send your message, click on the Options button in the New Message window. Select the Return Receipt option. When the recipient receives and reads the mail, her mail program asks (most likely) her whether she wants to send you a return receipt. If she says yes, that message is sent to you, and you get it the next time you read your mail.

Not everyone likes return receipts. If you request a return receipt but never get it, that doesn't necessarily mean that the message didn't get to the recipient. Instead, it may mean that the recipient decided not to respond to your request, or that she was using mail software that can't return receipts.

When you get a message with a return receipt request, Messenger prompts you about whether you want to send back the receipt. Simply select Yes or No in the dialog box, and Messenger takes care of sending back the receipt immediately.

Making the Most of Instant Messages

Not all messages come through Internet mail or Usenet. Communicator 4.5 comes with a feature called *AOL Instant Messenger* that allows you to find out whether someone is online and, if he is, to chat with him by using instant messages. These messages are not Internet mail, and they disappear when you leave AOL Instant Messenger. Some other services have similar instant messages, notably the popular "ICQ" service; however, the two services do not interact.

The basic idea behind AOL Instant Messenger is that when you log in to your Internet service provider, you tell the AOL Instant Messenger server that you are online. Then if one of your friends wants to chat with you, she can check to see whether you're online, see that you are, and then start sending you messages. You can even tell AOL Instant Messenger to let you know when your friends first come online.

Unfortunately, using AOL Instant Messenger is a bit of a disappointment relative to how fun it sounds. In fact, it has so many drawbacks that I know only a tiny number of Communicator users who use AOL Instant Messenger. I give you a brief overview here, but I suggest that you not get too excited about it until you have tried it.

To start the service, give the Communicator⇨AOL Instant Messenger Service command. You see the dialog box shown in Figure 12-7. If you already have an AOL Instant Messenger screen name or an America Online screen name, enter it in the dialog box and click the Sign On button.

Figure 12-7:
Signing on to AOL Instant Messenger.

If you don't have an AOL Instant Messenger screen name, you have to register for one. Select <New User> in the screen name list and click Sign On. Communicator takes you to the AOL Instant Messenger registration page, where you can apply for a screen name. You must choose a three- to ten-letter name that no one else has chosen to use as your screen name. You must also choose a password, so that only you can use that screen name.

Getting a unique screen name is the first of the major problems with AOL Instant Messenger: Almost every reasonable name has already been taken. Every name of an AOL user (more than ten million of them) is already reserved. When I was trying to sign up, I tried more than ten names, all of which were already in use. I finally just typed in some random characters and was able to use that. When you find a screen name that AOL Instant Messenger decides is acceptable, click the Sign On button.

When you are online, you see the window shown in Figure 12-8. The main AOL Instant Messenger window has two tabs. The Online tab tells you which of your buddies are online, and the List Setup tab lets you do things like add and delete buddies. The rectangle in the lower left of the window is actually a button that pops up the list of commands that you can use with AOL Instant Messenger.

Figure 12-8:
The main
AOL Instant
Messenger
window.

Here's another disappointing thing about AOL Instant Messenger: You need to know someone's screen name before you can add him to your list. Thus, you probably need to communicate with your friend by e-mail or phone in order to get his AOL Instant Messenger screen name so that you can add him to your buddy list.

While you are online, you can watch the list in the Online tab to see which of your friends is online. If you spot someone you want to send an instant message to, select her name in the list and click the IM button. This button opens a little message window into which you can type your message. You use this window to chat with your buddy until you or she stops responding.

Part IV
Who's Webbing Now?

The 5th Wave   By Rich Tennant

ORIGINAL VAN-GOGH-OF-THE-MONTH CLUB

"SINCE WE BEGAN ON-LINE SHOPPING, I JUST DON'T KNOW WHERE THE MONEY'S GOING."

In this part . . .

The best part of the Web is its content, and these chapters show you dozens of Web sites of interest to almost everyone. You can find all sorts of fun places; you can make — or lose — money; you can read online magazines; you can meet computer geeks; you can even learn more about your government. This part offers more than a bit of everything!

Chapter 13
Starting in the Library

In This Chapter

▶ Looking at places that attempt to organize the Web

▶ Discovering the best catalogs

▶ Poking around other collections

*T*he first two parts of this book show you what the Web is and the tools you need to explore it. Now's the time to start exploring. This chapter and the four that follow it are full of examples of the best and brightest spots on the Web. Something for everyone can be found here; with luck, you'll find dozens of "somethings" in these chapters.

Notice that these examples are not simply "good places to go." In fact, you may spend only a minute or two at a site before moving on to another one. Thus, many sites that are listed here are often "good places to start."

This difference is important, particularly on the Web. Some of the best Web content doesn't really contain very much content. Instead, much of the content consists of pointers (links) to other good content. This setup is one of the ways in which the Web differs from other electronic media, such as television and radio. Web sites that are high-quality collections of pointers to other Web sites are, in fact, quite valuable locations in and of themselves. In contrast, a television station that runs only listings for other stations, for example, may not be so valuable (although I know some people who watch this type of cable channel, so there must be a market there somewhere).

Getting In When There's No Front Door

People who come to the Web after using a service such as CompuServe or America Online are often confused because the Web doesn't have a hierarchical structure. To find information about Windows programs on America Online, for example, you must first go to the Computer area and then to the PC area under the Computer area and, finally, to the Windows area under the PC area.

No surfing allowed

A short note on vocabulary. By now, you may have noticed that this book uses terms such as *explore*, *traverse*, and *wander* to describe your movement around the Web, but never the term *surf*. In fact, *surf* is probably the most inaccurate and overused metaphor for the Web to date — even worse than calling the Web the "information superhighway."

Think about it for a moment: What do surfers do? They go to one place; they paddle out; they ride in; they paddle out; they ride in; and so on. Their movement is limited to about 100 yards, always going back and forth.

Now think about how you use the Web. You start in one place. You read a bit and follow a link to somewhere else. You follow a link somewhere else again. Maybe you return to the second place to go out again to a fourth place. Or you go all the way back.

Notice the difference?

The *surf* metaphor also breaks down in what makes surfing fun versus what makes using the Web fun. For most surfers, the goal is a really wild ride in which they barely hang on for dear life but get some great action. (Actually, a day full of such rides is the goal.) For a Web user, the ride itself shouldn't be wild. Maybe you want the destination to be wild, but getting there should be relatively painless.

The differences go on and on:

- Most surfboards look nicer than Web browsers.

- No Web-inspired clothing is anywhere to be found (well, at least none you'd want to wear in public).

- You don't need to wash off your feet after exploring the Web.

- Surfing causes your thighs and ankles to hurt; wandering the Web hurts the wrists and eyes.

- You don't get blonder by using the Web.

- So far, surfing has inspired many more songs than has the Web.

- People don't usually go "oooh, ahhh" while watching you use the Web.

So the next time you hear people saying something about "surfing the Web," you can assume that either they haven't used the Web that much or they have never gone surfing.

The Web has no "ceiling" and no single, agreed-on beginning location. The owners of a few Web sites would like you to believe in a Web top — namely, their sites. By now, however, you know that ain't so.

But don't get the impression from this lack of a Web ceiling that you have nowhere to start. As you see in Chapter 4, Communicator lets you type any URL you want in the File menu's Open Location command. This command enables you to start wherever you want by entering a URL that you see in this book, in a magazine article, in an advertisement, and so on.

Communicator also lets you specify your *home page* — the page displayed when you first run the browser. Netscape, of course, would love for you to keep Netcenter as your home page because it makes money when you wander around Netcenter. Few home pages, including Netcenter, have everything you'd want on them, because every Web user wants something different. Thus, you will probably find yourself moving around the Web by entering URLs into Communicator, not just clicking on links that you see on the screen.

The term *home page* can be somewhat confusing because some people also call the first page you see when you enter their Web site a "home page." Thus, two different things are called home pages: the first page you see when you start your Web browser and the first page you see when you enter a particular site.

Collecting because it's there

People and companies who collect lists of pointers often have many motivations. Some people may need to have good collections of pointers for their jobs. If your job concerns forestry, for example, you may want access to all the information about forests on the Web that you can get. If you have such a list and you publish it on the Web, you are assured to get mail from people who appreciate your effort but want to point out that you forgot a particular Web site. What a great way to do research!

Other people who publish lists of pointers do so because they just love to have lots of information. These people are often the same people who collect antique encyclopedias, who get excited when they find a reference book that they don't already have on a favorite subject, and who would rather hang out in a university library than at a university sporting event. These folks are good to have around if you're doing a difficult crossword puzzle, or if you can't find anything on the Web about a particular topic.

Both kinds of people do, in fact, perform a valuable service for the Web community. Well-organized people produce well-organized lists that can make the difference between finding the information you want and missing a great resource. Not-so-well-organized people produce lists that may not be so well organized but often contain nuggets that you can't find in other places.

Further, many companies also collect lists of pointers and publish them on their corporate Web sites. Publishing these lists makes good sense for many reasons. It makes the company look knowledgeable about the subject, which is usually related to the kind of business the company is in. If the page is popular enough, the list also causes people to come to that site first when looking for other sites, which gives the company another chance to advertise its products or services.

Netscape's Netcenter is an excellent example of why a company would consider spending money on creating lists of links. The better Netcenter is, the longer Web users will keep using it. More use means more money for Netscape, some of which it plows back into making Netcenter better.

Picking the best

"I'm busy," you may be saying. "Just tell me which list of lists is the best." Nope. There's no such thing. Good ones certainly are there to be found, but none is "the best" in all circumstances, just as no one television channel is best to watch for all kinds of shows.

For some people, "the best" is the biggest. (Texans are often said to have this belief.) But even for these people, no single best Web pointer site can be specified. Which is "bigger": the site with the most pointers in a few categories or the one with the most categories of pointers? In this chapter, I have listed some of the ones that *I* think are the best, and I hope you find them at least good, but please don't think that this is a comprehensive list, or even that you're supposed to like what I like.

Virtual Libraries

Some of the major starting point sites on the Web are organized loosely as libraries by subject. In other words, the pointers are grouped by topic, just like the books on the shelves at most libraries are grouped by topic. Of course, the method for grouping by category is different for each site, just as it is for the various library cataloging methods.

The term *virtual library* indicates that these libraries don't actually contain much content. Virtual libraries are sets of *pointers* (links) organized by category, like a real library's card catalog. Using these libraries is almost like going into a building marked "Library" and finding a catalog where the cards just point to the contents of other libraries. At first, that card catalog doesn't sound so useful, but if it is really complete and well organized, you can still benefit greatly from it.

World Wide Web Virtual Library

`vlib.stanford.edu/Overview.html`

One of the first major attempts to organize the Web was the World Wide Web Virtual Library. In fact, it's still one of the best places to look for a categorized view of Web sites. Each subject is maintained by a different volunteer, usually a specialist in the area. As you can see in Figure 13-1, the categories are listed alphabetically. The library currently has more than 100 categories, and new ones are being added all the time. (Of course, when you are talking about organizing all the information on the Web, even deciding what is a "category" is hard.)

As with the other libraries described in this chapter, you can search the top level of the World Wide Web Virtual Library for words and phrases. Other libraries that contain more information kept at a single site usually have better response to searches. Most of the individual libraries pointed to by the World Wide Web Virtual Library, however, are individually searchable, which usually is sufficient if you know which topic you want to look in first.

Yahoo!

`www.yahoo.com/`

Some of the best libraries start off as whims or short-term projects and then take on a life of their own. Yahoo! is such a site. Containing hundreds of thousands of links, Yahoo! has quickly become one of the most popular libraries on the Web. Figure 13-2 shows the top of the hierarchy, but don't be fooled by the lack of listings: Each level has many levels beneath it, and the maintainers add hundreds or thousands of links every day.

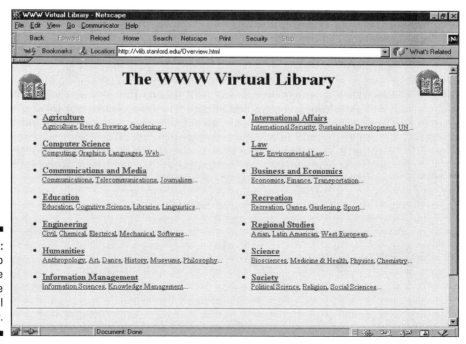

Figure 13-1:
The top level of the World Wide Web Virtual Library.

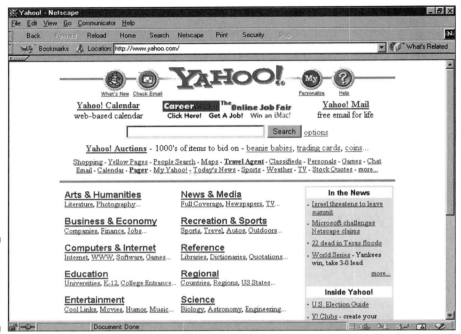

Figure 13-2:
Just the tip
of the
iceberg in
Yahoo!.

The folks who run Yahoo! actively solicit new links from people on the Internet. They supplement those links with ones that they get from their own program that automatically looks at various parts of the Web. This two-pronged approach to collecting resource pointers has helped Yahoo! grow to an incredible size in a very short time and become one of the most-visited sites on the Web.

Note that Yahoo! is *not* a "search site" like other popular Web spots. The links in Yahoo! are collected and checked by people, not by some program. To me, this distinction makes all the difference in the world. Yahoo! can organize its links in a fashion that you and I can understand. For example, Figure 13-3 shows the first level under the Recreation and Sports section. Notice how it is organized so that sports fans can find what they want quickly, and dance enthusiasts can find what they want without wading through sports information.

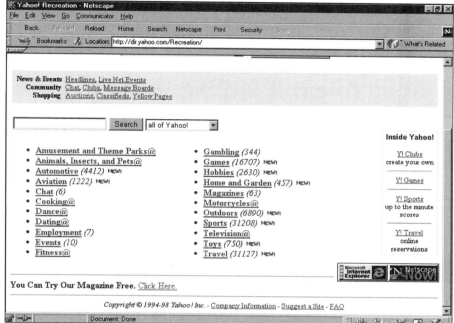

And, yes, a silly story lurks behind the name. *Yahoo!* stands for (are you ready for this?) *Yet Another Hierarchically Organized Oracle.* Yeah, right. More likely, the name appeared before the decision about what the name stood for.

I find Yahoo! to be one of my favorite sites. It's more complete than most of the other libraries; it has a much nicer feel to it; and something new is always going on there. If you're looking for a "first library," I recommend Yahoo!.

Argus Clearinghouse

www.clearinghouse.net/

If you like libraries because they are organized by librarians, you'll probably love the Argus Clearinghouse. It was originally from the University of Michigan and organized by the University Library and the School of Information and Library Studies. Figure 13-4 shows the top level of the current Clearinghouse.

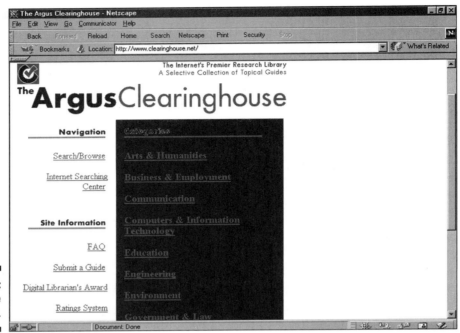

Figure 13-4:
Entering the
Clearinghouse.

As you may imagine, the Clearinghouse is about as much like a university library as you can get on the Web. Many of the subtopics are collected by librarians; the others, mostly by academics. As such, it has a very academic slant to it, making it different from the other large pointer sites. The pointers in the Clearinghouse tend to be to universities, although plenty of non-university pointers are there as well. Figure 13-5 shows a typical listing from the Clearinghouse.

Inter-Links

alabanza.com/kabacoff/Inter-Links/

Previously known as NovaLinks, Inter-Links is more of an overview of the Internet, particularly the Web, than are the other virtual libraries. The intent of Inter-Links is to help beginning users get a feel for all that is on the Internet. In that, Inter-Links isn't as complete as some of the other libraries. The simple introductory page is shown in Figure 13-6.

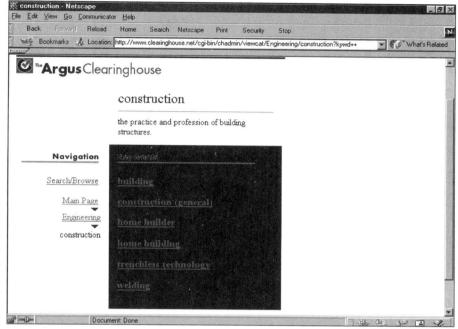

Figure 13-5:
Information
on
construction
in the
Clearinghouse.

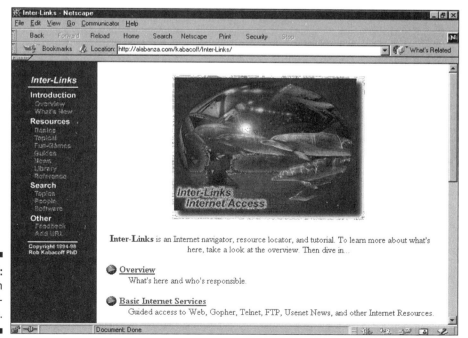

Figure 13-6:
Introduction
to Inter-
Links.

The trade-off of designing a Web site for beginners, compared to trying to be complete, may be lost on some people, particularly if you forget how overwhelming it is to be presented with dozens of pointers when you first start using the Web. The links in Inter-Links are generally of higher quality than those on the "we-list-everything" type of sites.

Anointers of Pointers

Beyond the large libraries are dozens of smaller collections that are very valuable for people wondering what's out there on the Web. Most of these libraries are created by individuals or companies hoping to convince people coming to their sites looking for pointers to check out the other services they offer.

As described in Part V of this book, almost anyone can create Web lists. Not all lists, however, are created equal. If you are not terribly thorough, for example, pretending to have a complete list on a particular subject may mean that you are doing a disservice to someone searching for information. To be helpful, these kinds of lists need to be both complete at the time they are created and updated often with new pointers as they arise.

WebRing

```
www.webring.org
```

So you're at a Web site you really like, but you've gone all the way through it and you want more. How do you find a related site easily, without having to go back to a search site? If the site you are at is part of a WebRing, finding related sites is easy. Participants in a *WebRing* on a particular subject have links to other sites in the same WebRing. A site can get into a WebRing via a simple process, and Figure 13-7 shows the main page for the WebRing organization.

The "ring" in WebRing is the fun part. Each WebRing has an order to it, with every site being part of a circle of links. Thus, when you are at one site in WebRing, that site has links to the "next" and "previous" members of the ring. A ring that has 10 or 20 sites on it is easy to traverse by selecting "next" at each site. You can find related sites, especially the one you like best, quickly and easily.

For example, Figure 13-8 shows part of a typical page that is part of a WebRing. Notice how the WebRing portion of the page has pointers both backwards and forwards, as well as to the central list. Most WebRing participants have similar sections on their Web pages

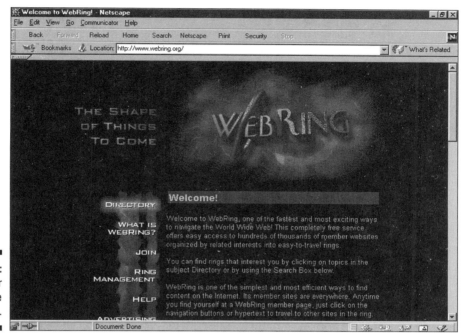

Figure 13-7:
The center
of all the
WebRings.

Figure 13-8:
Part of a
WebRing
site.

Business Web

www.bizweb.com/

BizWeb is an attempt to organize the business side of the Web. Although it is not terribly large, it is probably one of the best listings of products and services on the Web, pulled together in one place. Figure 13-9 shows some of the categories on BizWeb.

BizWeb is far from perfect, mostly due to companies not registering with it. As more and more companies find out about BizWeb, however, it may become even more useful for searching for products and services.

Microsoft Library

library.microsoft.com/

Since Microsoft entered the market for selling information and not just software, it has done an admirable job of collecting data on all sorts of computer-related topics. It sells some of this data in various Microsoft CD-ROM packages but also gives plenty of it away free. The Microsoft Library, shown in Figure 13-10, is an example of the latter.

Figure 13-9:
BizWeb covers many categories of businesses, particularly shops and malls.

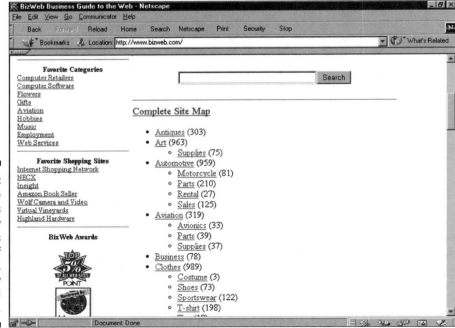

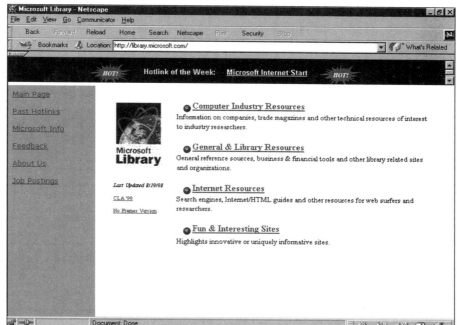

Figure 13-10:
Microsoft's
free library.

The Microsoft Library provides many great references, including a very complete list of library-related sites that should be of interest to most teachers and parents. Its list of computer magazines, shown in Figure 13-11, is also pretty impressive, given how many of those magazines are not overly fond of Microsoft.

Larry's InfoPower Pages

`www.clark.net/pub/lschank/home.html`

Some librarians can't get enough of the library at work. Larry Schank is one such librarian. His InfoPower Pages are an excellent source of pointers on a small list of topics. The top level of his pages is shown in Figure 13-12.

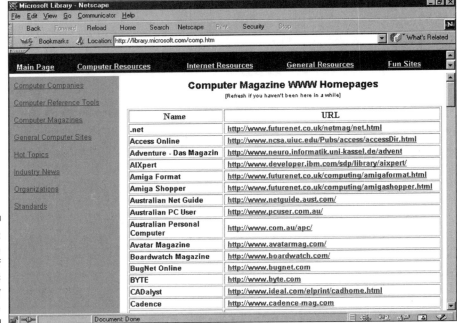

Figure 13-11:
Some of the
hundreds of
magazines
listed by
Microsoft.

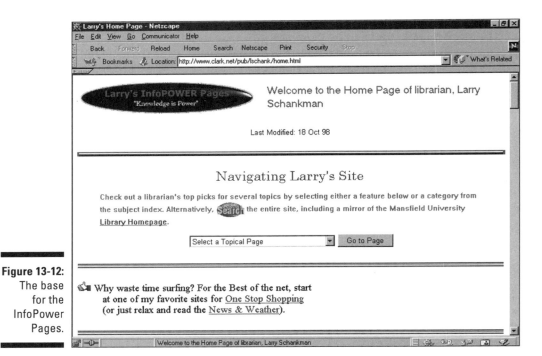

Figure 13-12:
The base
for the
InfoPower
Pages.

Larry's set of resource lists is pretty impressive for a single person. Among the topics for which he has collected pointers are the following:

- ✔ Behavioral sciences
- ✔ Library and librarians
- ✔ Business and economics
- ✔ Law and legal resources
- ✔ Humanities
- ✔ International and country studies
- ✔ Education
- ✔ Geography and environment
- ✔ Health and medicine
- ✔ Internet and computing
- ✔ Government and political science

Figure 13-13, for example, shows part of his political science resources.

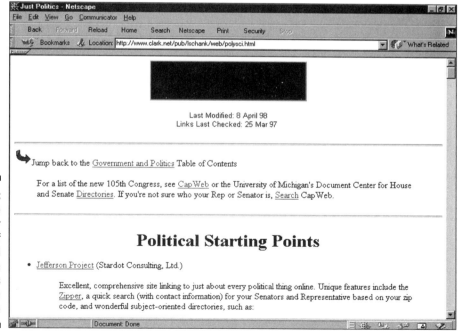

Figure 13-13: The InfoPower Pages' list of political science resources available on the Web

Chapter 14

Finding Fun, Fun, Fun

. . . .

In This Chapter

▶ Finding people on the Web

▶ Exploring Web game resources

▶ Humming along with Web music resources

▶ Using the Web to help turn into a couch potato

. . . .

*A*s many of the Web pages in this book show, the Web is more than research, business, and commerce. People create the content on the Web, and people tend to act like, well, people when they get creative. Thus, many of the best Web resources are not all that serious or high-minded.

All This and People, Too!

If you're a people person, you probably like to see what people on the Web are doing when they're not being so serious. Some are just trying to make contact with other people out there in the universe; others are trying to keep themselves amused; and others are trying to hide. (Of course, the ones trying to hide should probably not create Web home pages.)

You can find people being people at hundreds of places on the Web. This section shows just a few, but finding many more is easy. Much of Usenet consists of people trying to make one-to-many contacts; in fact, Usenet is a good place to do people-in-public watching, if you can get used to all the unpleasant parts (as I describe in Chapter 9).

Who's who on the Internet

```
www.yahoo.com/Society_and_Culture/People/
            Personal_Home_Pages/
```

Chapters 18 through 21 discuss how to create your own Web pages. Of course, people hav2e been putting together Web pages for quite some time, with varying degrees of success. Many people can get the hang of HTML but may miss the mark with respect to, shall we say, interesting content. Others have good content but need a few lessons in design or even basic HTML use.

Still, you may want to take a look at what ordinary Web folk have for home pages. Figure 14-1 shows the Yahoo! Personal Pages Web site. Here, tens of thousands of people have registered their home sites with short descriptions of what kind of content they offer (if any). Anyone can register for free, so it's quite the egalitarian listing.

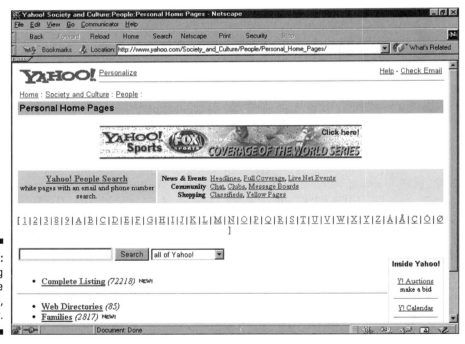

Figure 14-1:
Finding everyone on the Web, made easy.

A surprisingly high number of these pages are published by ordinary people who freely admit that they don't have much to say on their home pages. They're mostly there to watch, but they may pipe in every once in a while. If you end up creating your own home page, even if it isn't anything special, you should probably register it with this site so that other people can find you, giving them the same browsing opportunities that you are taking advantage of; that seems only fair in the people-watching game.

Going other places

```
news:rec.travel.misc
```

If you like to travel, the newsgroups with names that start with `rec.travel` (such as `rec.travel.misc`) are a great place to chat with other people who travel and who live in the places where you want to go. Figure 14-2 shows some of the articles in `rec.travel.misc`. You can find many travel groups, including the following:

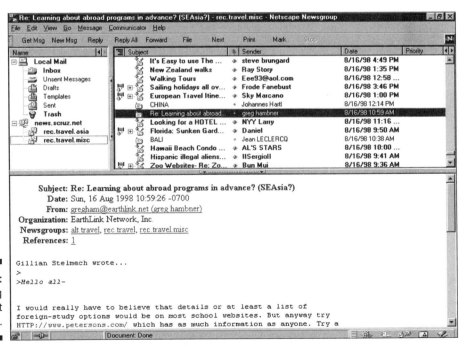

Figure 14-2: Chatting about traveling.

✔ rec.travel.africa

✔ rec.travel.air

✔ rec.travel.asia

✔ rec.travel.australia+nz

✔ rec.travel.caribbean

✔ rec.travel.cruises

✔ rec.travel.europe

✔ rec.travel.latin-america

✔ rec.travel.marketplace

✔ rec.travel.misc

✔ rec.travel.usa-canada

The kinds of conversations you see in the Asia, Europe, and USA-Canada newsgroups often fall into either the "have you been to so-and-so before" category or the "when you go to so-and-so, be sure to see such-and-such." These kinds of conversations are good ways to see what people find important when they travel and what natives find important to show others. The other newsgroups are good places to talk about bargains and warnings, but the main discussion groups are excellent for people who like to get around.

Making things

```
news:rec.crafts.misc
```

If you're interested in crafts, you can probably find a newsgroup that interests you. Of course, not everyone has a craft to play with, but those who do tend to want to tell others about their favorite finds, what they've made recently, the best stores for supplies, and so on. Figure 14-3 shows the rec.crafts.misc newsgroup. Many craft-related groups are around, including the following:

✔ rec.crafts.beads

✔ rec.crafts.brewing

✔ rec.crafts.carving

✔ rec.crafts.dollhouses

✔ rec.crafts.glass

✔ rec.crafts.jewelry

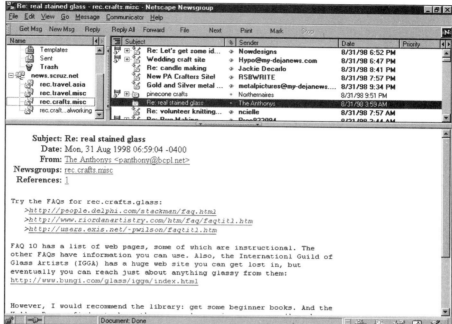

Figure 14-3:
Craft topics
in
rec.crafts.
misc.

- rec.crafts.marketplace
- rec.crafts.metalworking
- rec.crafts.misc
- rec.crafts.polymer-clay
- rec.crafts.pottery
- rec.crafts.textiles
- rec.crafts.winemaking

The newsgroups with names that start with rec.crafts. are usually much easier to read and follow than many other Usenet groups. You certainly run into fewer flames and inappropriate postings here than on other newsgroups. However, because many of the newer users of these groups haven't the faintest idea of what Usenet is or how to post messages, you see fewer messages in these groups than you might expect for popular hobbies. People-watching is easy here, and you may actually find yourself picking up a new hobby. For example, Figure 14-4 shows some of the kind of talk you can see on rec.crafts.metalworking.

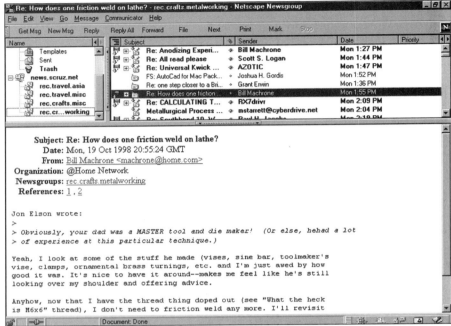

Figure 14-4:
The folks
who love to
work with
metal.

Yahoo! People Search

`People.yahoo.com/`

You may not be as interested in watching random people chat as you are in finding specific people. For that, a great service is Yahoo!'s People Search, shown in Figure 14-5, which lets you find tens of millions of people's e-mail addresses. The search facility is a free service, like all of Yahoo!.

Using the search function is easy, and you can specify as much or as little as you know about the person. If you want to find a person who has an uncommon last name, for example, knowing the last name is probably sufficient.

AnyWho

`www.anywho.com/`

The AnyWho directory service is another great place to find people and businesses. However, it's aimed at finding phone numbers and street addresses, not e-mail addresses (although some people have chosen to list their e-mail addresses there as well). Figure 14-6 shows the main AnyWho page.

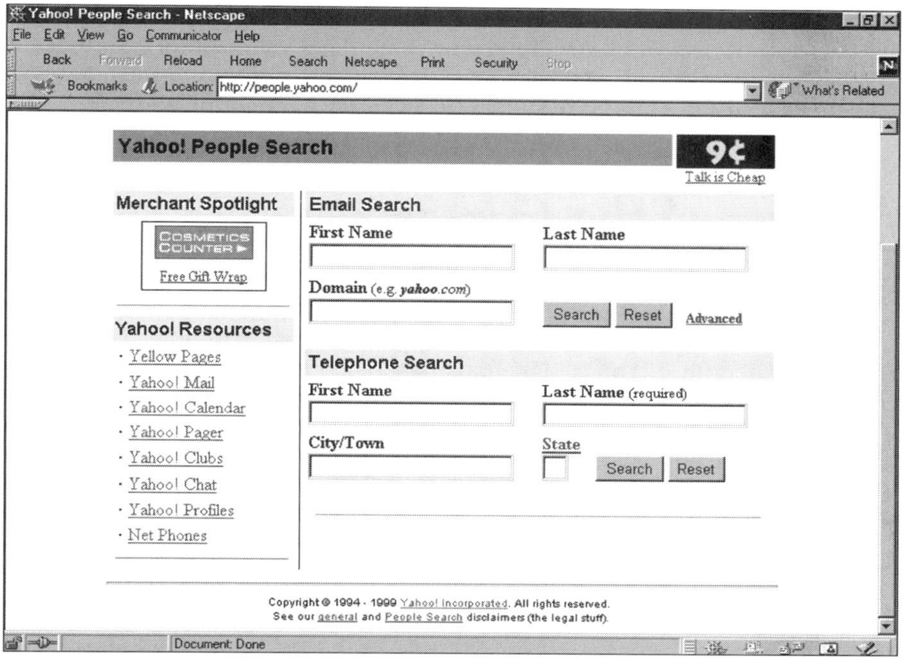

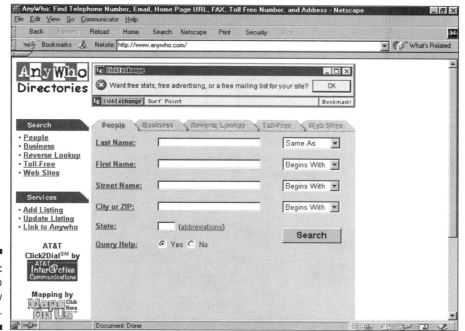

Figure 14-5:
Finding
folks with
Yahoo!
People
Search.

Figure 14-6:
Getting to
know
AnyWho.

One of the best features of AnyWho is that you can get an instant map of an address you have found. For example, if you look up IDG Books, the wonderful folks who publish the *...For Dummies* series, and then click on the Map button, you see where all these books come from, as shown in Figure 14-7.

Names of the Games

The nonwork activities that take up most people's attention are often sports and games. In the U.S., many more people are interested in sports as a spectator event than in actually participating in them, but tens of millions of people still play basketball, baseball, and golf. Multiplayer games such as bridge and Scrabble used to be much more popular than they are today, but millions still enjoy them.

Both sports and games have given way in the past decade to electronic games and video games that are for one or two people. Many people believe that the prevalence of Nintendo and Sega systems in homes, as well as the rise of similar computer games, has largely sapped the popularity of participant games and sports. Many Web sites cover all sorts of games and sports, including the now-popular video and home games.

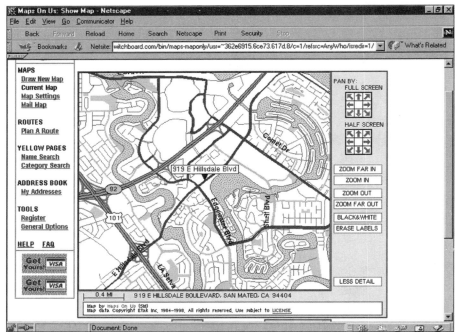

Figure 14-7:
Maps are just a click away at AnyWho.

Games Domain

www.gamesdomain.com/

By far the most complete Web site that covers games (but not sports) is Games Domain, shown in Figure 14-8. Games Domain has a worldwide view of the games realm. It covers all types of games, including video games and computer games, as well as traditional games such as chess and Go that can be played with a computer.

One of the best features of Games Domain is its collection of Usenet newsgroups and their affiliated FAQs. Games Domain was an early proponent of converting FAQs to HTML so that they could be easily viewed through the Web, and it now includes pointers to dozens of games-related FAQs (as well as, of course, to the Usenet newsgroups themselves). If you haven't encountered them yet, *FAQs* are files that contain the answers to many *f*requently *a*sked *q*uestions; they can be an incredibly valuable resource.

Figure 14-8:
The top
level of
Games
Domain.

Sport Virtual Library

www.justwright.com/sports/

Leave it to the British to come up with the consummate sports site, one that not only is complete but also fairly funny as well. The Sport Virtual Library, shown in Figure 14-9, puts most American sites to shame by having more of an international view (no surprise there) and less of an "all sports are good" attitude. The Web site also has an impressive set of pointers to information about international sporting events such as the Goodwill Games and the Olympics.

The sports are categorized loosely by the devices used in the sports, such as ball sports, wheel sports, and water sports. The topic headings also give a flavor of the prejudices of the authors, who are, after all, rabid sports fans. A few topics that should otherwise probably go on the Games and Recreation Virtual Library, such as juggling, also appear on the Sport Virtual Library.

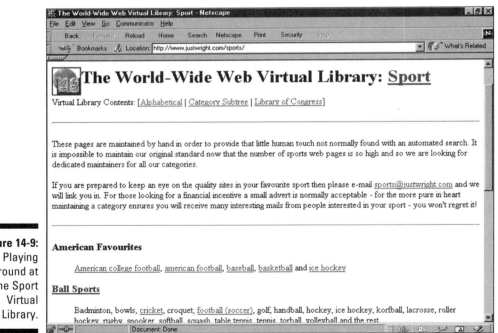

Figure 14-9: Playing around at the Sport Virtual Library.

Funky Web Groove Thang

The Internet was a center of musical chatter well before the Web came into existence. The multimedia aspect of the Web, largely unrealized as it is, makes the Web a bit more enticing for music lovers, but it is still in its infancy. That said, the music-based areas of the Internet have pretty much moved over to being Web-specific, with the exception of the dozens of fan mailing lists that still thrive.

Internet Underground Music Archive

`www.iuma.com/`

For the last 20 years, the modern music scene has always relied on bands starting small, getting local coverage, and growing slowly to national and international presence. Many bands and artists spend their hard-earned cash on making tapes and CDs, trying to get them distributed in local stores, and so on. Independent music labels usually have between only one and ten bands on them and often fold as fast as they arrive.

The folks at the Internet Underground Music Archive (IUMA), shown in Figure 14-10, started their careers by letting bands publish songs, promotional literature, and so on for free. Now they charge a small amount, but the purpose of IUMA is still the same: to enable unknown bands to promote themselves on the Internet.

The IUMA site has hundreds of artists in a variety of genres, although most would be classified as rock and roll. Some artists are selling CDs and tapes; others are just trying for a bit of recognition. If you want to sample music from bands you don't know (and have time to download large files), IUMA has the variety.

Listening to Indigo

`www.geocites.com/SunsetStrip/Frontrow/8979/`

One of the best musical experiences you can have on the Web doesn't involve any sound. Tens of thousands of sites are created by music fans for their favorite groups. These sites aren't just for rock and roll superstars, either: You can find sites for classical music, country, world music, and folk of all sorts. Most of these personal sites have a homey, excited feel to them.

If you're a fan of the Indigo Girls like I am, you are fortunate to have over a dozen Web sites that cover all aspects of this folk duo's career. For example, Figure 14-11 shows Indigo Universe, a typical fan site. These fan sites let you find tour dates, what songs they played at earlier concerts, pictures, e-mail addresses of other fans, and so on. The Indigo Girls' music has had a big impact on many of our lives, and being able to keep in touch with other fans (or just see what you missed at recent concerts) is great. Of course, the same is true for fans of the thousands of other bands who have also inspired unofficial Web sites.

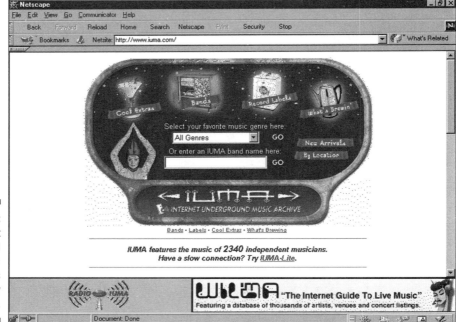

Figure 14-10:
Internet
Underground
Music
Archive's
introductory
page.

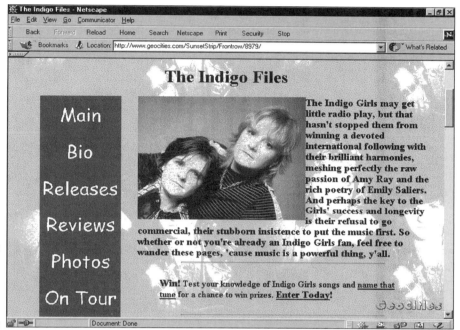

Figure 14-11:
A personal
view of the
Indigo Girls.

TeeVee via TCP

The Internet may be a haven for music lovers, but it's also a haven for couch potatoes who want to chat about their favorite television shows. Dozens of Web sites have (usually unauthorized) picture and script archives for the most popular shows. As you may imagine, science fiction shows are over-represented among these sites, but you can also find Web sites for everything from soap operas to Saturday morning cartoons.

Star Trek: Voyager

```
www.paramount.com/tvvoyager/
```

Many sites on the Web come and go, and publishing the addresses of such sites is always a risk. Television shows come and go even more quickly, however, doubling the risk. The newest series in the Star Trek universe, *Star Trek: Voyager,* has its own site that is sponsored by its producers (see Figure 14-12). The show is quite popular, so the Web site may stay around longer than the ones for some here-today-gone-tomorrow sitcoms.

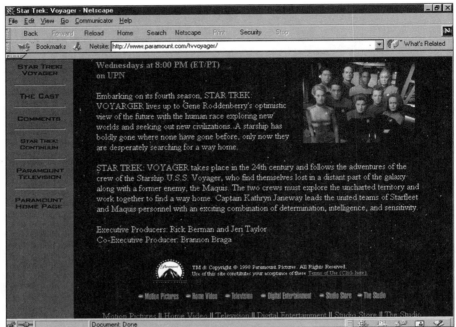

Figure 14-12:
Entering the
starship
Voyager.

You can find summaries of story lines, look at biographies of the characters, download pictures, and so on. The site is set up to keep current fans interested, although it is also a good model for how future television and movie promotions may appear on the Web.

The Tonight Show

www.nbc.com/tonightshow/

The Tonight Show with Jay Leno, shown in Figure 14-13, is another example of an official Web site that is supposed to keep people's interest in a particular show. Of course, the fans of *The Tonight Show* are quite different from fans of *Star Trek: Voyager,* so its Web site is much more low-key.

The Tonight Show Web site lists who's going to appear in upcoming shows, a few of the recent jokes, and so on. It also has quick video clips of some of the sight gag spots. In all, it's a pretty sedate Web site for a pretty sedate television show.

Figure 14-13:
The home
site for *The
Tonight
Show.*

Chapter 15
Web Ways to Shop

● ●

In This Chapter

▶ Cruising the shopping centers

▶ Looking into the little stores

▶ Checking out the services

▶ Finding business associations

● ●

A few years ago, barely any real commerce existed anywhere on the Internet. Sure, a few companies had their advertising available by FTP or by mail response systems, but by and large, you didn't have much reason to keep your wallet handy when you were on the Internet.

The Web has changed all that. As the Web became a popular medium for publishing, some people saw the dollar signs appear and wanted to make parts of the Web safe for shopping. All other media have advertising, and because the goal of advertising is to entice people to spend their money, why shouldn't the Web do the same?

So far, the reality of the Web as a shopping medium is not nearly as grand as merchandisers had hoped for. The speed of the Web prohibits catalogs from having very many full-color pictures in them, and many people still prefer to buy from a human, even if it's a disembodied person in the middle of who-knows-where at the other end of a toll-free 800 number. Nevertheless, more and more stores are on the Web every day.

The commercial side of the Web is still in its formative stages. Television advertising took decades to get into a profitable pattern, and newspaper advertising is still hit-and-miss; no one should expect to understand how best to sell things on the Web for at least another few years. Plenty of early adopters of Web advertising have made an incredible variety of things (also known as "stuff") available for purchase on the Web.

Doing the Mall Crawl

Many early Web entrepreneurs had the idea that, by making the Web seem like a place, people would want to come to a part of it to do their shopping. Parts of the Web could be like suburban shopping malls, they thought, in which people go wandering around from store to store for all their shopping needs.

This picture, of course, doesn't work well with the Web. Clicking a link that is supposedly "in" a mall can just as easily take you to another mall — maybe on a different continent. The early attempts at making malls on the Web failed for lack of tenants for the malls and lack of desire on the part of Web users to stay in one place. (Maybe the lack of frozen yogurt shops had something to do with it as well.)

This early lack of success, however, hasn't stopped many people from trying to make the ultimate Internet mall (or one that just makes money for the owners). I believe that there will probably be a small handful of Internet malls that succeed in the long run, but far fewer than is popularly believed these days. I list here a few that I think have a good shot of staying in business long enough to be listed in the next edition of this book.

DealerNet

```
www.dealernet.com/
```

One kind of mall that is having some success is the Web commercial site where every store sells similar items. This setup seems to work well if the mall also offers free, noncommercial information that Web users find attractive enough to justify putting up with the commercial aspects of the stores, or if the stores sell merchandise that is so compelling that people come just for the merchandise.

DealerNet is such a mall, specializing in car dealers. Figure 15-1 shows DealerNet's main entry point. From there, you can look for a car by manufacturer or see what particular car dealers who are participating in DealerNet have to offer. You can also get information on various new cars, repairs, and other car-related subjects.

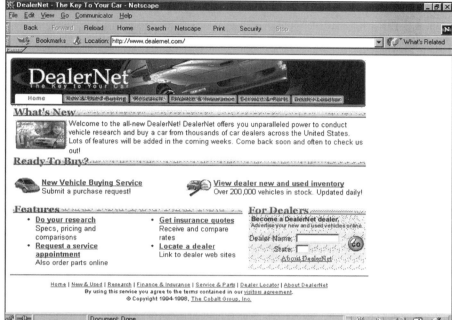

Figure 15-1:
The main
showroom
for
DealerNet.

The Internet Mall

www.internet-mall.com/

One mall that survived the early Web mall shakeout is, appropriately enough, The Internet Mall, a project of Internet pioneer Dave Taylor. It lists tens of thousands of places that you can shop on the Web. The mall is a good first place to look in your search for great places to shop on the Web.

The entrance to The Internet Mall is shown in Figure 15-2. You can almost hear the elevator operator saying "Fifth floor: clothes and sporting goods." Many of the items you see are available through the mall itself, while others can be found at Web sites pointed to by the mall. In this way, the mall feels like a combination of a department store and a mall, without the annoying background music.

Figure 15-2:
The
entrance to
The Internet
Mall.

WebAuction

www.webauction.com/

You're shopping, you want to see something of everything, and you want the lowest prices. Where do you go? Some people like malls, others like auctions. Recently, dozens of auction sites have sprouted up on the Web. One of the best and largest is WebAuction, shown in Figure 15-3. Much of what WebAuction offers is computer-related, but plenty of other items are also available (such as the two-line portable telephone I just bought for $40 less than the same one in the local electronics store!).

Auctions cater to people who like to haggle and shop. Bidding on an item you don't really want is easy, but very low prices on things that no one wanted to bid on that day are also readily available. WebAuction makes bidding simple, and you can even bid low and tell WebAuction to keep upping your bid if other people out-bid you. What a way to go broke!

Figure 15-3:
Tons to choose from at WebAuction.

One Shop Towns

In most places off the Web, finding a shop to spend your money is easy. Finding a place on the Web to spend your money may be a bit more difficult, particularly if the places are competing with other kinds of stores. If shopping on the Web is tedious, the merchants quickly lose your business.

Today, most stores on the Web compete directly with mail-order catalogs that offer toll-free 800 numbers for ordering. On the other hand, many of the best stores on the Web are mail-order stores that are experimenting with the Web as an additional way to get customers.

Music Boulevard

```
www.musicblvd.com/
```

CD shoppers fall into two categories: those who know what they want and those who don't. For those who don't, record stores are great. For those who already have a good idea of what they want to buy, mail-order CD stores offer lower prices and usually have a larger selection. Music Boulevard has made quite a reputation as a leading Web discount CD dealer.

Music Boulevard's site, shown in Figure 15-4, is meant to attract some of the buyers who like to browse in the record store, looking at CDs one at a time. Most of the CDs display complete song lists; some have additional information. As you browse and order CDs, the Web page tells you how much you've already ordered so that you don't get out of control. In this way, the experience is somewhat of a cross between going through a catalog and browsing in a record store.

Internet Shopping Network

www.internet.net/

If computer hardware and software is what you're shopping for, the Internet Shopping Network (ISN) may be the place you want. It's a discount mail-order store with tens of thousands of items, categorized and easier to find than in any paper catalog. Figure 15-5 shows that ISN has two parts, one for buying directly and the other for auctions.

ISN has big plans, particularly to branch out beyond the computer market. In fact, the shop-by-television Home Shopping Network (HSN) cable channel bought ISN as a way to get more into the Web world. ISN started with more funding than many other Internet stores, and it has a good chance of growing into many areas where large volume can lead to lower prices.

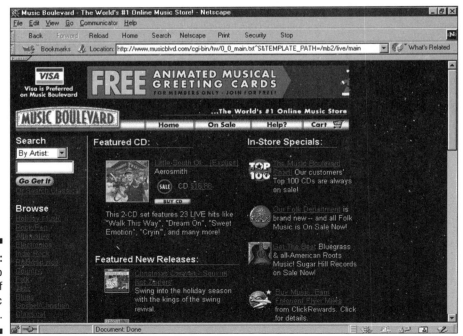

Figure 15-4:
The top
level of
Music
Boulevard.

Figure 15-5:
Shopping at
the Internet
Shopping
Network.

Computer Literacy Bookshops

www.clbooks.com/

Computer users like computer books, and no store anywhere is quite like Computer Literacy, a small chain of bookstores that has been around for much longer than the Web has. It has an incredibly huge collection of books and magazines on computer topics and has a very active mail-order department. Visitors to Silicon Valley often make trips to Computer Literacy on their way to the airport, leaving with many hundreds of dollars of books that can't be found in the regular bookstores in their home towns.

As part of its mail-order business, Computer Literacy has quite an active Web site, as shown in Figure 15-6. Because so many computer books have similar titles, being able to search for a particular word in a title or for an author can make all the difference in finding a specific computer book. After you select a book you are interested in, Computer Literacy's search feature also enables you to search for all books on the same topic.

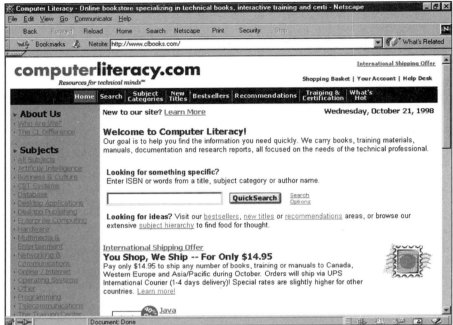

Figure 15-6:
Computer
Literacy's
starting
page.

Amazon.com

www.amazon.com

If a regular bookstore is more your style, you can find many from which to choose on the Internet. Probably the most popular bookstore is Amazon.com, which is shown in Figure 15-7. It has a phenomenal selection of books in many categories, and it also sells CDs and tapes. Although Amazon.com offers many computer books, its strength is in its "regular" books and audio tapes.

Like shopping for music CDs, shopping for books online is not as pleasing for most people as is browsing in a bookstore. On the other hand, online bookstores can have a much greater depth of stock than normal bookstores, and searching for a particular book that you want can be much easier. The trick is to find a Web bookstore (or record store, and so on) that matches your desire for convenience with reasonable additional features, in exchange for the desired feel of a real-life bookstore.

Figure 15-7:
The main
entrance to
Amazon.com.

Wits' End Antiques

www.tias.com/stores/witsend/

Even small stores have Web pages. In fact, telling the difference between a
small store and a big one just by looking at their Web pages is almost
impossible; you must look at what the stores carry. Small stores that understand the culture of the Web and understand their customers can do well on
the Web.

Wits' End Antiques, shown in Figure 15-8, for example, could exist anywhere.
It has the kind of merchandise that is usually bought in person but can be
bought by mail order. It has added a few nice touches to its Web page, such
as pointers to other antique dealers and Web sites that cover antiques,
resulting in a feel that a plain "buy from us"-style Web page lacks.

Figure 15-8:
Wits' End
Antiques.

Services with a Smile

When you think of shopping, you may think of getting stuff you can hold in your hand or put in your garage. You can buy many other types of things, however, including services. For example, many people spend more on services such as insurance and financial advice than they do on merchandise such as CDs and books.

The Web offers an opportunity for service companies to give plenty of free information to prospective and current customers, thereby seeming like the good guys of the Information Superhighway. It also enables them to transact business in a way not allowed by telephones and regular mail. Service companies are far behind merchandise companies in using the Web for commerce, but you can expect them to begin catching up soon.

Homebuyer's Fair

`www.homefair.com/`

Many people spend thousands of dollars using real estate agents. In any town, you can often find dozens of agents, and choosing one who meets your needs is often a hit-and-miss proposition. Of course, no one would buy a home just from looking at its Web page, but the Web is a good way to choose an agent, find an area to move to, or preview homes in a particular area.

Homebuyer's Fair is a general marketplace for people looking at homes. Its Web site, shown in Figure 15-9, gives oodles of good advice about finding homes and also has many commercial listings. It has multiple collateral sections, including information about mortgages, finding apartments, and so on.

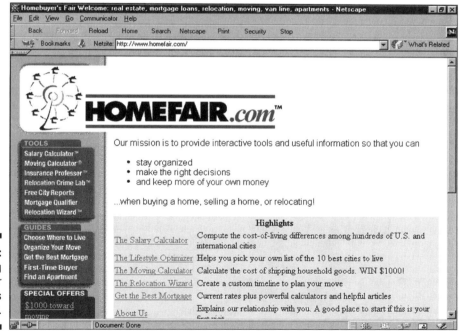

Figure 15-9: Starting location for Homebuyer's Fair.

BookWeb

www.bookweb.org/

Another type of service becoming popular on the Web is that of trade organizations. These groups often provide lists of all their members, give background in what the groups do, and so on. The Web is a good medium for trade groups who normally don't get much coverage. For example, the American Booksellers Association (ABA) has a Web site called BookWeb, shown in Figure 15-10.

BookWeb enables ABA to do more than just list the location of its members, which for bookstores isn't all that interesting because most people know where a local bookstore is located. For example, BookWeb highlights recent bestsellers, trends in book selling, and so on as an inducement for Web users to go to their local bookstores more often. Another feature, the lists of author tours, also has the same effect: Get people to go to bookstores more often.

Figure 15-10:
The entrance to BookWeb.

The Business of Business

Given that commerce is fairly new to the Internet, and particularly to the Web, many companies are just now feeling their ways through the maze of challenges. Some are trying to emulate other companies; others are trying new things to differentiate themselves from their competitors. The goal for most of these companies, however, is the same: attract customers by using the technologies available through the Internet.

CommerceNet

`www.commerce.net/`

CommerceNet was one of the first business groups to get publicity for bringing together commercial interests on the Internet. Its charter, "to develop, maintain, and endorse an Internet-based infrastructure for electronic commerce in business-to-business applications," pretty much means that it wants the Internet to be safe for commerce. At the same time, it is investigating ways to promote commerce on the Internet by looking at how to publicize commercial vendors.

CommerceNet's Web site, shown in Figure 15-11, describes its goals as well as its progress. You can also find a list of pointers to the Web sites of its members and subscribers. Like many other business groups, CommerceNet's work moves forward slowly, but its Web site has also been a place where Web-phobic companies can start to look at the methods they will be using in a few years to collect money and promote themselves on the Web.

CEO Express

`www.ceoexpress.com/`

Today's businesses have many different kinds of people running them. Most companies have a chief executive officer, or *CEO,* who is in charge of most of the management decisions. This is quite different from the chief financial officer, or *CFO,* who cares much more about the money than the ways that it is made or spent. Of course, many companies also have a gang of vice presidents who have a variety of tasks.

CEO Express, shown in Figure 15-12, is aimed at the CEO who knows how to use the Web but doesn't have the time to go wandering around. It has links to dozens of different business news services, business research, and other kinds of information that are typically wanted by CEOs. Of course, the site doesn't exclude people who aren't CEOs, but the content is definitely slanted toward business executives.

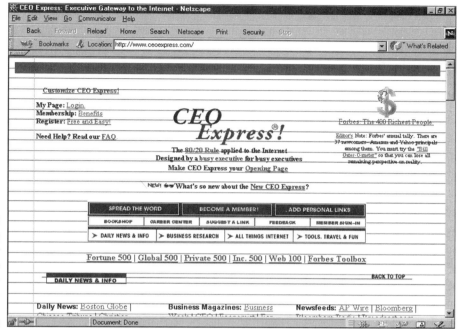

Figure 15-12:
A place for
busy CEOs
(or people
who wish
they were).

Chapter 16

Self-Reference: Computers on Computers

In This Chapter

▶ Getting help when you need it most
▶ Talking to the big companies
▶ Doing the dweeb thing
▶ Reflecting on the Internet

*E*verybody on the Web has a computer. This statement may seem a tad obvious, but it means that everybody on the Web has something in common: computers. Although not all computers are alike, their commonalty has led to large areas of the Web being devoted to discussions of computers.

Actually, people on the Web certainly have more than computers in common, but people don't seem to want to talk about the nature of the human condition, spirituality, impending death of the body, and so on as much as they want to talk about computers. Maybe next year. . . .

Emergency Road Crews for Your Computer

Every computer user is familiar with becoming dependent on a computer and then having it fail at the wrong moment. For some people, such failures are a nuisance; for others, they are nerve-wracking. If my computer doesn't work, I want help, and I want it *now*.

Of course, you can always refer to the manual or the books (such as this one) that you have bought to help you. However, if none of these printed materials have what you need to fix the problem, you can turn to online resources. The Web is still a bit weak in this area; commercial services such as CompuServe and America Online have much better forums for getting problems resolved quickly. Some places, however, do exist on the Web where you can search for answers and even ask questions if you can't find what you need.

Capital PC User Group

www.cpcug.org

Many local user groups have Web pages. Calling the Capital PC User Group a "local user group" is a misnomer, however. The group is an international support organization that just happens to have a location (Washington, D.C.) implied in its name. The CPCUG is one of the biggest computer groups in the world.

The most interesting part of the CPCUG Web site (and for many people, the most interesting part of the CPCUG) is the myriad user groups that are part of CPCUG. Figure 16-1 shows this part of the Web site. Some of these groups consist of just a few people who share a specific interest; other groups have hundreds of members.

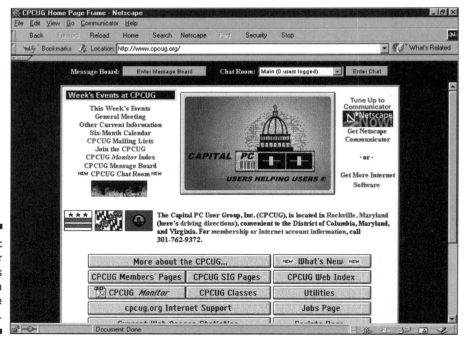

Figure 16-1: CPCUG user groups cover a wide range of interests.

PC questions

```
news:comp.sys.ibm.pc.misc
```

Usenet is not a good medium for getting an instant response in an emergency, but thousands of people have gotten help from other users in some of the newsgroups. One of the most active groups is comp.sys.ibm.pc.misc, the catch-all group for questions about PC systems. Figure 16-2 shows a few of the messages that go by every day.

Because of the often overly broad range of topics at this site, one of the dozens of other Usenet newsgroups that also discuss the PC may be the best place for specific queries. For example, more than a dozen groups have names that start with comp.sys.ibm.pc. Similar Usenet newsgroups that relate to parts of the PC, such as comp.os.ms-windows.misc (which covers Microsoft Windows) also are available.

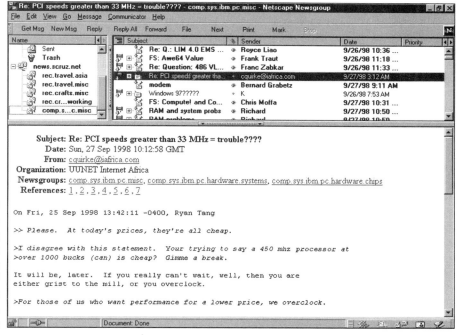

Figure 16-2:
This PC newsgroup often gets hundreds of messages per day.

MacInTouch

`www.macintouch.com/`

Macintosh users can tap a different set of resources. The MacInTouch site, maintained by Ric Ford, is a superb source for news about the Macintosh. It is usually updated daily, and it also has links to dozens of other good Mac pages. Figure 16-3 shows the top level of the site.

To many people, the Macintosh community seems more tightly knit than the PC community. Given Apple's ups and downs in the past few years, you can understand why Mac users feel like they need to keep up to date more than PC users. This site caters to both novices and wizards and also helps track the general Mac business.

Support in Your Court

Calling the tech-support department of most companies is an exercise in frustration. You wait on hold for, typically, ten minutes. You pray that the hold music they have isn't horrible. Instead, you get used to the horrible music or, worse, a constant stream of advertising for the product that isn't working.

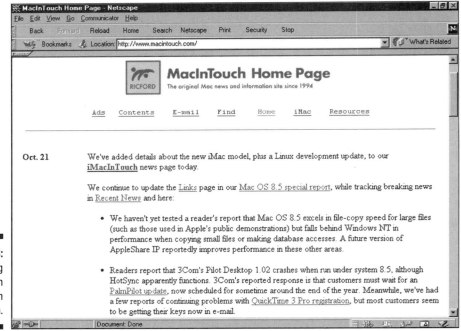

Figure 16-3:
Getting
Macintosh
news from
MacInTouch.

A few companies have started to put much of their product-support information on the Web in hope of keeping customers off the phone and happy. Of course, lots of questions that can be answered by humans at the company can't be answered by the material at the Web site, but a "frequently-asked questions" document on a manufacturer's site has a reasonable chance of having what you need. On the other hand, the Web site is free, it's available after hours and on weekends (which is when products seem to break, isn't it?), and it has no hold music.

If you are a company, keep in mind that putting your support database on the Web isn't really technical support; it's more like *presupport*. Presupport is a good way to reduce the number of people who need to call you, and it enables you to keep your customers happier for a very small price. The sites shown here are for the largest manufacturers, although dozens of other smaller companies also have presupport sites on the Web.

Microsoft

`www.microsoft.com/`

They're big. They're bold. They own the market. And, in a nice twist, they have one of the best tech-support Web sites you can find anywhere. Even before it became The Monopoly That Ate the Software Industry, Microsoft published its database of tech support information on many services such as CompuServe. Now that database and numerous gigabytes of support information are available for free on the Web. Figure 16-4 shows part of the Microsoft Web site.

Microsoft's Web site mixes technical support with sales, marketing, and news. The tech support part of the Web site contains a large set of searchable databases. The searches return information on bugs, common problems, "workarounds," and so on. Of course, the material is written by Microsoft, so don't expect the reports of bugs to be at all apologetic.

Microsoft also maintains a huge collection of files that you can download from its Web site. These files are updated device drivers, sample code for its programming packages, fixes for some software, and so on. Again, all these files are free, and for most people, finding these files is easier than waiting on the phone to Microsoft. In fact, most of Microsoft's newer products have links in their Help menus that take you directly to the right page on the Microsoft support site.

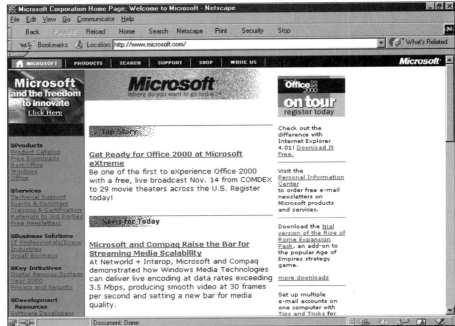

Figure 16-4:
A portion of
the wide
world of
Microsoft.

Apple

www.apple.com/

Macintosh users also have a very good Web resource for them: the Apple
Web site. Like the Microsoft site, the Apple site offers a plethora of software,
fixes, and so on; you can even buy a new Mac there. Figure 16-5 shows the
top level of the Apple Web site.

Like many other companies, Apple is somewhat of a bureaucracy, and many
divisions have overlapping responsibilities. Thus, finding the best place on
the Apple Web server to look for answers to specific questions isn't always
easy. On the other hand, Apple is very familiar with presenting information
in a variety of fashions, so you can often find what you're looking for in more
than one place.

Novell

www.novell.com/

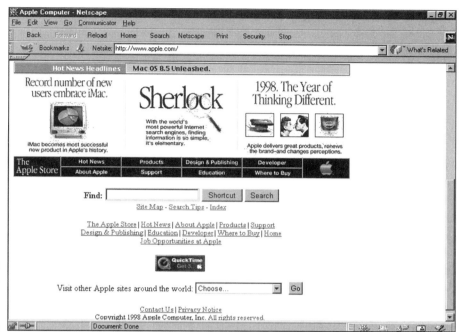

Figure 16-5:
Apple's
Web site.

If you work on a LAN that operates using Novell's NetWare or intraNetWare products, you're familiar with the problems that a network crash can bring. And because so many manufacturers sell software that works on NetWare, finding conflicts and problems is all too easy. Novell's Web site, as shown in Figure 16-6, can be an answer to many of your problems.

Because network problems are notoriously hard to track down, Novell has worked hard to make the technical support database easy to search. People who support NetWare networks report that they have found incredible nuggets of information while looking through the support database, and regular users should feel reasonably at home as well.

Dweeb Talk

If you like computers, you probably like to talk to other people who like computers. For the first decade, the Internet consisted of almost nothing other than people talking to each other about computers or sending each other files that related to (you guessed it) computers.

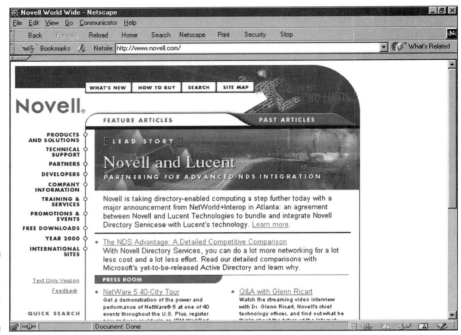

Figure 16-6:
Novell's
support
Web page.

Like the rest of the Internet, the Web is full of computer talk. Some of the talk is idle chatter, but the best of it is very helpful to people who rely on their computers for their work or, um, their pleasure. This section shows a few places that you may find interesting if you want to know just what people who talk computers talk *about*.

Seidman's Online Insider

`www.onlineinsider.com/`

Because the growth of the online world has been so quick, many print magazines have cropped up to try to help you make sense of the Internet industry. If you're already using the Internet, however, these magazines are mostly full of things that you either already know or have no interest in. Another problem with monthly magazines about the online world is that they are out of date by the time you get them in your hands.

Seidman's Online Insider is a free electronic magazine that you can have sent to you through e-mail. The magazine is written by Robert Seidman, who has a very eclectic view of the online world. It covers all parts of the Internet delivery and content businesses. Figure 16-7 shows the home page for *Seidman's Online Insider,* where you can also look at back issues and find subscription information.

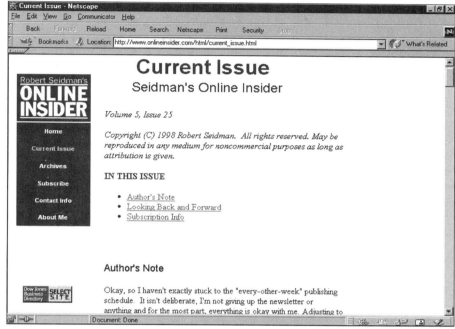

Figure 16-7:
The
Seidman's
Online
Insider
home page.

HotWired

www.hotwired.com/

If you cross *People* magazine with *Rolling Stone* with *BYTE* and put it online, you get *HotWired,* the online sister to the oh-so-hip *Wired* magazine. *HotWired,* shown in Figure 16-8, is free, but you must use a Web form to subscribe to it. This stipulation means that you can read *HotWired* only if you have a Web browser that supports forms and security.

The content on *HotWired* is all over the map. Different areas of *HotWired* include the following:

- ✔ Large multimedia files, such as music and pictures
- ✔ Computer industry news overlaid with lifestyle coverage
- ✔ Technical posturing about the future of the Internet
- ✔ Advertising
- ✔ Discussion about the articles
- ✔ Interactive entertainment

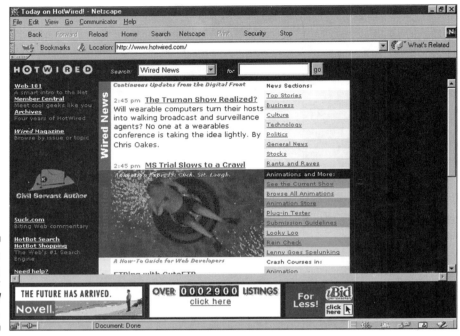

Figure 16-8:
The starting
page for
HotWired
subscribers.

The feeling on *HotWired* is cutting edge (possibly *over* the cutting edge),
immediate, and trendy. For example, Figure 16-9 shows another, typically
overstimulating page on HotWired.

If you like this type of trendy graphics, *HotWired* is certainly an interesting
Web site to visit over and over.

Perl

```
www.perl.org/
```

Programming languages are not everyone's cup of tea. People who don't use
computers much often look at programming languages as if those languages
were forms of black magic that they could never master. Even if you're a
regular computer user, you may feel more than a bit of trepidation if you are
asked to train in a programming language such as C or Basic. I'm quite fond
of Perl, enough so that I have written *Perl 5 For Dummies*. It's a great starting
point for getting the hang of Perl, in my not-so-humble opinion.

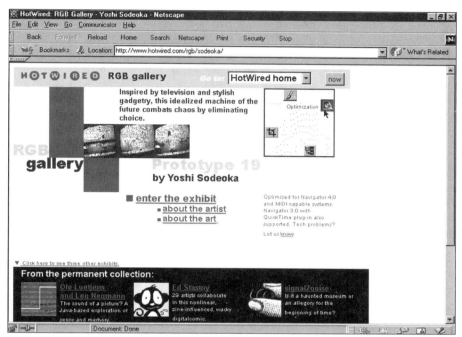

Figure 16-9:
Design
gone mad
at
HotWired.

Perl is a relatively new programming language that has many features that make it particularly attractive to people writing quick-and-dirty programs that can process text. Familiarizing yourself with Perl is fairly easy: Perl is between Basic and C in difficulty. After you soak up even a little bit of Perl, however, using it is a breeze.

Best of all, Perl is completely free. Most Perl programmers use it on UNIX systems, but versions for MS-DOS, Windows NT, and the Macintosh also are available. Figure 16-10 shows one of the best sites, which contains many pointers to other Perl resources. Perl has garnered a near-fanatic following of users, and quite a bit of sample source code is available.

The Internet in the Mirror

What could be more self-referential than using computers to talk about computers? Using computers on the Internet to talk about computers on the Internet! Does life get any better?

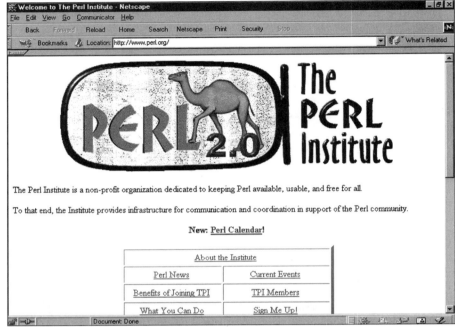

Figure 16-10:
The Perl
Institute is
the leading
professional
group for
Perl
programmers.

Actually, the Internet can evolve in no better way than through online discussions about what is happening, what people want, and so on. For example, Usenet news was started as an experiment. As the experiment succeeded, Usenet also became the medium for discussion about itself. Almost every new Internet service has come out of heavy discussion, followed by experimentation, followed by revision based on feedback.

IETF

`www.ietf.org/`

The main group that coordinates the standards on the Internet is the *IETF* (*Internet Engineering Task Force*). The IETF is a voluntary group that meets only three times per year. Almost all the work of the IETF is done through the mailing lists of its Working Groups.

Figure 16-11 shows the IETF's home page. It leads to Working Group lists, descriptions of upcoming meetings, and the archives of documents and standards called *RFCs* (*Requests For Comments*). RFCs are the written understanding of the underpinnings of the Internet. They have no force of law, but everyone on the Internet pretty much agrees to try to abide by them.

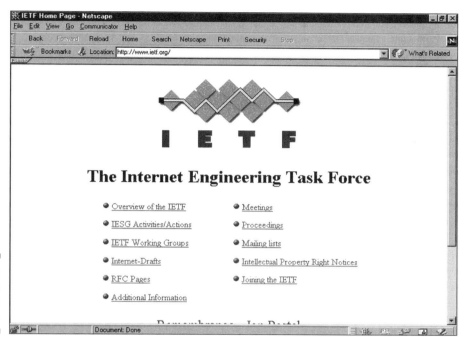

Figure 16-11:
Here is the
gateway to
the IETF.

If you're interested in the human side of the IETF, you should look at some of the Working Groups. Figure 16-12 shows the Working Group area of the IETF server. Each Working Group has its own mailing list, and many of the Working Groups have Web sites that have collected all the old mail from the mailing lists. The Working Groups are also where RFCs originate.

Because people don't need to do anything to join the IETF other than participate, the number of people in the IETF is unknown. IETF's loose structure has served the Internet and the Web well so far, and there is no need to change it now.

Usenet Info Center

```
sunsite.unc.edu/usenet-i/
```

Usenet has become so large and diffuse that finding out what's new and what's happening in the Usenet world is difficult. Kevin Atkinson has put together an excellent Web page, shown in Figure 16-13, that pulls together a wide range of resources about Usenet, such as a searchable list of all newsgroups.

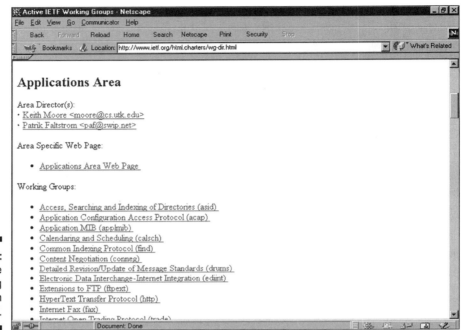

Figure 16-12:
Some of the
Working
Groups in
the IETF.

Figure 16-13:
The Usenet
Info Center
Launch
Pad.

The Center's list of FAQs (documents with answers to frequently asked questions) concerning Usenet is particularly useful. If you are new to Usenet or want to go a few levels farther into it than you already have, these FAQs are excellent places to start. Also check out the descriptions of the various Usenet news readers. If you're a Netscape Communicator user, you'll find the description of some of the older news readers particularly humorous, given their arcane syntax and rules.

Security Reference Index

    www.telstra.com.au/info/security.html

The Internet is not all fun and games. You've probably heard about some of the more notorious break-ins that have happened on the Internet, but you probably haven't heard about the hundreds of others that happen all the time. Security is a big issue for administrators and users everywhere on the Internet.

Telstra has put together an excellent Web page that covers almost every aspect of security on the Internet. The site, shown in Figure 16-14, actually covers more than just the Internet; many of the pointers lead to LAN security discussions as well. For an overview of what's being discussed and done about security on the Internet, however, this site is an excellent place to start.

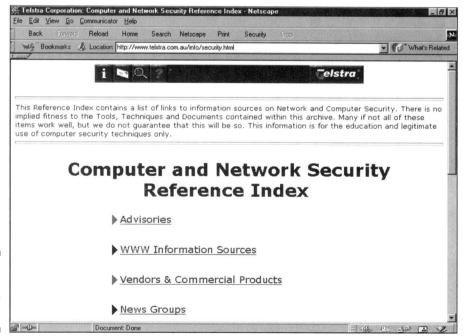

Figure 16-14:
Telstra's
security
Web site.

Consummate Winsock Apps List

`cws.internet.com/`

If you use a Windows system and TCP/IP, you are probably aware of the myriad choices you must make. First, you need to choose a Windows TCP/IP driver, commonly called *Winsock,* of which there are more than a dozen. Then you must choose all the TCP/IP applications, such as your Web browser. The choices go on and on. Fortunately, a single Web site collects information on all the known Winsock drivers and applications. The Consummate Winsock Apps List, shown in Figure 16-15, is a godsend for system administrators and end users who just want to know what is available. The pages have links to the manufacturers or, in the case of freeware or shareware, links to the programs themselves. Lists of helper programs, such as HTML editors, also are available.

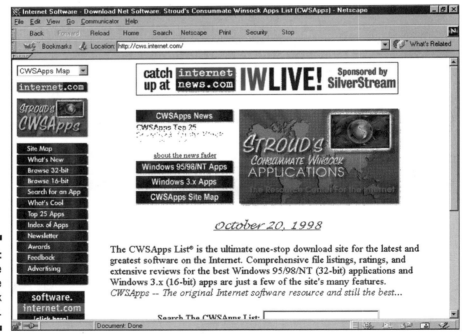

Figure 16-15:
The
Consummate
Winsock
Apps List.

Chapter 17

Your Government: At Work?

In This Chapter

▶ Finding nationwide government resources

▶ Getting more local with state governments

▶ Finding help for schools and parents

▶ Using the Web to get laws changed

*A*lmost everyone has a love/hate relationship with the government. We love it when it provides services we want and need; we hate it when it charges us for those services or for services that we don't want or need. As Thoreau put it, "Government is at best but an expedient; but most governments are usually, and all governments are sometimes, inexpedient."

More and more governments are using the Web in the same way as many companies are. These governments and their agencies use it as an advertising medium, a way of giving out information, and a method for keeping their clients (that's us, the citizens) happy. People have responded by setting up Web sites that are based around either supporting current laws or changing them, much like normal political activities are organized.

The Feds Are Ahead

In the United States, few people think of the federal government as being at the forefront of communications technology. In fact, few people believe that they can communicate at all with their elected representatives or most parts of the federal bureaucracy, such as the IRS or the Social Security Administration. Many federal agencies, however, have recently latched onto the Web as a way to tell the online world about themselves.

The U.S. federal government has zillions of departments, many of which are still stuck in the paper era. Now that funding cutbacks are becoming more common, many of these departments are getting on the Web as a way to protect their turf, letting the taxpayers know what the agencies actually do with their tax dollars.

U.S. House of Representatives

www.house.gov/

The most direct way to affect federal legislation is by contacting members of Congress. Most newspapers list the addresses of all the local congresspeople, but few citizens ever write to their representatives about the issues that are important to them. The small but vocal minority that do then gets the most say with the representatives.

Congress has taken steps to reverse this trend by making more information about itself available free on the Web. Figure 17-1 shows the House Congressional Web site, a central repository of information on such things as the name of every representative, what committees they serve on, and the internal congressional bureaucracy. Don't expect to find much creativity here, but at least the information is up to date, and you can find out how your representative voted on important bills.

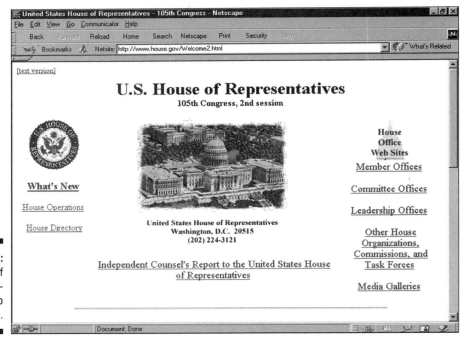

Figure 17-1:
The House of Representatives Web site.

Federal legislation

thomas.loc.gov/

If you're more concerned about legislation that is moving through Congress than the people moving it, the THOMAS system, run by the Library of Congress, is probably for you. THOMAS, shown in Figure 17-2, tracks all laws as they are amended and passed through the two houses. (The name THOMAS always appears in all capital letters even though it doesn't stand for anything; the system is, in fact, named for Thomas Jefferson, a strong believer in open public debate.)

The Library of Congress, which is traditionally thought of as the place where you send books to copyright them, has taken a much more activist role in enabling people to find legislation in which they are interested. The search feature of THOMAS enables you to access the text of legislation by searching for the bill number or words that appear anywhere in the bill. You can also quickly find out where in the congressional process the bill is, who has sponsored it, and so on.

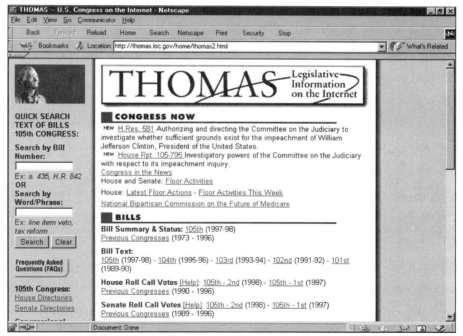

Figure 17-2:
The top
level of
THOMAS.

FedWorld

`www.fedworld.gov/`

Congress isn't the only one getting into the Web. Many agencies of the Administration have Web sites. FedWorld, shown in Figure 17-3, is the best central spot to look first if you want to see which part of the Administrative branch is doing what on the Web. FedWorld usually has the most up-to-date pointers of any Web site.

The main part of FedWorld is a search engine that has many different ways to find what you want. FedWorld also contains lists of sites and databases that are part of the federal government. For example, Figure 17-4 shows another federal site, the site for the Internal Revenue Service. Don't scream: It's actually a very useful Web site where you can download any tax form imaginable and get plenty of tax help.

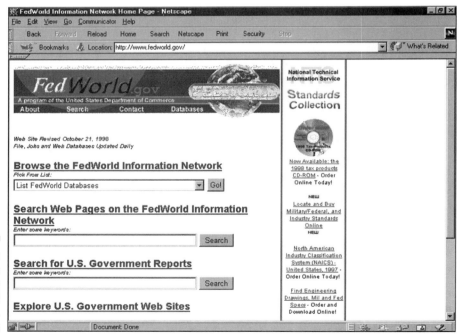

Figure 17-3:
The beginning of FedWorld.

Figure 17-4:
Tax
information
at your
fingertips.

National Science Foundation

www.nsf.gov/

The National Science Foundation (NSF) has always been on the forefront of Internet use. For many years, the NSF paid for many of the main Internet links so that scientists around the country could pass data quickly, thereby helping their research. Although the NSF is now much less involved with the Internet itself, it is still very active in sponsoring scientific research.

The NSF's Web site, shown in Figure 17-5, is one of the best you can find in the U.S. government. Part of this superiority, of course, has to do with NSF's Internet legacy, but another part has to do with making sure that NSF projects continue to get funded. The NSF does an excellent job of promoting its funded projects, particularly the expensive ones, to reduce the chance that it will lose congressional funding.

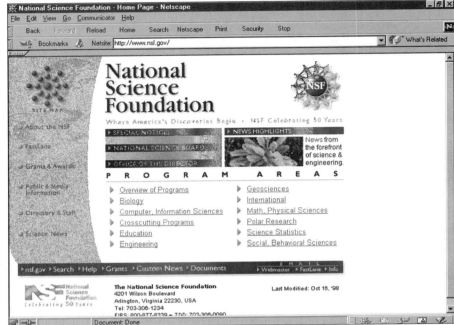

Figure 17-5:
The central
Web site for
the National
Science
Foundation.

U.K. Government Information Service

www.open.gov.uk/

The U.S. federal government isn't the only national government on the Web. Many European countries, as well as the European Union itself, are starting to publish Web sites for pretty much the same reasons as those of the American government.

Figure 17-6, for example, shows the central Web site for the federal bureaucracy in the United Kingdom. A surprising number of federal agencies in the United Kingdom have set up their own Web sites, many of which are better designed and have more information than their American counterparts. This site also has pointers to federally supported agencies such as museums and research labs.

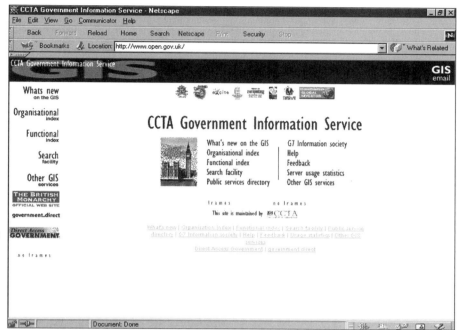

State and Local Folk

If you move down from the federal level, you find many fewer Web sites. A handful of states have systems, some of them as extensive as FedWorld, but most states with a Web presence have only one or two experimental pages that don't say much other than "Come visit our state; we need the tourism."

On the other hand, state bureaucracies have the same need for advertising and information distribution that federal bureaucracies do. In fact, with the current trend in Washington toward canceling federal programs and giving the money to the states, many state agencies will probably start promoting themselves more so that people within their states know more about them.

California

```
www.ca.gov/
```

California has one of the more online governments. With so many computer activists living in the state, the legislative and executive branches have had little choice but to put much of its most important information online. Figure 17-7, for example, shows the list of state departments that have Web sites.

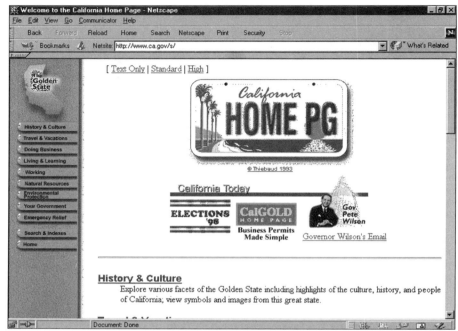

Figure 17-7:
California
agencies
with Web
sites.

In many ways, the California government is trying to make the Web part of its daily affairs. Election results are now reported on the Web as they appear on election night, and the state legislature has the text of many of its bills available online.

Oregon

`www.state.or.us/`

Other states also have Web sites that contain a great deal of public information. Oregon, another computerphilic community, has a very complete Web site, as shown in Figure 17-8.

The Oregon server is a good example of how state Web sites often grow from disconnected servers into a central site. Many of the sites that you can reach from the main page clearly are not designed by the folks who designed the page you see in Figure 17-8. A single central agency can help bring all these servers together into one Web page and still let each of the agencies run its own server and manage the information on it. This setup differs from many company Web sites, in which the entire server is run by one person, usually a system administrator or other technical person.

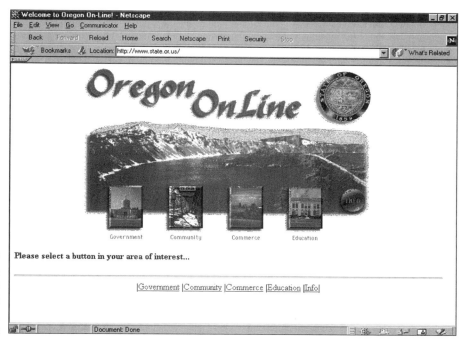

Figure 17-8:
Oregon's
government
site.

K through 12 through the Web

Home computers are widely touted for their capability to help kids in school. Whether or not you believe that computers can be used to enhance education (and plenty of folks don't), you can find plenty of resources for parents and students on the Web — everything from lesson plans to science project ideas to homework helpers.

Many of the kindergarten through 12th grade resources you find on the Web are pretty much the same as you find in magazines and books aimed at kids and parents. The advantages of the Web are that you don't need to go out and search for the magazines and books; the content on the Web is often more up to date; and it's almost always free.

Web66

web66.coled.umn.edu/

A few Web kindergarten through 12th grade sites are aimed specifically at parents; many more, however, are aimed at teachers. In the current educational funding environment, parents are often helping teachers with everything from buying computer equipment to staffing computer labs in schools. Thus the Web sites aimed at teachers are usually quite appropriate for parents as well.

Web66 is a great service that is meant to help teachers work with the Internet in general and the Web in particular. It's a service of the University of Minnesota College of Education. The folks at Web66 advocate that K through 12 schools set up their own Web sites so that schools can share information with other schools.

The Web66 site, shown in Figure 17-9, contains plenty of good information about how to set up a Web server, how to structure pages so that kids can share and get good information, how to deal with appropriate use of computers, and so on. It also includes links to all the known K through 12

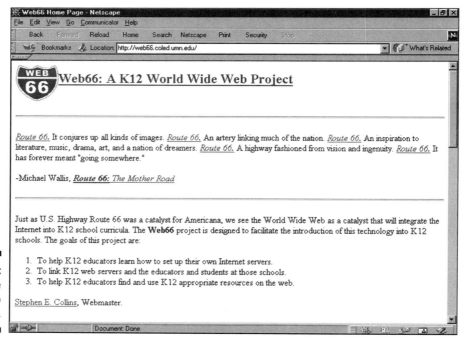

Figure 17-9: The entrance to Web66.

schools that have Web pages. Some of these pages are cute, and some are barely usable, but many look better than some of the commercial Web sites you encounter. Figure 17-10, for example, shows a typical school site.

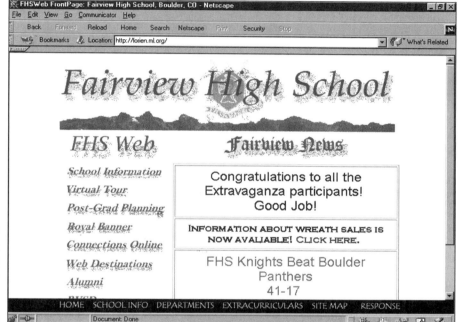

Figure 17-10:
A typical home page at a high school.

ERIC

`ericir.syr.edu/`

ERIC, the *E*ducational *R*esources *I*nformation *C*enter, has been around for many years, providing information to teachers about how to deal with computer and technology issues. Its popular AskERIC service enables teachers to ask questions of a board of people who can give personalized answers or direct them to existing materials that they may need.

ERIC's Web page, as shown in Figure 17-11, leads to all of ERIC's services, including AskERIC. The collection includes pointers to many other Web sites as well as lists of conferences, publishers, and so on.

Figure 17-11:
A section of
the Web
page for
ERIC.

Change That Law: Advocates Get the Word Out

You may have heard how the power of the Internet has helped prevent bad laws from being passed. For example, a legislator introduces a bill with some extreme changes; people on the Internet hear about it; a flurry of e-mail and postings to various Usenet newsgroups results; and many people then get in touch with their legislators, who put the kibosh on the bill. The press then notes how the Internet has changed things.

Unfortunately, this scenario is still relatively uncommon and usually has little to do with the Web because most of this type of action occurs in mailing lists and Usenet newsgroups, which are usually not available to people who aren't already participating. Face it: Hundreds of bad laws are passed every year, and only a handful get the kind of publicity described here.

The Web is quite useful for groups of people who want to make long-term political statements and to track the laws that affect them. Oddly, it is not yet being used much for these purposes, but that will probably change as the Web grows in the next few years.

NRA and NOW

```
www.nra.org/
```

and

```
www.now.org/
```

The National Rifle Association, commonly called the NRA, was one of the first major political groups to put up a Web site. This site, shown in Figure 17-12, includes information about current legislation, how to join, group benefits, and so on. Figure 17-13 shows a similar kind of site, this one for the National Organization for Women, better known as NOW.

In many ways, the NRA and NOW Web sites look like the Web sites for a company selling products. Political groups have products, just like commercial organizations have products. They want you to stay interested, to feel like you want to keep in contact with them, to give you a sense of urgency about their products, and so on.

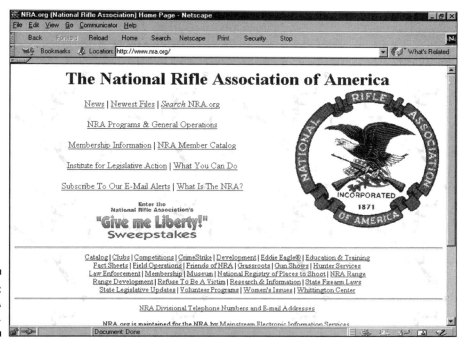

Figure 17-12:
The NRA
Web site.

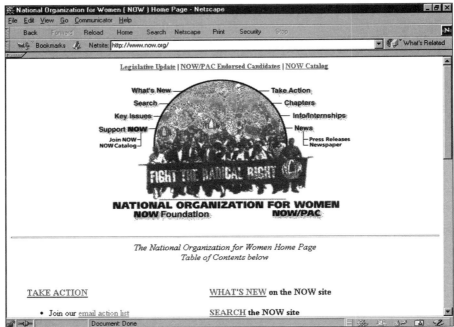

Figure 17-13:
NOW's
Web site.

Tibet liberation

www.tibet.org/

To many people, the NRA is part of the right wing of a "left-versus-right" debate, and NOW is part of the left wing. These people try to shoehorn local and national issues into the Republican/Democratic membership division or the liberal/conservative conceptual division. Issues such as social welfare, national defense, governmental power, and so on all get split up along these imaginary lines.

Many political groups and struggles lie pretty much outside of the left/right spectrum. For example, millions of people from all political persuasions have been trying to pressure China into allowing Tibet to exist as an independent country ever since China invaded Tibet in 1950. Figure 17-14 shows the home page for a group that is trying to keep the debate about Tibet alive.

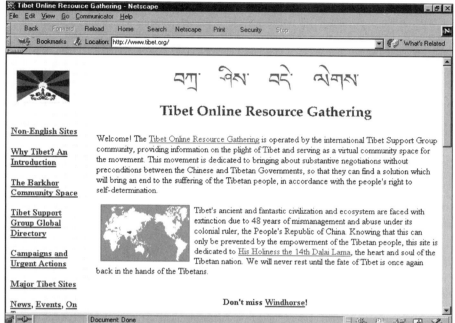

Figure 17-14:
The Tibet
Online
Resource
Gathering
page.

Computer Professionals for Social Responsibility

`www.cpsr.org/`

Many other political groups also fit outside the left/right spectrum. Some groups, such as Computer Professionals for Social Responsibility (CPSR), are mostly concerned with educating people about their current rights so that those rights are not taken away. Figure 17-15 shows the CPSR Web site.

Like many political groups, CPSR's interests revolve around more than a single issue. For example, CPSR is using the Web to publicize privacy issues that the growth of the Internet affects. The Web site also has pointers to other computer-affiliated political groups.

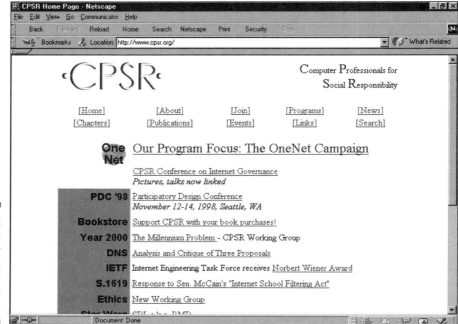

Figure 17-15:
The
Computer
Professionals
for Social
Responsibility
Web site.

Part V
Your Name in Lights

"I COULDN'T SAY ANYTHING—THEY WERE IN HERE WITH THAT PROGRAM WE BOUGHT THEM THAT ENCOURAGES ARTISTIC EXPRESSION."

In this part . . .

1f you're one of those people who isn't content to just sit back and read what's on the Web, these chapters are for you. Composer is the tool you use to create Web pages. The chapters in this part explain how you, too, can use Composer to publish your own Web pages, and they provide guidelines on exactly how to do it as well as a solid grounding in the technical stuff you need to know. Beyond all that, these chapters give you advice on how to publish content that is not only attractive but also compelling.

Chapter 18

So You Want to Be a Producer

In This Chapter

▶ Deciding to publish on the Web

▶ Exploring individual and business publishing on the Web

▶ Finding a Web provider

▶ Thinking about legal issues with Web pages

*U*p to this point, you have pretty much been reading about other people's content. You have seen dozens of pictures of places on the Web that have interesting things on them: fascinating ideas, humorous snippets, and so on. If you're like most people, you have probably said, "Hey, I can do that!" Of course you can.

As discussed way back in Chapter 2, you need a Web client like Navigator to browse around the Web; to put your content on the Web, you need a Web server. That last part isn't completely true: Actually, you just need *access* to a Web server. That is, each site on the Web needs to have a server, but each user at the site needs only to be linked into the site's content to have something published.

This chapter and the following three chapters cover how you can become a Web publisher using Composer, which is part of Netscape Communicator. Putting your content on the Web is similar to putting your content on paper. In the print world, publishers range from people who photocopy a few pages to massive publishing houses. On the Web, you may publish a hundred words, or you may create a huge site consisting of thousands of pages. No matter how much or little you add, you need the same technology, the same design choices, and the same talent for figuring out what to say and how to say it.

Home Sweet Home Pages

Don't be put off by the highfalutin sound of the word *publishing*. At its simplest, putting content on the Web is no more like publishing than typing up a page of some of your thoughts, printing a dozen copies, and sending them to a bunch of friends is like publishing. Publishing can be simple, cheap, and low-key.

If you have explored some of the sites shown so far, you've probably come across some areas that seemed incredibly trivial, leaving you to wonder why someone bothered to create those pages. On the other hand, you've probably also come across other areas that seem a bit rough but quirky in a way that *you* like, even though you know most other people may not like them.

In other words, Web pages can be like the people who create them. If you're lucky, you can publish Web pages that are a great reflection of yourself. Maybe you aren't ready to write a full book about your thoughts and views, but you really want to communicate one special idea, and you can summarize this idea on one or two pages. Or you want some songs that you wrote to be published, but you aren't ready to share them with a record company. Or you are a painter or photographer, but you have only a dozen or so paintings or photographs that you think the whole world deserves to see, not enough for a gallery showing.

If what you want to publish — be it a treatise on politics, your band's latest tune, or your newest photo of the pond out back — isn't ready for primetime, the Web may be just the outlet for your creative expressions.

Personal Webtop Publishing

The cost of publishing content on the Web is essentially $0. No paper is involved, and no transportation costs are charged. You can create the content on your computer using Composer and spend a few cents uploading it to your Internet provider; after that, the electrons just float around the Internet. If your intent is simply to have your words, sound files, and pictures available to the world, or at least the part of the world that has a Web account, the solution is incredibly simple: Create Web content.

Of course, creating Web content is different from getting your book published and making it available in bookstores or getting a record deal and getting your CD into record stores. In most parts of the world, many more people have access to bookstores and record stores than have access to the Web. But face it: How many people buy books that aren't best-sellers or that aren't on topics that they are particularly interested in? How many people buy CDs or tapes from artists they haven't heard on the radio? The next time you're in a bookstore, look at the shelves of novels and think about how many of them no one will buy. Check out the unsold stacks of CDs and tapes from independent-label artists.

Publishing on the Web is quite different from publishing in the mainstream media in that the Web's possible audience is smaller. (Maybe a hundred million people can access the Web, whereas billions of people can read books.) On the other hand, today's typical Web users are often more curious than today's typical book and music buyers; you can see this by the fact that they go to so many Web sites in their search for entertainment. Web users poke around more. They look into places that may lead them nowhere on the off chance that something interesting may pop up. Of course, this curiosity is true for some book and music buyers, too, but not in the same proportion as Web users.

Keep in mind, too, that the Web's audience is more widespread. Even if you get your book published, it's probably only distributed in your own country. If you get a local gallery owner to show your paintings, your audience is limited to the people in your local area. Put your thoughts or paintings on a Web page, however, and your content is available to Web users worldwide.

One of the advantages of publishing your stuff on your Web page is that you don't have to convince a publisher (or anyone else) that enough people will buy your stuff to cover the cost of publishing and to earn everyone involved a profit. Nor do you need anyone to approve of your content in order to publish it.

The teeny cost of gigantic storage

The economics of publishing on the Web are really amazing. Suppose that you've written what you think is a terribly interesting book, but you haven't found a publisher for it. You decide to put it out on the Web for free, forgoing the chance to get rich in exchange for the chance to be appreciated (and maybe courted for your next novel).

Typical novels run from around 80,000 to 100,000 words, which translates roughly to 500 kilobytes (half a megabyte) of hard disk space. Today, the folks running Web sites can buy hard disks for roughly $50 per gigabyte, meaning that the space your novel takes up on the hard disk costs them about 2 cents. (If the Web site is smart enough to store your story in compressed format, squeezed into a teensier disk space, we're talking a penny.) And the cost of disk storage goes down every year.

Of course, not everyone is a writer. You may be an artist, and pictures certainly take up more disk space than words. Moderate-sized photos, however, usually take less than 1 megabyte each, and a good collection of photos rarely runs to more than 100 megabytes, which is about $5. If you're a musician, full stereo, CD-quality music takes up about 10 megabytes per minute, so a few songs for your sampler shouldn't run more than the same 100 megabytes.

Compared to standard publishing, storage on a Web site isn't a significant expense. In fact, the cost is almost trivial relative to just the beginning costs of publishing a book or a CD. Of course, storage isn't the only cost for Web sites, but it is often one of the major costs that book and CD publishers must deal with.

Communications cost more than storage

The communications cost for an Internet provider is usually quite low. Of course, the cost depends on the location of the Web space provider, the provider's overhead, the number of other people like you who want to publish Web pages, and so on. For most Web providers, however, the communications cost is less than $1,000 per month.

At first, communications cost may seem like the biggest part of the costs of being a Web provider: If a Web provider has only ten people who are publishing on its service, it must charge each of them $25 to $100 per month just to cover its communications cost. Very few companies, however, are just Web providers; they are also general Internet providers, which enables them to spread the communications cost over a much larger number of people.

Administration can be cheap or expensive

One of the hardest things for Web providers to predict is the cost of getting you, the novice, on the Web. If you read this chapter and the three that follow it, you can find out almost everything you need to know about putting your information on the Web in a well-formatted manner. Your Web provider won't need to help you much at all.

On the other hand, if you tried to publish your content right now without having read these chapters, you'd probably have a zillion questions, and the chances are good that you'd take up a great deal of the Web manager's time. Web providers need to factor the amount of hand-holding you may need into the cost of the service; hand-holding time is usually quite difficult to predict, so providers often guess high.

If you aren't actually changing any of your Web content on a regular basis, don't pay money to the Web space providers that charge you a monthly fee for maintaining your Web content unless the rate is very low — for example, about $5 per month (although even that is somewhat high). To maintain a static Web site takes no effort. You should be charged a monthly fee only for those months in which you add or change your content — and even then the fee shouldn't be very high.

You may get it for free

As a potential content provider, you probably want to go with a Web provider that has many, many people already using its service so that the communications cost to you is low.

Many Internet providers let you publish on the Web for free as long as you have an account with them and as long as you don't bug them for too much help in your Web publishing. Today, thousands of providers offer this kind of arrangement.

This arrangement makes a fair amount of sense. An Internet service provider already pays the communications cost and probably has loads of disk space just sitting around. The Internet service provider may limit the amount of space you can take up on the disk to 5 or 10 megabytes, but you're unlikely to fill that up with text, and the provider probably will let you run over the maximum for a small amount of money.

Web providers can be found in many ways, although you can't find one for yourself in the pages of this book. Any list we put in this book would be out of date before you got a chance to read it. One way is to ask your own Internet provider whether it offers Web services. Another is to look in your local Yellow Pages or in the advertisements in the back of almost any Internet-related magazine.

Business Publishing on the Web

As you have seen from the many figures throughout this book, the Web is much more than a personal publishing medium. Companies big and small have been posting Web pages for a few years, and more are rushing to the Web all the time. You may even be reading this book because your company wants to be part of the stampede.

The differences between Web pages for companies and Web pages for individuals often boil down to the following four areas:

> ✔ Style and design
>
> ✔ Payment
>
> ✔ Purpose
>
> ✔ Promotion

That professional look

A business is much more likely than an individual to spend time and money getting the look of its Web content just right. Most companies, even small ones, pay designers and artists to create advertising for them. Designers and artists have a good understanding about what does work and what doesn't work in ads, and they know how to avoid the cheesy look of some ads you see in places such as the telephone Yellow Pages.

For a business with plenty of competitors, the particular "look" that business presents to the world can be everything. For individuals who are merely publishing their writing or some art they have created, the presentation isn't nearly as important because their competition all looks pretty much the same.

Think for a moment about how you would select an insurance salesperson by looking in the Yellow Pages. A badly designed ad, a blurry photo, or awkward wording in the listing can easily make you pass over one salesperson's listing in favor of any of the other zillion listings.

Selling it

The Web is promoted as the future of retailing, enabling people sitting in their homes in front of their PCs to buy things they see on-screen. Actually, the home shopping cable channels use the same scenario, and those channels are making more money than most companies selling products on the Web. Face it: For most people, sitting in front of a TV is much more fun than sitting in front of a computer.

This is not to say that you can't make money selling products on the Web. In our consumer culture, you can sell products almost anywhere. The Web has the advantage over most other mediums in that the user can buy something without leaving the medium (by using Web forms like the ones illustrated in many earlier chapters). Even TV home shopping channels force you to pick up the phone to place an order; on the Web, you're only a click or two away from ordering.

Businesses that want to achieve direct sales through the Web must make online ordering as easy as possible for people, or else shoppers will continue to shop the old, familiar ways — such as by calling toll-free numbers. Furthermore, because most people don't enjoy doing too many new things, businesses must give them an additional reason to shop on the Web, perhaps by offering online shoppers more features, such as sales that are open only to Web shoppers or instant information on out-of-stocks and delivery dates.

So far, businesses seeking retail sales on the Web haven't done much to make online shopping better or easier than shopping by telephone. Ordering items on the Web is just getting out of the novelty stage. Placing an order by using a Web form is often slower and more confusing than simply picking up the phone, calling a toll-free number, and speaking with a human. (A few Web stores have broken out of this rut, notably Amazon.com and Dell.) The Web is fine for giving things away, and a great deal of effort is being put into using it as a sales tool, but it doesn't work well quite yet for bringing in the sales directly.

Getting people in the front door

Even if you are trying only to advertise on the Web, not to sell directly to consumers, you still want your Web area to be seen by as many people as possible. Advertising is notorious for *not* being seen. If you keep your finger on your television's remote control, for example, you are likely to see far fewer ads than someone who watches just one channel for longer periods. All those ads you miss by zipping through the channels are failing to sell you whatever they were designed to sell you.

Many businesses on the Web are trying to get people to see their pages by having the pages' URLs mentioned in the many lists of commercial Web sites. Those lists have become increasingly crowded, however, and their value has been decreasing lately because they contain just too much information. Other businesses are sponsoring some of the free newsletters on the Internet so that their URL appears in each issue of the newsletter. Others are paying to be part of the many Internet malls in hopes that people who visit the mall site see the business's site and check it out (but I don't think that's going to do them much good).

Still, having people find you is one of the most difficult tasks of any business. Only so much money is available for advertising; if getting listed in the "better" Internet lists and malls costs you, you can spend only so much on other forms of advertising.

In this way, business Web sites have some of the same desires as individuals who publish on the Web — namely, to get noticed. If you've published your collection of short stories for anyone and everyone to see, you want it located in a place where people will see your short stories or can at least find them through other means. The question is whether you are willing to pay for more and better exposure for your Web presence. For both businesses and individuals, the answer is based on their budgets and how much they believe that the service will actually increase their exposure.

Where to Hang Your Shingle

If you were reading a book on how to start up your own Web site, this would be the section containing all the nasty details about buying a computer, setting up the communications connection to another Internet provider, setting up the Web server software, and so on. Be thankful that none of that tedious technical detail is found here.

Most individuals who want to publish on the Web, as well as most companies that want a small Web presence, have absolutely no reason to set up their own Web server. The hardware costs are high, a huge amount of technical savvy is necessary to set up the software and hardware, the communications costs are great, and on and on. This isn't to say that you should never consider setting up a Web site — just that you can probably save a great deal of time and money by going with an existing Web site provider.

The Web providers that charge for their services offer myriad price structures. Some charge a flat fee based on how many pages you have; others charge based on how frequently people access your content; and still others charge a flat monthly fee. Most of these structures are geared toward businesses and are way too expensive for the individual who just wants to put up a page or two of political views or sports predictions.

The free services usually don't offer you any help in creating a good-looking Web area, but some do offer this kind of help. If you're going to publish your own work, you should check with your Internet service provider about whether you can publish through its service, whether it charges you anything for publishing, and how much (or how little) the service provider is willing to help you make a good-looking Web area. If the Internet service provider indicates that it doesn't allow any Web publishing, you need to look around for a different Web provider, which may entail having to establish a second Internet account.

Think Twice, Then Think Again

Web content consists of more than just the text and pictures you see as you visit a site. Some Web sites have good style, nice design, and an enjoyable layout; others are ho-hum, and their design makes them a bit hard to read; still others are just plain awful.

Beyond the issues of design, however, are questions about what is good or not good to put on a Web page. In the excitement of publishing on the Web, you can easily forget that some of your readers may have cultural, political, religious, or geographical points of view that may cause them to be offended by some of what you decide to publish. This is not to say that you should not publish your views; if your intention is to make your site attractive to as many people as possible, however, you certainly need to think about more than just the appearance of your content.

You probably have many topics to consider when putting your Web pages together. Still, the best way to see what works and doesn't work is to explore the Web with an eye toward how others have made their sites attractive. If you find yourself drawn to a particular kind of site, consider emulating it. Of course, you don't need to simply copy what others have written on the Web: You can be creative and generate inviting Web pages at the same time.

When the Web Is Slow, Small Is Fast

One of the biggest temptations of creating your own Web pages is the desire to publish a lot of content as quickly as possible. You've got a hard disk full of pictures and written material you've found interesting, and you're just dying to let the world at it. After all, Web access is almost free, and your Web provider isn't charging much for you to publish this content, right?

Maybe. The fact that the Web has flourished is partially based on the custom of people publishing loads of information and entertainment that wasn't available on the Internet before. You should feel free to continue that trend, but you should also consider how you can do so without wasting the overall bandwidth of the Internet (that is, the amount of information the Internet can carry comfortably).

As you have been using Communicator, you have probably already discovered Web sites that have huge inline graphics that take more than a minute to download. Face it: Huge inline graphics are usually a pain. Yes, they're sometimes nice to look at; and yes, they may even be useful. If you own a 28.8 Kbps or faster modem, however, or if the Internet (or your Internet provider) is slower than usual at the moment you are accessing a Web page, viewing a huge graphic can be frustrating and time-consuming. And don't forget that many people still have 14.4 Kbps modems!

If you don't like huge graphics that other people create, why create them yourself? You have many ways to make smaller graphics: You can use fewer colors in your pictures, show smaller pictures, or use pictures that are created at lower resolutions. Various paint and graphics conversion programs include options that enable you to create smaller files; use those features whenever possible.

Of course, graphics files are not the only ones that can be extremely large. Even a very useful 50K text file can seem huge to someone using only a 14.4 Kbps modem or who lives in an area where Internet connections are always slow. If you post a long text file at your Web site, consider breaking the file down into smaller chunks. Often, a long file can be broken into chapters or sections.

For now, most people don't pay much to access the Web, and the Internet is running fairly rapidly in most parts of the world. To assume that this state of affairs will be the case even two years from now, however, is dangerous. If the Internet, and thus the Web, becomes expensive or slow (or both!), large files will be shunned. We all may as well start looking at conservation so that the resources of the Internet are not squandered.

Just Because It's Cool Doesn't Mean It's Good

Then there's the delicate subject of taste. Similar to what you may find in many forms of media, much of what is on the Web is junk. Just because you *can* put some content on a Web page doesn't mean that you *should* put it there.

The wild freedom of Web publishing is a double-edged sword. Easy access to publishing on the Web means that some people who want to publish for a small audience can now do so at low cost, and the small target audience can access the material easily and cheaply. On the other hand, the same material is also being presented to a much larger audience that is uninterested in it; and many in that audience may be very offended, outraged, or hurt by what is said or how it is said.

Even if you can publish for free, remember that publishing is a privilege. If you are writing something that is likely to provoke strong reactions in people outside your intended audience, try to think of ways to dissuade outsiders from visiting your Web site (or at least from reading the parts that will provoke strong reactions). This strategy is simple courtesy, and it provides a bit of self-protection as well. If you publish an article that attacks the beliefs of a particular religion, for example, you may want to precede the article with a page that describes the tone of the article and suggests that people who may be offended by such an attack not follow the link to the article.

At one time or another, every one of us has said things that have angered other people. Sometimes that was our intended result; other times, it was an unanticipated side effect. Particularly when we were children, most of us were punished for some of the things we said. As adults, some of the ways we speak and the things we speak about in public can cause reactions in others so strong as to make them want to silence us. Every country in the world has dealt legally with how much expression to allow and to disallow.

The Web is basically no different than most other publishing media. Like everything from magazines to television, parts of the Web are of general interest, and other parts are of very narrow interest. All publishers deal with the same issues of rights, responsibilities, freedom, and costs.

Pay Attention to the Law

As you can tell, nothing in this book tries to discourage thoughtful publishing on the Web. Keep in mind, however, that not everyone is so generous. Legal restrictions are placed on a wide variety of publishing applications in many countries, and Web publishers can run afoul of the law in many ways.

For one extreme example, consider the statement "I would like to kill the President of the United States." Publishing that statement on a Web site in the United States could easily be considered illegal, and you could end up in jail within hours of putting it on your Web page. In other countries, such a statement may be discouraged and even condemned, but would be perfectly legal. In still other countries, such a statement would be applauded. (A statement such as "I would like to kill the President of *fill in the country*" can have different legal repercussions depending on where the statement is made and where it is read.)

Now, consider the fact that all three of these types of countries are on the Internet. A Web page published in the United States is readable in more than 150 countries. A Web page published in any of those countries is readable in the United States.

The law adapts very slowly to new technology. In the United States, it is not clear how the law deals with the fact that someone can read content published in other parts of the country (and other parts of the world) without physically "importing" the content. Already, cases are in the courts that raise this question relative to pornography, and it is likely that other forms of currently restricted speech (such as death threats, slander, and fraud) will soon follow. Many countries are experiencing movements to ban from the Internet some types of speech that are acceptable in other media, and many countries are actively moving to ban types of speech that are currently legal.

Sadly, no legal guidelines currently exist for what you can and can't publish safely on the Web. Of course, you should assume that anything that is illegal to print on paper is probably illegal to distribute on the Web, although even that assumption isn't always a foregone conclusion. The kinds of content that are often prohibited in various states and countries include, but are not limited to, the following:

✔ Disparaging various religions and beliefs

✔ Encouraging insurrection

✔ Sexually explicit material

✔ Threats against leaders

✔ Descriptions of how to make weapons

✔ Trade secrets of companies

Of course, every one of these areas has shades of gray; that's one reason we have judges and lawyers to sort these matters out. Given the newness of the Web, it's likely that something that may have been considered legal on paper could be considered illegal on the Web — or vice versa. In other words, be careful.

Chapter 19
That's Why They Call It Composer

In This Chapter

▶ Thinking about HTML
▶ Creating Web pages
▶ Formatting characters
▶ Getting paragraphs to look right
▶ Making tables

*A*s you look around the Web, you probably notice that some Web pages have complex designs, and others are simple and uncluttered. Composer, the part of Communicator that lets you create Web pages, lets you design your pages to be either way. Personally, I prefer the uncluttered look, and that's what I emphasize in this chapter.

The preceding chapter describes how to get started creating your own Web pages. The next step in the process of creating your own Web content is to find out enough about HTML, the hypertext language used on the Web, to understand what Composer does. For many people, HTML isn't the easiest thing to learn because it is certainly more than just a few commands, so very little is shown here. Instead, you are shown how to use Composer, which creates HTML for you without forcing you to know much about the HTML it creates.

By the way, in case you've forgotten, HTML stands for *H*ypertext *M*arkup *L*anguage. You'll see what the *markup language* part means very soon; see Chapter 20 for the *hypertext* part. Chapter 21 has more about HTML for those who want to go further. However, keep in mind that you don't need to know much about HTML to create your own Web pages with Composer.

This chapter gives you enough of a grounding in HTML to use Composer. If you want a much more in-depth lesson in HTML, however, check out *HTML For Dummies,* 3rd Edition, by Ed Tittel and Steve James (IDG Books Worldwide, Inc.). This chapter also gives you an overview of how to use Composer. If you want a full book on the subject, you should check out *Netscape Composer For Dummies,* by Deborah S. Ray and Eric J. Ray.

It's Just Like a Word Processor — But Completely Different

If you've worked with computers at all, you're probably at least somewhat familiar with using a word processor to perform such tasks as formatting text. These days, most people use (or have at least seen) word processors that display the formatting as the text is entered. For example, most people have used a word processor such as Microsoft Word or Corel WordPerfect. Well, you can think of Composer as a kind of a word processor.

Programs that show formatted text as you enter and change it are humorously referred to as *WYSIWYG*, which stands for *What You See Is What You Get*. (Consider yourself an old-timer if you remember which character on the late-'60s hit television show *Rowan and Martin's Laugh-In* made that line popular. *Hint:* She was played by Flip Wilson.)

Each word processor is different and has different user interfaces, but almost every modern word processor has certain capabilities in common. They all can add formatting attributes (such as italics and boldface) to characters, they can indent paragraphs, and so on. Even simple word processors such as the WordPad program in Windows offer these capabilities.

Assume, for example, that you create the following sentence in your word processor:

The second word in this sentence is emphasized.

Then assume that you want to make the word *second* appear in your text in boldface characters. In most word processors, you select the word and issue a command (probably the Bold command). Again, word processors differ, so the act of selecting a word and the act of giving a command can entail different actions on your part (such as choosing a menu command, pressing a key combination, clicking an icon on a button bar, and so on). The result of selecting the word and giving a command, however, is a sentence with the word *second* in boldface. The sentence on-screen now looks like this:

The **second** word in this sentence is emphasized.

Word processors differ even further from one another if you format entire paragraphs. To indent a paragraph in one program, for example, you may need to specify the indentation by using a Paragraph command; in another, you move markers on a ruler; in still another, you may press the Tab key.

In many ways, Netscape Composer is like a word processor. You type plain text in, and you can select and format that text in many ways. What you see on the screen is the formatted text with the boldface, underline, paragraph formatting, and so on. I assume that everyone reading this chapter has used a word processor, even a simple one, and knows how to do things like select text and make it bold.

HTML WYSLCDFWYG (Say What?)

Okay, now forget all that stuff about formatting text in word processors. Documents created with HTML look completely different from how they appear on the Web (*ergo,* the heading for this section: *What You See Looks Completely Different From What You Get*). You create HTML documents by using *text editors* or HTML creation programs like Composer, and sometimes word processors.

A text editor enables you only to add, delete, and change text; unlike a word processor, text editors do not enable you to change the formatting of the text you enter or edit. The Windows Notepad program, for example, is a text editor because it uses no formatting commands. If you have a character-based interface to the Internet, you may be familiar with a text editor on your host system. Some people prefer to make HTML pages with a text editor.

Netscape Composer is a glorified text editor that knows a lot about HTML. That is, Composer produces HTML files, which are really just text files on steroids. Composer actually does a bit more than this, but its basic product is text files.

HTML enables you to convert or create documents by using a plain text editor that Web clients then display as nicely formatted pages. The formatting consists of two parts: the formatting commands you put into your HTML documents and the interpretation of these commands by the particular Web client that someone uses to view your document.

Every HTML document has two kinds of things in it: *content* and *HTML commands*. The content consists of most of the words that you type. (Chapter 20 describes how to add pictures and hypertext links as content.) The HTML commands are also text, but they are labeled in a special way so that a Web client reading the document can say, "Oh, an HTML command; I'm supposed to do some formatting."

The correct term for HTML commands is *tags* because they aren't really commands in the same sense as, say, Windows commands. Instead, these commands mark areas of your text where the Web client performs some formatting or takes some other action. You can imagine these tags as markers that "hang on" the text to tell the Web client what to do.

You really need to understand the difference between content and HTML tags before you delve farther into HTML. Your HTML document itself doesn't look nice after it's complete. In fact, it may be barely readable. That's why

Composer (and other Web site creation packages) exists: to make it easier to create HTML documents by hiding the HTML ugliness (unless you want to see it). If that document is accessed by a Web client, however, the Web client knows how to read the HTML part and then interpret it as formatting commands. This action alters the appearance of the text by formatting it with fonts, boldface, blank lines between paragraphs, and so on.

What HTML looks like

If you're still confused, here's a short example. Remember that sentence from the section on "It's Just Like a Word Processor — But Completely Different"? If not, here it is again:

The **second** word in this sentence is emphasized.

HTML tags consist of the character <, the text of the tag, and the character >. (The < character is also known as the *left angle bracket* or the ever-popular *less than symbol*. The > character, as you can probably guess, is called the *right angle bracket* or *greater than symbol*.)

Now, to start making your text bold, you use the HTML b tag; to stop the text from being bold, you use the /b tag. Adding the HTML tags to your sentence make it appear as follows:

The <b>second</b> word in this sentence is emphasized.

If you view this sentence by using Communicator, the browser removes the <b> and the </b> and formats the text between them, the word *second,* as boldface type.

Now you can see what the *ML* in HTML stands for. HTML is a *markup language* because you use the language to mark up regular text with tags. If you look at a document and you don't see any tags, it isn't marked up and, therefore, it isn't an HTML document.

HTML documents

Again, you need to keep in mind that HTML documents are text documents with no inherent formatting. All the formatting you see on the Web is done by using HTML tags that are imbedded in those text documents. Without the formatting, the document would be a plain text file.

The difference between a standard HTML document and its formatted view is quite striking. Figure 19-1 shows a typical HTML document. Notice how many tags are in the document relative to the amount of text. If you view this same document by using Communicator, you see something more like the screen shown in Figure 19-2.

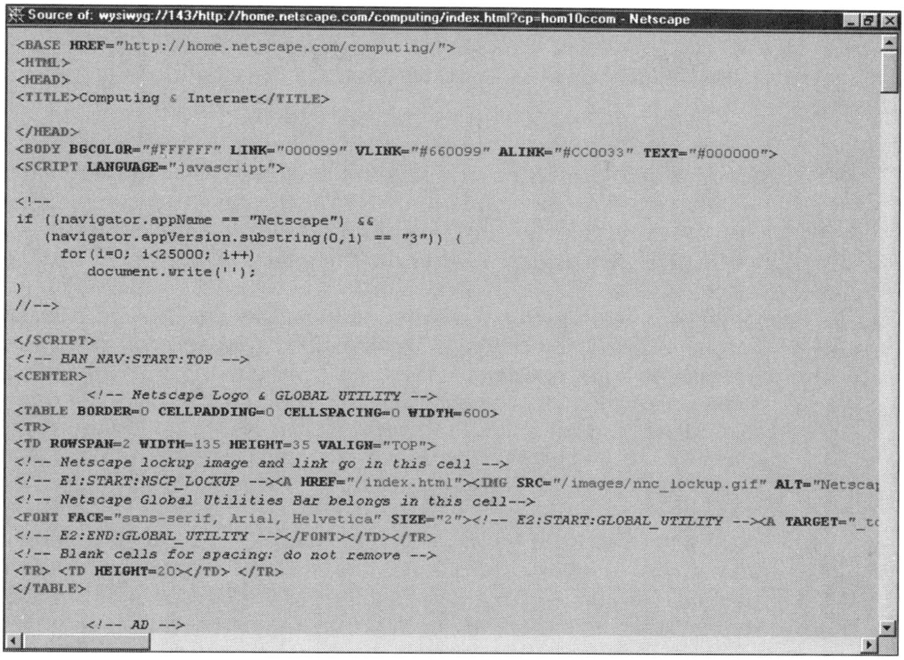

Figure 19-1:
A typical HTML document with many markup tags.

Figure 19-2:
When viewed in Communicator, the tags disappear and the formatting is added.

You can create HTML documents with a text editor in two ways:

- ✔ You can start with a complete text file and add HTML tags.
- ✔ You can add the tags as you enter the text.

Many people prefer the first method because they can see what the content looks like before they add all the HTML clutter. Other people choose to add formatting as they go along. Either method produces a text file with content and HTML tags, which is, after all, the goal.

However, you can create HTML documents in a third, and easier, way: with a Web site creation tool like Composer. In Composer, you don't see the HTML unless you want to. Most of the time, you're using a WYSIWYG screen that looks much like a word processor, showing you how your text will be formatted. You can, of course, also see the HTML document that you're creating, but most of the time, you just use the WYSIWYG tools and trust Composer to do the HTML correctly.

 Although Composer helps you create simple Web pages, it is definitely not enough for creating professional-looking Web sites. Because of the complexities of HTML and the number of different Web browsers available, you have to hand-tweak your HTML for anything other than the simplest of Web pages. Composer is a good way to start creating pages, but you shouldn't consider it sufficient for real Web site creation.

Getting into Composer

You start Composer with the Communicator⇨Composer command or by clicking the fourth icon on the component bar, the one that looks like a pencil on a piece of paper. Figure 19-3 shows the Composer window. You can also launch Composer with the File⇨New⇨Blank Page command.

Before you start creating a Web document, you should probably check the Composer settings by choosing Edit⇨Preferences to open the Preferences dialog box. Figure 19-4 shows the main Composer settings.

 Enter your own name for the author name. I suggest leaving the "Automatically save page every 10 minutes" setting selected, because checking this option causes Composer to save your work for you in case you forget to. The External Editors section lets you specify the name of your favorite text editor for editing your HTML text directly and an image editor for creating graphics. You can leave both of these boxes blank if you won't be doing any direct HTML editing or creating your own graphics, but you can fill them in if you plan to do serious HTML or graphics work. I also suggest selecting the middle option of the Font Size Mode choices, although this setting isn't all that important.

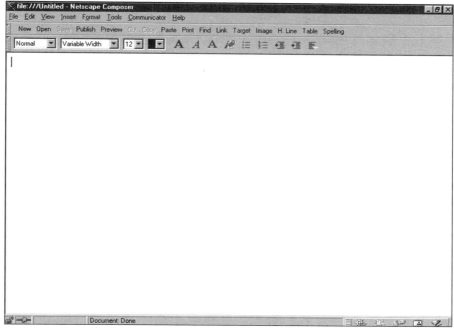

Figure 19-3:
The
Composer
window,
ready to
compose.

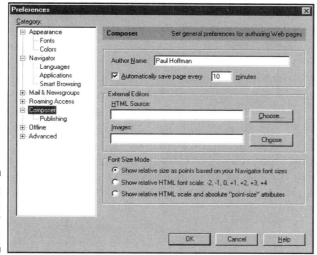

Figure 19-4:
The basic
Composer
settings.

Other ways of starting Web documents

You don't have to start with a blank sheet when you create a Web document in Composer. In fact, many people like to model their documents after other documents they have found on the Web. Doing so is easy. Just go to the Web page you want to use as a template for your new page and choose File⇨Edit Page. This command opens up a new Composer page with the current Web page already filled in. You can then edit the text and change the formatting.

Of course, editing someone else's Web page for practice with HTML is very different from publishing the page (even with edits) as your own. Republishing something that someone else wrote is probably illegal, much less unethical. In fact, many people claim that using someone else's page formatting ideas is also unethical. You should think about the consequences of copying other people's work before you republish anything that you started from a template.

Netscape also has a Web page "wizard" that steps you through the process of creating a Web page. You have to be online to do this, because the wizard requires many interactions with the Netscape corporate site. However, many users have found the wizard to be slow and cumbersome compared to just starting from a blank page or with an existing Web page. To start the wizard, choose the File⇨New⇨Page From Wizard command.

Okay, so you have a blank page in front of you. How do you start? Just start typing. Composer is like a word processor, and the way you enter text is to type it. If you can't imagine what you would want to type, you can type in some of the text from this book (and, for now, don't worry about the formatting, like the boldface or lists).

Levels of Formatting

HTML has three types of formatting: character formatting, paragraph formatting, and page formatting. These three kinds of formatting are the same as you find in most word processors. *Character* formatting is the kind of formatting you find on individual characters or groups of characters, such as boldface, text size, and text color. *Paragraph* formatting applies to a whole block of text and usually involves vertical spacing and indenting. *Page* formatting in HTML affects the color and pictures you see on the background of the page.

Formatting styles appear in two places in Composer: on the formatting toolbar and in the Format menu. The formatting toolbar is the second toolbar in the Composer window. Its elements are shown in Figure 19-5.

Remove formatting ┌─Numbered list

Figure 19-5:
The many
tools on the
formatting
toolbar.

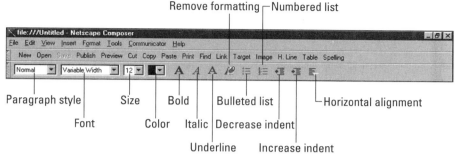

Paragraph style │   Size   │   Bold │   Bulleted list   └─Horizontal alignment

Font   Color   Italic │ Decrease indent

Underline   Increase indent

Composer gives you many choices for formatting that may not show up in the pages that you put on the Web. That is, many kinds of HTML formatting only work in Communicator 4.5; they don't work in earlier versions of Communicator or don't work with other Web browsers, such as Microsoft Internet Explorer. If you plan to make your Web pages available to anyone, not just Communicator 4.5 users, you should stick with the formatting that works with all browsers.

Formatting characters

Adding character formatting in Composer is identical to the way you add character formatting in any word processor. You simply select the text you want to format and choose one or more of the formatting styles. For example, type some text into the blank page, select it, and click the underline button on the formatting toolbar; you see that the text is now underlined. To format as you type, you set the insertion point, choose a formatting style, and type: The text you type has that format.

The first four submenus of the Format menu specify character formatting. They are as follows:

✔ **Font:** Specifies the name of the font to be used. Specifying a font is not standard HTML, and you should avoid doing so.

✔ **Size:** Specifies the size of the text. HTML doesn't use point sizes like standard computers but instead uses *relative sizes* to specify the size of the font shown on the screen. The values you see in this submenu (and in the size list on the formatting toolbar) are based on your choices in the Edit➪Preferences dialog box described earlier.

✔ **Style:** The type of additional character formatting to be added to the text. In this submenu, only bold, italic, and underline are standard HTML. The other choices may or may not work with older (or future) versions of Communicator.

✔ **Color:** The color of the text. You can choose one of the predefined colors from the submenu.

The Format⇨Remove All Styles command (and the associated button on the formatting toolbar) takes away any character formatting you have added to the selected text. Note that if the text has inherent character formatting (such as boldface for some of the types of headings), this command won't remove that formatting, only formatting that you have added.

Formatting paragraphs

HTML paragraphs come in three general categories:

✔ Basic paragraphs

✔ Headings

✔ Lists (bulleted or numbered)

You specify the kind of paragraph you are formatting in the Format menu or from the drop-down list at the left side of the formatting toolbar. Figure 19-6 shows examples of the types of paragraphs.

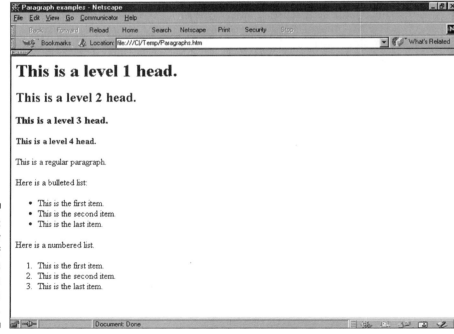

Figure 19-6:
The many kinds of paragraphs you can make in Composer.

Basic paragraphs are the kinds of paragraphs you use in day-to-day work. They can be *normal* or *formatted* (which is properly called *preformatted,* but Netscape chose to give it a more confusing name). Normal paragraphs have automatic line-wrapping for long lines; preformatted paragraphs use the line endings you apply yourself by pressing the Enter key at the end of each line.

Headings in HTML are numbered, like they are in most word processors. A level-1 heading is the most important, a level-2 heading is subordinate to a level-1 heading, and so on. Communicator and other Web browsers usually show level-1 headings as bigger and bolder than level-2 headings.

Composer also allows you to indent your paragraphs and set the alignment for them. However, the method it uses for indentation is definitely non-standard and creates HTML that looks lousy in some Web browsers. The alignment choices for paragraphs allow you to specify whether a paragraph is left-aligned, right-aligned, centered, or justified. To specify this, Composer uses an HTML tag that is part of the most recent version of HTML but that is not supported by older versions. Because of these problems, I suggest that you don't use either of these features.

Learning to love lists

HTML's list features help you make nicely formatted lists with very little muss and fuss. Five kinds of lists are available, although only two are commonly used.

In other chapters of this book, you come across the two most common types of lists: *ordered lists* and *unordered lists*. Ordered lists are often called *numbered lists* because each item in the list starts with a sequential number. Unordered lists are often called *bulleted lists* because the items have a bullet before them.

Ordered lists are usually used for steps in a process, as in the following example:

1. **Find the remote control.**
2. **Turn on your television.**
3. **Sit down.**

Unordered lists are used to list items that have equal value but no particular order, as follows:

- Potato chips
- Soda
- Pretzels

Lists are trickier to create than other paragraphs because they involve two types of paragraph formatting — bulleted and numbered.

1. **Specify where the list starts and ends, and then specify each list item.**

2. **When you start a list, click either the bulleted list button or the numbered list button on the formatting toolbar.**

   This action both starts the list and creates the first list item. As you fill in the list, Composer creates each additional item.

3. **When you're done with the list and you want to create other types of paragraphs, click the same button that you used to start the list.**

Formatting pages

HTML allows you to specify the background and color of your HTML page. In Composer, you use the Format⇨Page Color and Properties command to set these features. The first tab of the dialog box for this command also lets you specify the title for the page (which appears at the top of the Communicator window when you are viewing the page), as well as your name and other descriptive items (which don't appear on the page but can be found by people searching the Web).

The dialog box's second tab, shown in Figure 19-7, lets you specify how the document background and text look. If you choose to use custom colors, you can specify the colors for normal text (which, as you discover earlier in this chapter, can also be specified with character formatting), for the text that has links, and for the background. I suggest leaving the defaults alone, because they are what most Web users expect when they view your page.

If you want to get fancy, you can use a picture for the background instead of a single color. The picture must be in JPEG or GIF format (these formats are described in Chapter 20), and the picture that displays the page is *tiled* in the background, meaning that it is duplicated over and over to fill up the entire background of the Web page.

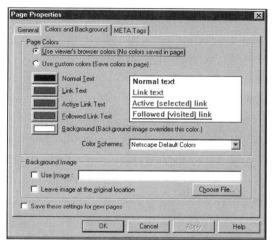

Adding Horizontal Lines

You often want to break up the content on your Web pages into visual chunks. The easiest way to do so is to add horizontal lines between paragraphs. (The formal HTML name for horizontal lines is *horizontal rules.*) To insert a horizontal line, put the insertion point where you want the line and click the H. Line button on the composition toolbar or choose the Insert⇨Horizontal Line command. This step inserts a paragraph with a horizontal line that goes across the page.

Although Composer inserts the line all the way across the page, you don't have to leave it that way. If you carefully move your mouse pointer to either end of the line, you see the pointer change to a double-pointed arrow. You can then drag the end of the line in to make it cover less of the width of the page. In HTML, horizontal lines are centered, so Composer automatically shortens or lengthens the other side of the line for you when you change its length on the page.

Fun with Tables

HTML tables are a mixed blessing: You can create very nice-looking information with them, but the HTML tags needed are quite complicated. Composer makes creating and formatting tables a breeze.

To start a table, click the table icon in the composition toolbar or choose the Insert⇨Table⇨Table command. Doing so brings up the large dialog box shown in Figure 19-8. Don't be daunted by its size; choosing what you want is actually quite easy.

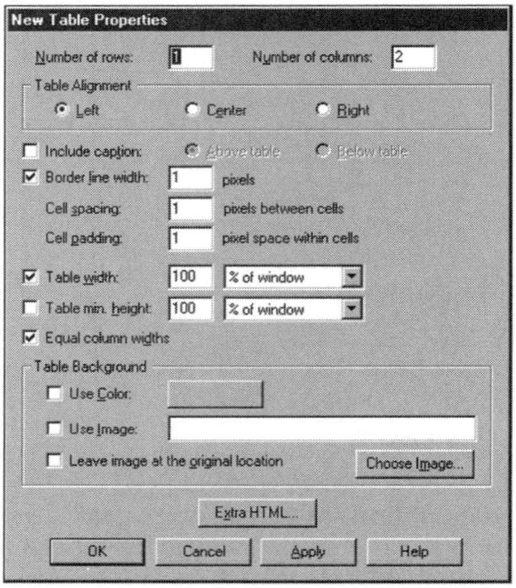

Figure 19-8: Choices for creating a new HTML table.

The main choices you have to make are how many rows and columns you want. Don't worry about this choice too much, for that matter, because you can always add or delete rows and columns later. The other choices you can make include the following:

✔ The alignment of the table relative to the Web page.

✔ Whether the table has a caption, and if so, whether the caption is above or below the table.

✔ Whether the table has a border around the cells, and if so, how thick the line is.

✔ The spacing around the text in the cell.

✔ How wide the table is, either relative to the page or as an absolute width.

✔ The minimum height of the table.

✔ Whether the columns maintain equal widths.

✔ The background for the table (a color or a picture).

After you create a table, you can fill in the cells just by typing into them. You can enter and format the text in table cells just like you can in the rest of your HTML document.

For example, Figure 19-9 shows a typical table after it is created. It has five rows and two columns, is centered in the page, and has the default borders.

Composer also lets you manipulate tables in many ways to get exactly the look you want. The most convenient method for making these changes is in the Table Properties dialog box. Select any part of the table and choose Format⇨Table Properties. The first part of this dialog box looks just like the Insert Table dialog box, but the Properties dialog box also has tabs for the current row and current cell.

A few of the interesting things to experiment with are cells that span a few columns and cells that have different widths than the other cells in the table. Both of these settings are easy to change with the Table Properties dialog box.

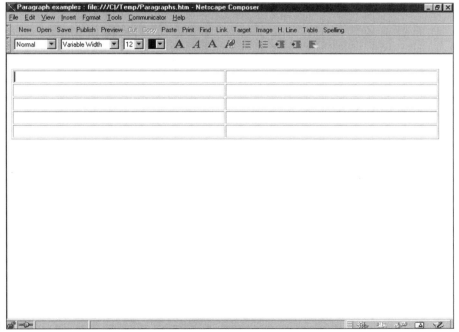

Figure 19-9:
A new
table,
ready to
be filled in.

You can even have tables inside tables. This arrangement is particularly visually attractive if the tables have no borders. Create a table, put the insertion mark in one of the cells, and insert another table. For example, you can use tables-inside-tables to align the edges of pictures. The possibilities are endless.

You Created a Web Page: Now What?

Of course, you want to be able to take the work you have done in Composer and make it available somewhere else. Otherwise, why would you use Composer at all? Save the page on your hard drive. Of course, Composer saves pages like all other programs: via the File⇨Save and File⇨Save As commands. You should save your work with the file extension .html because that is the extension most Web sites expect your HTML files to have.

You can also print your page with the File⇨Print command or simply view it in Communicator with the File⇨Browse Page command.

If your Web site administrator has set things up for you to *publish* your pages from Composer, you can upload the pages to the Web site automatically. Unfortunately, you can't just assume that publishing has been set up for you; in fact, many Web sites have complicated methods for getting your HTML files to them. Composer allows you to automate this process, but only if the Web site administrator has taken some steps first. If your administrator hasn't made arrangements for you to publish your pages, you have to bug her or him so that you can start.

By all means, check with your Web administrator about publishing directly from Composer. If doing so is allowed, the administrator can tell you what you need to put in the Composer preferences (choose Edit⇨Preferences to access the Preferences dialog box) to make direct publishing work.

At that point, you can then put your finished Web page on the Web site with the File⇨Publish command. This command's dialog box prompts you for some information about where you are publishing the page, and then it automatically uses some Internet protocols to get the page to your Web server.

Chapter 20

The Best Parts: Hypertext and Graphics

In This Chapter

▶ Understanding links

▶ Creating links to other documents

▶ Linking within a document

▶ Including pictures in your HTML documents

Chapter 19 describes how to use HTML formatting in your documents. The HTML formatting in that chapter is useful for making your documents more readable, but it ignores the two most popular parts of the Web: links and images. Both of these concepts are covered in this chapter.

Thinking about Linking

As discussed throughout the book, jumping from one document to another by using hypertext links is the basis for the Web. Many documents act as guides to other documents on the Web, enabling you to access those additional documents with a single click. Other documents use links to point to parts of the same document.

Before you start merrily linking your Web documents to other documents hither and yon, a good idea is to first step back and think about what you really want to do with hypertext and the best way to do it. If you've been bopping around the Web as you read this book, you may have come across some Web sites that just didn't feel right. Maybe the links from the first page at the site weren't what you expected, or maybe some of the links were bad.

As you write, your best course is always to work from an outline or at least an overview of what you want to say. As you create Web documents, think about where you will link to and how those links may look to the casual Web user who has just breezed into your document but is unfamiliar with other related Web documents. Your outline or plan doesn't need to be anything formal — just a nudge to think about how your creation looks to the rest of the world.

The name of the link

In most fields, you need a consistent way to discuss the topics encompassed by the field; setting certain standards for the names of these topics, therefore, is important. Unfortunately, that's not true on the Web. If you create a link from one document to another, you can name the link whatever you want. The Web community has come to no consensus about the best way to name links, and this inconsistency has caused all sorts of problems.

Web search utilities do not work nearly as well as the ones for Gopher because cataloging all the HTTP universe is impossible, whereas the Gopher universe is easily cataloged. Everything on a Gopher server is either the name of a menu or the name of a document. Because each Gopher menu is a list of names, people who publish at Gopher sites have adopted somewhat standardized strategies for naming menus: The names are all descriptive of what is in each menu. (Search utilities are described in more detail in Chapter 7.)

Not so on the Web. Some Web search systems index their text by the names of the links, while others index based on the content of the entire HTML document. Indexes based on the names of links rely on one style of naming, whereas indexes based on the content of the whole document rely on a different style of naming.

For example, imagine that you want to put a link in a document you are writing to another Web site that has a really fantastic collection of snail pictures. You may phrase the link as follows:

```
You can see lots of great photos of snails on the Web.
Click here to access Professor Kapha's
collection of snail photographs.
```

The underlined word *here* is the link to the other site. Another way to phrase the link is like this:

```
You can see lots of great photos of snails on the Web,
such as Professor Kapha's photo collection.
```

Notice that the link the user clicks is now the words *Professor Kapha's photo collection* (not including the period at the end of the sentence).

For search systems that index their content only by the names of the links (not by the content), neither of the names tells the index anything about what is really important. To make the Web searcher's index useful, you really want the word *snail* in the title of the link, such as in the following example:

```
You can see lots of great photos of snails on the Web,
such as Professor Kapha's photo collection of snails.
```

This approach, however, makes the sentence redundant. Furthermore, you don't really want to base all your link name choices on what some search indexes may or may not do. Instead, you want the sentences you use to link to be easily readable and to get the Web user your information in the clearest way possible. This usually means that you should avoid the "click here" kind of descriptions because Web users know that if they see a link, they "click here" to access it.

This may seem obvious, but you're best off avoiding link names that don't refer to the object of the link at all. As you traverse around the Web, however, don't be surprised if you find links such as this:

```
You can see lots of great photos of snails on the Web,
such as Professor Kapha's photo collection of snails.
```

Choosing good link targets

Another major problem with many of the links you may create in your Web documents is that, after a period of time, your links may point to servers whose names have changed, servers that are no longer on the Internet, servers that don't allow access to the general public, or servers that are very slow. As you make links, think about whether the same information may be available at different sites, and choose the site with the best availability.

For example, you may have noticed that it takes a very long time to get documents from the site you intend to link to. If so, you probably don't want to send thousands of other people to that site without first asking the keeper of those documents for permission. Before linking to a slow site, send mail asking permission. You may get a reply telling about a better place with the same information or that the address of the site is about to change.

As a service to all users of the Web, you need to periodically check all the links in the Web pages you create. If you have many links that were valid when you wrote the document but later went bad (such as if the name of the host changes), you may be sending hundreds or thousands of people on a wild goose chase for naught. Make a habit of checking your resources and updating your Web pages if the resources move or disappear.

Linking to the Outside World

Creating links in Composer is a snap. Simply select the text that you want to be the link and then click the Link icon on the composition toolbar (or choose Insert⇨Link). In the dialog box that appears, shown in Figure 20-1, enter the URL for the place that you want to link to and then click OK.

You can link to a location on the Internet or to a local file. If you are linking to somewhere on the Internet, simply enter the URL of that location, such as `http://www.isoc.org/`. If you are linking to a file on your computer, you don't have to type the full URL yourself; you can click the Choose File button and use the standard File Location dialog box to find the file that you want to link to. Selecting the file in this dialog box causes Composer to fill in the proper URL for that file.

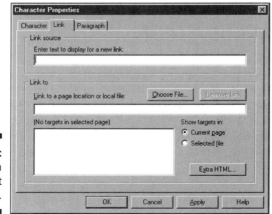

Figure 20-1:
Creating a
hypertext
link.

Linking within a Document

So far, all the links you have seen have been to other documents on the Internet. You can, however, also make links to specific spots in a document. These spots are called *targets* because they are the target location for other links. A target can be a single point or some selected text. For example, it is common to have headings as targets and then link to those targets from a table of contents.

To specify that a point or some selected text in a document is a target, click the Target button in the composition toolbar or choose Insert➪Target. A small dialog box appears, asking you to name the target. Each target in an HTML file has a name, and all the targets in a file have to have different names.

Linking within a file is easy in Composer. When you create a link, Composer lists all the targets in the current file or the file you specify, and you just pick one out of the list. I have a tendency to give my targets similar names, and misspelling is always an issue for me, so this feature is pretty handy.

Mixtures with Pictures

Okay, it's time for pretty pictures! Well, pretty is in the eye of the beholder, but pictures seem to be one of the most compelling parts of the Web, and you may be itching to include them in your Web pages. Composer makes adding the images to HTML files easy; the hard part is getting images that enhance your pages without looking tacky or taking too long for users to download.

On the other hand, not everything is so automatic outside of HTML. Dozens of different formats exist for graphics files, and most Web browsers understand how to display only one or two of these formats. By far, the two most popular formats are GIF, a format popularized by CompuServe almost a decade ago, and JPEG, which is a newer standard that was created by many companies together. Other formats exist, but most Web browsers understand only one or both of these two; Communicator handles both just fine.

Two types of images can be found on the Web: those that are part of HTML documents and those that you download just like other files. The ones that are part of HTML documents are called *inline images* because they appear in the same line as text. Downloadable images are no different than any other downloadable file.

You've probably already guessed how Composer lets you insert images. In case you didn't, you choose the Insert⇨Image command or click the Image icon on the composition toolbar. Doing so brings up the Image Properties dialog box, shown in Figure 20-2, where you can specify the location of the graphic and various formatting. To later edit this information, simply double-click the graphic, or select it and choose Insert⇨Image again.

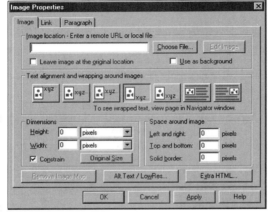

Figure 20-2:
Inserting an image into your Web page.

Where images go on the line

Most images are much taller than a single line of text, and you may want to vertically align the text after the image with the top, the middle, or the bottom of the image. You can also specify whether the top or middle of the image aligns with the bottom of the text or the *baseline* of the text — that is, the bottom of the text without *descenders* (lines that extend down, such as on the letters *y* and *g*).

You can also cause text to flow around an image instead of having the text on a line by itself. The two right-most buttons in the Image Properties dialog box let you specify that the image should be either aligned with the left side or the right side of the page, with text flowing around the image. (Text flowing does not work in all Web browsers.)

Images as links

Inline images can act just like text in that they get wrapped by Web browsers, can act like links, and so on. Of course, you can't add formatting such as bold or italics to an image (although it would be kind of fun if you could). In fact, many Web pages use small inline images as links to other documents. Although these images act similarly to buttons in dialog boxes, they are just simple inline images.

To make an inline image into a link, follow these steps:

1. **Insert the image as described in the previous section.**

2. **Select the image and click the Link button on the composition toolbar or choose Insert⇨Link.**

   These actions turn the image into a link.

Where do images come from?

Like most things in life, you can take images from someone else, or you can create your own. If you aren't artistically inclined or don't want to take the time to design your own graphics, you can use GIF or JPEG files that already exist. You can find many places on the Web from which you can download small icons and buttons for your Web pages. You can also include larger pictures that you get from the many FTP sites that have graphics collections.

On the other hand, if you like to create your own graphics, many paint programs save their output in GIF or JPEG format. If your paint program doesn't save files in these formats, you can easily find graphics conversion programs that take the output of your paint program and convert it to GIF or JPEG format.

What about character-based browsers?

Instead of joining the rush toward the all-graphical Web, you should remember that millions of Web users can't view the images in your Web pages. These people are already quite familiar with being frustrated by thoughtless Web page designers who blithely assume that everyone can see graphics. Remember, too, that many people turn off automatic image downloading as they browse around the Web so that they can get information faster.

Fortunately, HTML enables you to put text where an image would have appeared, providing that the Web browser allows this feature. Character-based browsers show this text, enabling their users to at least get a hint of what the image may have looked like. To specify alternative text for the image, click the Alt. Text/LowRes button in the Image Properties dialog box and enter some descriptive text for the image in the dialog box that appears.

Chapter 21

In Case You Need HTML

In This Chapter
▶ Discovering the basics of HTML
▶ Figuring out HTML's structure
▶ Designing good-looking Web pages

*U*sing Composer means not needing to learn about HTML . . . as long as you are willing to live with Composer's restrictions. As handy as Composer is at creating Web pages, it is fairly limited when it comes to doing good design. For that, you need to know how to do your own HTML. This chapter covers HTML in more depth than the previous two chapters and shows how you can use a text editor to add HTML in Composer and change the HTML that Composer has created.

What Does Composer Compose?

Composer creates Web pages that are formatted with HTML. However, Composer doesn't show you the HTML that it creates. Instead, you have to view it yourself in a different window. You have two ways to view the HTML:

✔ Have Communicator show you the *page source* — that is, the HTML that goes into a Web page.

✔ Edit the Web page with a text editor.

If you just want to look at the HTML source for a page but not edit it, choose View➪Page Source. This command brings up a window showing the HTML as text. However, if you want to edit the HTML directly, you need to use a text editor such as Notepad, which comes with Windows 95 and 98.

To edit the source text, choose Edit➪HTML Source. This command causes Composer to start another program on your computer, namely the text editor

that you specified as the HTML editor when you set Preferences with the
Edit⇨Preferences command. (This procedure is described in Chapter 19.)

To repeat the example from Chapter 19, you may see text in Communicator
that looks like this:

The **second** word in this sentence is emphasized.

The HTML that created that sentence looks like this:

```
The <b>second</b> word in this sentence is emphasized.
```

The <b> and </b> are the HTML tags that cause the word to be emphasized.

< and > Are Your Friends

HTML is one of those funny systems in which bunches of rules exist for
some things, while other things have almost no rules. Certain tags, for
example, must appear between certain other pairs of tags, but they can't
appear between other, different tag pairs. On the other hand, you can place
tags anywhere you want on the line of your text document — even on lines
by themselves. The following two examples, therefore, result in identically
formatted text:

```
<b>second</b>
```

and

```
<b>
second
</b>
```

Both versions give you the bold word **second** on your page.

As you get to know HTML's rules, keep in mind that this markup language
was originally written for a much smaller audience than it has reached.
Many folks contend that forcing people who want to set up simple Web
pages to learn a text markup language is inappropriate, particularly if that
language has so many structural rules. In a more perfect world, people
reading this book would not need to be concerned about editing text files by
using arcane symbols and then checking their work by hand, but we don't
live in that perfect world; we live in this one.

Because parts of HTML are quirky and overly technical, only the parts of the
language that you commonly use are described here.

Starts and stops

As described in Chapter 19, every tag starts with a < character and ends with a > character. So far, you've seen only two tags, the <b> and </b> tags, which turn the boldface formatting on and off. Most HTML tags work similarly to the <b> and </b> tags, in that you put one tag at the beginning of what you want to format and the same tag with a / in front of it at the end. These pairs of tags are called *start tags* and *end tags*.

As noted in Chapter 19, one of the most common errors you can make in adding HTML tags is to forget to add the matching end tag with the start tag. For this reason (among others), you really need to check your work carefully *before* putting it on the Web. To do this, simply open the HTML file on your hard drive using Communicator.

Capitals don't count

The *case* (whether capital or lowercase) of the letters in tags is not significant, meaning that you can do whatever you want with it. Either <b> or <B> means exactly the same thing to every Web browser. This book uses lowercase characters for its tags simply because they're easier to read, but you can do as you please. The example we've been working with can just as easily appear as follows:

```
The <B>second</B> word in this sentence is emphasized.
```

For that matter, it can also appear as follows and still be treated the same:

```
The <b>second</B> word in this sentence is emphasized.
```

Where does the line end?

Another nice informality of HTML is that you can put HTML tags next to the text that they modify or on separate lines. Web browsers interpret line breaks as a space between words when they look through an HTML document. Although this convention may seem a bit odd to you, creating Web documents this way is much more flexible than having to keep tags on the same line with the text that precedes or follows it.

One side effect of this flexibility means that you can have very short lines in your HTML document and they will appear at the full width of the Web browser's window. This feature also means that you don't need to guess how long to make the lines in your paragraphs. That is, the lines in your HTML document adjust themselves to the full width of the Web browser window, whatever width that window may be.

Check out the following example:

```
One side effect of this means that you can have very short
lines in your HTML document and they will appear at the
full width of the Web browser's window.
```

The preceding text looks the same in Web browsers as the following example:

```
One side effect of this means that you
can have very short lines in your HTML
document and they will appear at the
full width of the Web browser's window.
```

Another nice advantage of this line-length freedom is that you can choose to put your HTML tags on the same line with the text they refer to or on separate lines. The following two examples, therefore, appear exactly the same when viewed in a Web browser:

```
One side effect of this means that you
can have <b>very short lines</b> in your HTML
document and they will appear at the
full width of the Web browser's window.
```

```
One side effect of this means that you can have
<b>very short lines</b>
in your HTML document and they will appear at the
full width of the Web browser's window.
```

Notice how the second example has the boldface characters on a single line in the HTML file, making the phrase stand out better. Many people prefer to add HTML tags to their documents in this fashion so that they can find the tags more easily if they later revise the documents.

Adding Your Own Tags in Composer

Chapters 19 and 20 show how to use Composer to make Web pages without having to insert your own HTML tags. You can, however, insert your own HTML tags if you want. Many reasons may prompt you to dig into tags yourself, such as if you are adding an HTML form (covered later in this chapter) or other HTML markup that Composer won't produce.

To insert any HTML you want in Composer, simply put the insertion point where you want the tag and choose Insert⇨HTML Tag. Composer displays a dialog box into which you can type the desired HTML tags.

Composer also recognizes that sometimes you want to add HTML *attributes,* which are subparts of HTML tags, when using standard Composer commands. You may have noticed that some of the Composer dialog boxes you have seen so far have a button that says something like "Extra HTML" (the Insert⇨Table dialog box is a good example). These buttons bring up another dialog box that allows you to enter parts of an HTML tag, which Composer adds when it inserts the formatting that you just specified.

Remember that you can also add and change the HTML in your document by using a text editor and editing the HTML source itself. To edit the source text, use the Edit⇨HTML Source command.

Top of the Doc

HTML documents have an overall structure that was intended to be mandatory but has, due mostly to people's laziness, become optional. Knowing about the structure, however, is important because you can create more useful HTML documents if you use the structure. For example, a structured HTML document can have a title, which an unstructured HTML document can't.

Every HTML document should begin with an `<html>` tag and end with an `</html>` tag. These tags mark the part of the document that is in HTML. For our purposes, the entire document is in HTML, so you would put these tags at the very beginning and the very end of the document.

Here's a place where using Composer makes life much easier. Every time you start a new document in Composer, it puts the `<html>` and `</html>`# tags in the document for you. You never have to worry about them.

Two parts exist between the beginning and end of the document. These parts are the head and the body, and they are marked by the `<head>`, `</head>`, `<body>`, and `</body>` HTML tags. This structure tells Web browsers what material applies to the entire document (the things in the head) and what applies to the body of what you want displayed.

Every document should have a title. Connecting to a Web page and having no idea what's being discussed can be disconcerting, to say the least. Fortunately, the `<title>` and `</title>` tags make creating titles easy. The `<title>` and `</title>` tags go in the head because the document's title applies to the entire document. In Composer, you use the Format⇨Page Colors and Properties command to insert these tags. Most browsers, like Communicator, show the title of a document in the title bar of the browser window.

Thus the structure of an HTML document really looks like this:

```
<html>
<head>
<title>The title of this document</title>
</head>
<body>
The content of the document.
</body>
</html>
```

A few other sets of tags can go in the head, but they are rarely used and fairly obscure. For now, assume that the head is there to hold the title.

Most Web browsers allow you to put the `<title>` and `</title>` tags at the very beginning of an HTML document without specifying the rest of the structure. Others ignore a title that is shown in this manner and assume that if you didn't specify a structure, everything in your document is the body. Therefore, if you want a title on your document that can be read by everybody, you should include all the structure tags as shown here.

Other Bits and Pieces

As you can see, HTML is a bit quirky in how it is used. Most tags come in beginning and end pairs; others don't. You need to pay attention to the overall structure for some features but not for others. I hope, however, that you have clearly seen that not too many details get between you and writing Web content. I have a few more details that I want to go over with you, though. A number of little HTML features exist that you should be aware of but that don't fit in any of the preceding categories. Consider this section the HTML junk drawer.

If only I were a programmer: Forms and image maps

One last bit of unfinished business that the more observant of you may have noticed: I've so far included no description of how to create HTML forms. Everything else in HTML is reasonably easy to grasp, but creating forms is not quite so easy. To create forms, you must be a programmer, and most Web sites that let you create your own documents don't let you create forms for just that reason.

Think for a moment about the forms you've seen as you moved around on the Web. Most forms have a few sets of buttons, and forms often have some fill-in fields as well. Every form has a button — usually labeled *Submit,* or *Send,* or *OK* — that causes the contents of the form to be sent to the host site for processing. Notice that word *processing.* To process the results, you need a program of some sort, and each program is tailored to a particular form.

Even if you know a bit about programming, you shouldn't think, "Hey, I can create the form and the program myself." On many systems, unless the program associated with a form is very carefully written, that program can become a huge security hole for the system. Hackers have already broken into various Web sites via badly written form programs, and it is likely that they will continue to do so.

Image maps are pretty much the same as forms. (By the way, the techies like to refer to them as one word, *imagemaps;* feel free to use either version.) After you click a certain part of an image map, the location of where you clicked is sent back to the host site for processing. The program at the host site then says, "Ah, he clicked at this spot; therefore, he wants to get this information," and sends it to you. Again, you need a program to determine what to do with that information, and those programs also are susceptible to hackers and crackers (although image map programs aren't likely to be as vulnerable as forms programs).

Comments

You can put comments into your HTML documents that serve as notes to yourself. These comments are not displayed by Web browsers, but anyone looking at your HTML file can see them. Comment tags are a bit different than other HTML tags. Comments begin with the `<!--` tag and end with the `-->` tag. Thus, part of your HTML document may look like this:

```
There are many things that I want to say to the world.
<!-- Boy, isn't that the truth...-- >
However, the world never listens to me anyway, so
what's the point?
```

Special characters

You can't include just anything in your HTML documents. Specifically, you can't include certain characters either because they confuse the Web browser or because they may have different meanings on different systems. Fortunately, HTML anticipates these circumstances and makes them easy to take care of.

The three common characters that you *can't* include in an HTML document by themselves are <, >, and &. These characters are special in HTML; Chapter 19 describes why the first two are so special (to hold formatting tags, remember?), and the use of the & is described in a moment. If you want to put the characters < or > or & in your HTML document, you must use the following text exactly as it appears here for each character: <, or >, or &.

To put it more simply:

`&lt; = <`

`&gt; = >`

`&amp; = &`

To represent the text x<y, for example, you would use the following text:

```
x&lt;y
```

As you can now see, the & sign (called the *ampersand*) is used at the beginning of special characters, which is why you can't just put it in your document on its own. You use a similar method for representing characters that differ between computers and operating systems.

Composer prevents you from having to know any of this arcane stuff. When you type a < character, for example, it puts the < in your HTML document for you and just displays the < on the screen.

The Web extends far beyond the United States, and HTML is an international language. Thus, it must also account for characters that do not appear in normal English use. Many European languages, for example, have vowels with marks over them, such as ö. American computers have no standard way to represent ö, so HTML uses a special symbol for it: &ouml ;. The German city Köln, therefore, would be represented as follows:

```
K&ouml;ln
```

Inserting special characters in Composer is cumbersome, however. On Windows, you have to use the Character Map program that comes with Windows; on the Mac, you have to use the Key Caps program.

Part VI
The Part of Tens

The 5th Wave — By Rich Tennant

"It's a letter from the company that installed our in-ground sprinkler system. They're offering Internet access now."

In this part . . .

This part gives you a few quick chapters containing lists of ten various things having to do with the World Wide Web: Ten things Communicator and the Web don't do yet, ten ways to have fun with Communicator, and ten charming Web sites to visit. Well, that's thirty, total, but you get the idea.

Chapter 22

Ten Things Communicator and the Web Won't Do for You . . . Yet

- -

In This Chapter

▶ Looking into many possible futures

▶ Imagining the Web that you want

- -

*E*ven though you may never have the fancy multimedia computer that you want, and creating attractive Web pages may never be easy enough for mere mortals to accomplish without help, the future of the Web looks bright. Many people today may look at Communicator and say, "So what?" But many things could change within the next few years to make the Web an even more exciting place to be.

This chapter lays out ten ways in which Communicator and the Web may improve. The future features described here are not based on miracles or any huge technical improvements. In fact, they could exist today if people a year or two ago thought that developing these features was important enough.

Depending on when you read this book, some of these "future" items may, in fact, be part of the present. One of the hard parts in writing about the future is that the future can come to pass before the book has a new edition. Remember, however, that all these features can keep improving, just as many parts of the Web have improved over time.

Publish Software That Never Gets Out of Date

The Web is usually more up to date than the disks we keep lying around. A company with a Web site can put information on it at any time, including new software and refinements of software. This process is very different from the traditional way of publishing software, in which the software is distributed on floppy disks and CD-ROMs. If that software is revised or the content on the CD-ROM is updated, the disks already sold are out of date. (In fact, even the disks still on the store shelves are out of date.)

Combining software publishing with the Web is starting to change the nature of the software industry. Netscape is on the forefront of this revolution, as you know if you've used the SmartUpdate feature on Netcenter to get updates of modules (although you still have to download major revisions of Communicator). Many other kinds of software would also benefit from having enhancements available on a Web site. Imagine a CD-ROM encyclopedia that automatically updates to include this week's news or a medical reference that adds new studies every month.

Put the Content Close to You

Looking at a Web site housed on a server that is physically far away almost always takes longer than looking at a site that lives closer to you. If you're in the United States, browsing sites in Asia or Europe can be tediously slow. Browsing distant sites doesn't have to be slow, however, because these sites can set up *mirrors* in the U.S. (and U.S. sites can set up mirrors in other parts of the world).

Mirror sites and future versions of Communicator can make getting information much faster and reduce the load on the Internet at the same time. For example, Communicator could sense that you were linking to a site in Taiwan, remember that a mirror is located much closer, and get the information from the mirror (possibly asking you for permission to do so first). This action would reduce both your frustration at slow browsing speeds and the amount of information traveling on the trans-Pacific Internet cables.

Use Names instead of Locations

Most URLs point to a location where information is stored (the notable exceptions are the `mailto:` and `news:` URLs). What if the same information is stored in many different places? Shouldn't a way exist to choose the "best" of many possible locations?

One of the next big advances on the Internet that will probably appear in a future version of Communicator is *URNs,* or *Uniform Resource Names.* If you link to a URN, you get back one or more URLs for the thing named in the URN. You can then choose the URL you want. Getting the list of URLs from a URN is called *resolving* the URN.

Asking for information by name (or URN) has many advantages over asking for it by its location (or URL):

✔ If the owner of a document moves the document, the owner must update only the pointer in the published URN, and everybody who later accesses that URN can find the information at its new location. (People who try to access the document by using an out-of-date URL won't reach it after the move, however.)

✔ URN client software can be smart. For example, when you request resolution of a particular URN, you can also tell the URN client where on the Internet you are, and the software can give you the closest URL that has a copy of the information. You may also specify a preferred language; if the information is available in many languages, the URN program can give you just the URLs of the document in the desired language.

✔ URNs are incredibly flexible. A good URN publisher can give you many URLs for a single URN request. For example, if a URN is *"Hamlet* in many languages," it may resolve to a set of many URLs, one for each language. That way, you don't need to specify a preferred language, and you can choose from the set of URLs returned to you via your URN client.

Let People Write Content Reviews

As the Web gets more and more content that costs money to access, you will probably want to start getting other people's opinions of the content before you access it. Services that support opinion polls and reviews of content will become as popular on the Web as they are in current paper media such as magazines.

Reviews of Web content will also be important even if the content is free, just because so much information is out there that you don't want to waste your time jumping around from site to site. These reviews may be free or cheap, but the most useful ones will cost more. Of course, given how easy linking is on the Web, the reviews will probably have links that take you directly to what is being reviewed, making them more useful than paper reviews.

Send You the Daily News

The "personalized newspaper" is a recurring theme in computers and communication. The idea is that each night a computer goes through all its available resources and creates a news summary based on your preferences. Many companies (including Netscape) have claimed to have created such publications, but none has come close to succeeding. So far, they have all been based on limited content from which to choose and unnatural methods for users to express their preferences.

Today, many Web sites pretend to be daily newspapers, but they are fairly anemic. Although they cull news from many different sources, presenting it in a way that lets you flip through it like you do a printed newspaper is still very difficult. If you've tried some of the newsletters available from Netcenter, you know what I mean. This deficiency is mostly due to bandwidth and screen size limitations, but you probably wouldn't put up with your regular newspaper being printed on tiny pieces of paper, either.

Enable Whole-Web Searching

The best catalogs on the Web right now are the ones created by individuals on particular subjects. Searching the entire Web, or even a significant portion of it, is still impossible. The Web search sites described in Chapter 6 are still primitive, incomplete, and of limited research value.

The technology to make the Web search sites better and more useful, however, is already available. Dedicated sites with advanced searching software, aided by the Web site administrators themselves, could lead to much better, searchable indexes. However, the Web is growing so fast that none of the popular search services can search more than a small fraction of the information available on the Web. Let's hope that Netscape devotes more time and money to this part of Netcenter in the future.

Tell You Where the Problems Are on the Internet

In many areas of the world, you can listen to news stations on the radio to find out the traffic conditions on the highways. This service helps drivers avoid areas congested by accidents or road construction, or at least lets them know that they need to plan on taking more time in their travels. Some areas even have toll-free telephone numbers with this kind of useful information.

Not so on the Web. You have no way to find out things like "the Web server at BigComputers is down," or "trying to get information from Web servers in Australia right now is twice as slow as it was an hour ago." Mind you, setting up such an information service wouldn't be hard. Netscape could even make such a service part of the next version of Communicator fairly easily. However, without a central authority on the Web, no one is really in the business of servicing Web users this way, and no standards exist for how a site might report its status.

Bring You High-Quality, Inexpensive Telephone Service

In the past year or two, plenty of people have talked about how you can use the Internet to make free phone calls. In fact, you can't, not unless you're willing to put up with phone calls where the other person's voice drops out for a few seconds or the sound breaks up regularly. Netscape announced free Internet phone calls as a feature of Netscape Conference but then realized that such calls require too much bandwidth to guarantee.

In the future, Communicator may come with software that lets you make phone calls from your PC. However, that software will have to be pretty smart, much smarter than the telephony programs are today. It will have to watch for lost bits of conversation and tell you what to do when they happen. Until then, you can still pick up the phone.

Build Real Communities

The talk about "virtual communities" on the Internet usually is well off the mark. Connection does not equal community. Just because you can chat with a group of people on the Web doesn't mean that you have the kind of long-term commitment to understand, support, and enjoy those people. Yet these commitments are requirements for real communities. Although very useful for many people, Usenet newsgroups can't be classed as communities because anyone can join them, no one must support anyone else, and understanding is often last on the list of importance.

This is not to say that communities can't be built on the Web. In fact, just the opposite is true. Real communities, however, take much more personal work than has been put into many Web sites to date. People must be committed; they must work within the limitations of the Web's communications capabilities; and they must keep at the relationship even when it doesn't work the way they imagined it might.

In the coming years, the Web is likely to help get some communities together that might otherwise never have been able to do so. Better chat software will be part of this process, but a bigger part will be a shift in what people expect from the Web. An even more important part will be a shift in what people expect from each other when they communicate without seeing or hearing each other. The outcome could be wonderful.

Bring Everyone into the Tent

Today, the main users of the Web are people in the major industrialized countries in North America, Europe, and Asia. The number of countries with almost no Web presence, either in terms of Web sites or Web users, however, is staggering. Smaller countries and poorer people are grossly underrepresented on the Web, more than on any other popular communication medium.

Web use doesn't need to be this way, however, and the tide is turning. The Internet Society is one of the prime movers in bringing the Internet to all countries of the world; it offers many programs that help countries share Internet technologies. Furthermore, many communities in the countries already on the Web are bringing Web access to more people by putting Web-enabled terminals in libraries and other public places.

The spirit of inclusion was one of the founding premises of the Web. Its open structure was designed to let as many Internet hosts as possible participate. The next step is to help as many users as possible participate. This step, if taken, will in turn certainly fuel the growth of the number of Web sites, as well as the depth and thought put into the current and future Web sites.

Chapter 23

Ten Ways to Have Fun with Communicator

In This Chapter

▶ Some things you may not have thought of that could be a gang fun

▶ Stretching your imagination while in front of your computer

*W*riting this book is challenging because different readers have different things they want to do with Communicator. Some readers are businessfolk who use Communicator in their daily work. Other readers plan to use Communicator for their personal interests. Still other readers don't know what they want to use Communicator for and are open to almost anything.

This chapter lists ten fun things you can do with Communicator that you may not have thought of. It's not just "ten fun Web sites" because Communicator is more than just a way to look at Web sites. As always, enjoy!

See What It's Like Around the World

Thousands of still video cameras are connected to the Internet. People with bandwidth to spare turn on the cameras, connect them to the Web server, and just leave them on. Many of these cameras take a picture every minute or ten minutes, so you get a fresh view of what is happening whenever you go to the Web page.

Some of these Web cameras are indoors, others are outdoors. I prefer the outdoor ones so that I can get a feeling of what the weather is somewhere far away. I even look at these sites when the weather is nice at my house. szym.com/cameras/ is a good starting place to look for Web cameras, but you can also find plenty of other Web camera sites.

Get Free Things in the Mail Every Day

People love the "something-a-day" desk calendars. Cartoons. Photos of cute cats. Jokes. New words. You name it — people look forward to their daily dose of it on their desks. The Internet has its equivalent of these calendars, and you don't even have to go out on the Web every day to get them. Instead, they are delivered to your e-mail box.

You can get a huge variety of daily mail. The In-Box Direct area of Netcenter lists dozens of one-way mailing lists, many of which deliver daily news and entertainment. You may also want to consider some of the many mailing lists outside the Netscape world. Yahoo! groups these lists under "X of the Day," and they are pretty easy to find.

Listen to Radio Outside Your City

As Web-based radio takes off, more and more radio stations are "simulcasting" their regular radio broadcasts on the Internet. Of course, some radio stations could be from almost anywhere, but good stations have local programming and news that give you a sense of the interests of the people in that area.

If you want to get a good feel for what's happening in another city, listen to the news in that city. Many stations have plenty of local-oriented news and even local talk shows. The best time to hear local news is during *drive time,* the commute hours for that area.

Unfortunately, finding out whether a particular radio station simulcasts is difficult. No universal radio guide lists all the radio stations you can tune into. I hope someone fixes this situation in the future, because plenty of people would love to find radio stations around the world that they can listen to.

Say What You've Always Wanted to Say

In Part V, I talk about how to use Composer to create Web sites. Some people find creating their own Web site intimidating because they don't feel comfortable with page design or creating art. However, you don't have to have a Web page to say what you want to say. Parts of Usenet news have always been a forum for people saying almost anything they want, and many chat rooms have the same kinds of openness.

Go ahead and try it. Go to a Usenet newsgroup that interests you (reading Usenet is covered in Chapter 9). Read what some others have said, and then contribute your own two cents' worth. Many people find that it doesn't take long to get comfortable with talking in an open forum. If you prefer to have direct interaction, go to a topical chat room, lurk for a bit so that you can read what is happening, and then jump in.

Collect Pictures for an Electronic Scrapbook

Some people stay away from the `alt.binaries.pictures` subgroups in Usenet news because so many contain objectionable material. However, dozens of subgroups exist simply as a place where people can post their favorite photos (and sometimes paintings) of everything from trains to airplanes to horses. Many of these subgroups get dozens of new pictures a day. You can also find plenty of pictures on a variety of topics on pages of clip art and on other people's home pages. Many WebRings are for people who are sharing their art or the art they have collected. Be sure to ask permission before reusing these pictures; you almost always get the okay.

Discover Different Kinds of Music

Most of us like only a few kinds of music. Maybe you like classical music and opera; maybe it's country and folk; maybe it's speed metal and hip-hop. If you want to find out about other kinds of music, you can flip through the radio dial, but you usually end up starting in the middle of a song, or even worse, a commercial.

If you want to find out more about a new kind of music, you can easily find sites that have a number of samples of a particular category. All the major record companies (and many of the minor ones) have sites that feature samples of the music of their artists. Trying out the samples makes it easy to see whether you want to expand your musical horizons without spending any money or searching the radio dial. You can find guides to different types of music sites at many Web portals, such as Netscape's Netcenter.

Watch What Other People Are Searching For

You never know what's going on in some people's heads. Imagine what it would be like to look over people's shoulders while they use a search service on the Web, seeing which links they click and which pages they linger on. You can't quite do that, but some of the search services let you see the terms that people have recently been searching for. The search terms paint an interesting picture of the psyche of the "typical" Web user.

For example, www.metaspy.com/ watches the searches that happen at the www.metacrawler.com/ search site, showing you the last ten searches that took place. It refreshes itself every 15 seconds. If you find a topic that you want to search for yourself, you just click on it, and you get the same results of the search as the person who entered the search term.

Share Your Instant Poems

Word magnets on refrigerators have certainly caught on in the past ten years, but they can be frustrating if the word set isn't big enough, or your refrigerator isn't big enough. Where there's a trend, there's a Web site, or in this case, many Web sites. Yep, you can play with the equivalent of a refrigerator magnet set or just read what other people have written.

One of my favorite refrigerator sites is at www.IEOR.Berkeley.EDU/~andryan/fridge/, also known as the *Virtual Fridge*. You can read poems going back well over a year, and if you're in a public mood, you can create your own on the spot. This site, like the other refrigerator sites, is a great example of how good Web programming and a silly idea can go a long way together.

Play the Stock Market

And I do mean *play*. Of course, you can buy and sell stocks for real on the Web; it's one of the hot areas of Web commerce. However, most of us don't have the time or the money to do serious investing, and even if we did, we wouldn't trust ourselves not to lose the whole thing. But that shouldn't stop you from having fun with stocks.

The Web sports dozens (if not hundreds) of sites that let you track portfolios of stocks for free. Well, go ahead and make up a portfolio! Make up different portfolios on different sites and see how they do against each other. You can feel rich as you watch your various investments go up (or feel poor as you watch them go down), and you never have to worry about losing the real thing. Most of the Web portals, such as Netcenter, let you do this kind of tracking.

Wander Around Aimlessly

OK, admit it: Sometimes you just want some mindless fun and you have no energy. If channel scanning on the TV doesn't do it for you, try the Web's equivalent, and just go from page to page clicking any old link. Too bored to know where to start? Go to a search site and search for a common word and see what comes up first. Hours later, your mouse finger may hurt and you may have a headache, but look at where you've been!

Chapter 24

Ten Charming Places on the Web

In This Chapter

▶ Remembering that the Web is more than just "information"

▶ Finding places you want to visit

The Web can be a restful, enjoyable place if you let it. Many of the sites described in this book are useful, informative, and so on, but there's more to life than useful information. The Web can help you find out about what is available off the Web, too, and sometimes it's nice just to sit and be while you're roaming the Web.

Bill's Lighthouse Getaway

zuma.lib.utk.edu/lights/

People travel, people have hobbies, and people take pictures. Some of the personal sites on the Web have wonderful pictures of what people do when they're on vacation, when they're doing their hobbies, and so on. The Web site in Figure 24-1 is your gateway to many pages of pictures and descriptions of lighthouses.

Zen Page

sunsite.unc.edu/zen/

Many people view Zen Buddhism as one of the most contemplative religions in the world. Whether or not that is the case, you can find many Web sites with Buddhist themes, particularly themes of quietude and tranquillity. The site in Figure 24-2 features many such Zen pages.

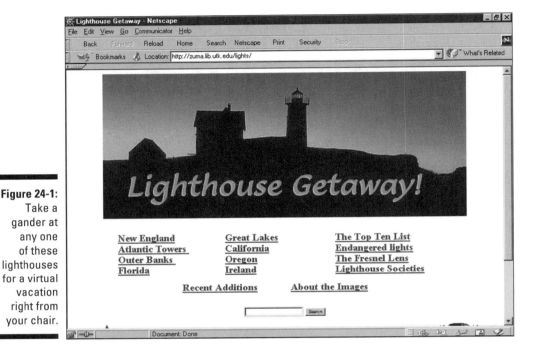

Figure 24-1:
Take a
gander at
any one
of these
lighthouses
for a virtual
vacation
right from
your chair.

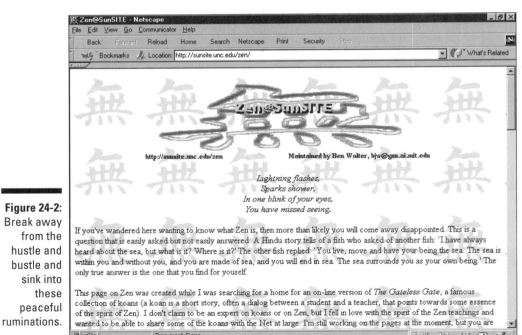

Figure 24-2:
Break away
from the
hustle and
bustle and
sink into
these
peaceful
ruminations.

Exploratorium

www.exploratorium.edu/

If you've ever been to the Exploratorium in San Francisco, you know that it is one of the least peaceful museums anywhere. Kids run around, trying all sorts of science experiments and teaching exhibits, generally having a wild, science-filled experience. Parents and teachers can often be found sitting exhausted on the benches.

The Exploratorium's Web site, however, is much more calm. It still provides much of the sense of wonder of the full Exploratorium; much of the magic of the museum has been translated to the many Web pages. Take a look at the site's home page in Figure 24-3.

Figure 24-3: Loads of educational entertainment await you at the Exploratorium.

Plugged In

www.pluggedin.org/

What do you get when you combine creative but financially poor kids with multimedia technology and training? Pretty amazing results. Artwork is just a fraction of what is created at Plugged In, a center in East Palo Alto, California, that is geared toward helping underprivileged kids learn to use multimedia equipment and facilities that are clearly beyond their financial reach. Figure 24-4 shows the main page of the site.

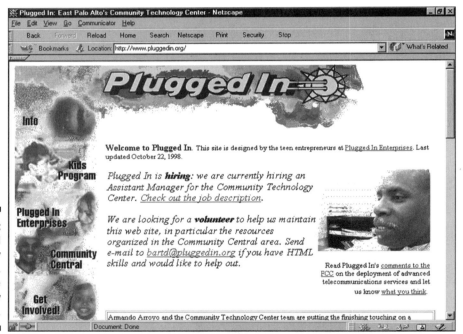

Figure 24-4:
If you build it, they will come. They've built it, now check it out.

The Peace Page

`www.ccnet.com/~elsajoy/index2.html`

Okay, call me an old hippie. A page about spiritual awareness and being centered touches my heart. The personal page shown in Figure 24-5 is one of my favorites, a testimony to someone who cares enough to tell the world that she likes things of the soul. What's so funny about peace, love, and understanding?

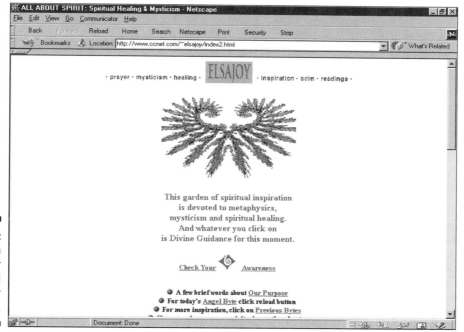

Figure 24-5:
Broaden your horizons and explore your spiritual self.

Positive Vibrations

`newciv.org/worldtrans/positive.html`

On a similar note, the page shown in Figure 24-6 has many links to other places around the Web that are positive. Yeah, sure, it's all relative, but I guess I like knowing that a few Web pages out there help to balance out all the pages extolling violent games, hatred, and just plain negative stuff.

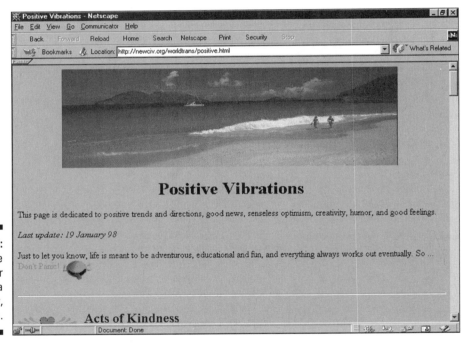

Figure 24-6: Add this one to your favorites for a longer, happier life.

Crossword Puzzles

```
news:rec.puzzles.crosswords
```

If you like to relax with a word puzzle or two, you probably do crossword puzzles. The `rec.puzzles.crosswords` newsgroup is a wonderful place to hang out when you're not putting pencil to paper. Some people post humorous clues; some point to other puzzle locations; and still others just like reading and writing about words. Get a preview of the newsgroup in Figure 24-7.

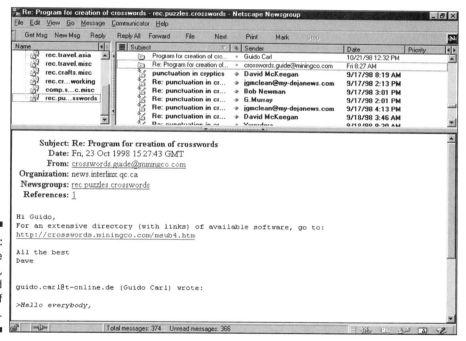

Figure 24-7: Learn the Whats, Whys, and Hows of crosswords.

GardenNet

www.gardennet.com/

Sitting in a garden is sometimes the most relaxing thing that many of us get to do during a busy week. Whether you like to tend gardens or just sit in them, the resources in GardenNet can be enjoyable in and of themselves. Check them out in Figure 24-8.

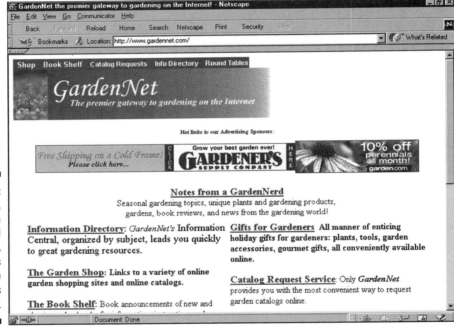

Figure 24-8:
Alright,
green
thumbs and
flora lovers,
here is
where the
best ideas
spring to life.

Bird Watching

www-stat.wharton.upenn.edu/~siler/birding.html

Another activity that is quite calming for millions of people is watching birds. You can find birding organizations all over the world whose interests vary from simply counting different varieties of birds to preservation and collecting. The Web site for one of these organizations is shown in Figure 24-9.

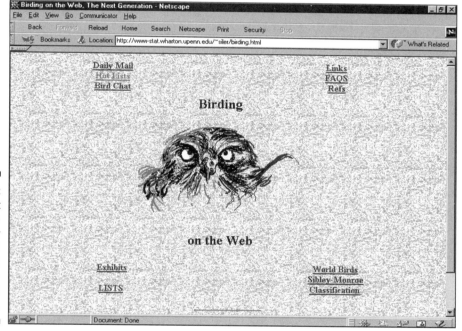

Figure 24-9: Find out more about our feathered friends on this well-developed site.

Pete's Pond Page

`reality.sgi.com/employees/peteo/`

Some folks are lucky enough to have a pond in their garden. This Web site is another one of those personal pages that serves as a resource spot for others with similar interests. No Web page can replace the tranquillity of going out and watching the goldfish, but the one in Figure 24-10 certainly helps if you can't go out and get the direct experience of a pond.

Figure 24-10: Sit back and relax with these beautiful pictures and innovative ideas.

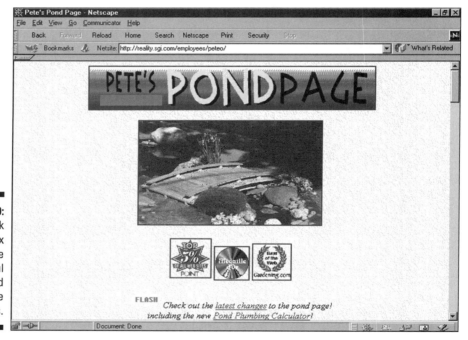

Glossary

The Internet is full of jargon, and much of it applies as much to the Web as it does to any other service. This glossary covers general Internet- and Web-specific terms that you may need to know. Many abbreviations are used on the Web, and you may also see these terms spelled out in places. Such terms are listed here with the more common usage appearing first — be it abbreviation or the full name — and the less common usage appearing in parentheses after it.

America Online

A large online service with more than ten million users. America Online, also called AOL, was the first of the big online services to have more than just a mail connection to the Internet. AOL introduced a Web browser in 1995.

anonymous FTP

The most common way to search for and download files. Hundreds of host computers on the Internet enable anyone to connect to their systems and look through directories for files they want.

Archie

A method for searching for files in anonymous FTP archives. Archie servers throughout the world enable you to log in or use Archie client software to search for files and directories by their titles. However, very few Archie servers still exist, and Archie is not a reliable means of finding files any more.

ARPAnet

The network run by the U.S. Defense Department's Advanced Research Projects Agency that was the original "backbone" of the Internet. The ARPAnet was originally intended as a research network that would also link Defense Department affiliates. ARPA handed the ARPAnet to the U.S. National Science Foundation, which turned it into the NSFnet.

ASCII (American Standard Code for Information Interchange)

Plain text characters. ASCII (pronounced *as-kee*) is a standard that says which computer-readable number is associated with each letter, digit, and punctuation mark. An *ASCII file* is a text file that can be read by almost any program.

BBS (bulletin board system)

A computer system that enables people to dial through modems and use their services. A BBS may be a single computer with a modem or a local network of many computers that can accept dozens of connections at a time. Most BBSs are on the Internet, although a few are not. BBSs often feature downloadable files, discussion areas, and other features that make them popular. You can use some BBSs for free, although others charge a monthly or hourly fee.

BITNET

A network of university computers that is separate from (but connected to) the Internet. BITNET is slowly fading away as the mainframe computers on which most of it runs are decommissioned, but it was a major force in academic computing until only a few years ago. BITNET computers are not on an active network but instead have intermittent connections.

bookmarks

Method of remembering specific Web sites. Communicator lets you store the names and locations of interesting sites in bookmark collections. You can use these collections to quickly get to the Web site you want.

browser

Software used for roaming the Web. Web browsers are client software that enable users to view the many kinds of information on the Web, such as HTML documents, Gopher pages, and FTP directories. Communicator is the most popular Web browser, followed in popularity by Internet Explorer. See also *client program*.

c shell

The most common user interface for people whose Internet providers run on character-based UNIX systems. The c shell is also one of the oldest user interfaces still widely used, and it shows. Unless you are a computer weenie, it is unlikely that you will enjoy using the c shell very much.

cache

An intermediate storage location that keeps a copy of information you have already seen. In Communicator, if you access a location that you have already been to and the information from that location is still in the cache, you don't need to get the information again from the Internet. Caches help reduce network traffic and make using the Web faster.

CERT (Computer Emergency Response Team)

A security force for the Internet. CERT is a clearinghouse of information about network security, known security problems on the Internet, and attempted (or successful) break-ins. Its FTP site, `ftp.cert.org`, has definitive versions of common Internet server software.

certificate

A statement from a trusted authority that a particular public key is associated with a particular name, such as an e-mail address. Certificates are used in S/MIME to help mail recipients be sure that they know who sent a message.

certificate authority (CA)

A company or department that acts as a trusted arbiter of identification. Users trust CAs to issue certificates only to people who have somehow identified themselves and proven that they have a particular public key.

CGI (Common Gateway Interface)

A programming standard used by most Web servers for handling forms. CGI helps one type of software (in this case, Web server software) present information to other types of software (the programs that handle Web forms) in a standard fashion so that the two don't need to know anything about each other.

chat

An old multi-user discussion system for the Internet. It has almost completely been replaced by Internet Relay Chat (IRC).

CIX (Commercial Internet Exchange)

The first major industry group for companies that provide Internet access. Because it is made up of competitors in a constantly changing market, CIX is a somewhat volatile group. CIX also lobbies the U.S. government on Internet-related issues.

client program

A program that a user runs to interface with server software. Client software often looks different on each computer it runs on, taking on the best features of that computer. Many different client programs can interact with one server program. See also *browser*.

client-server software

Software that is split between two programs: clients and servers. The term *client-server* has become widely used in the computer industry to describe database and information retrieval systems in which users run programs on their personal computers that interact with database programs on host computers. Most of the major Internet services (such as mail, Usenet news, and the World Wide Web) use the client-server model.

Communicator

A graphical browser for the World Wide Web, and the main subject of this book. Communicator is produced by Netscape Communications, which also produces other Web-related software such as server software.

CompuServe

The first major online service. CompuServe was bought by America Online, and its service will probably be folded into AOL's in the future. See also *America Online.*

digital signature

An attachment to a mail message that proves that the message was written by a particular person. The digital signature can only be created by someone who has a particular digital key. Another feature of digital signatures is that they prove that a message has not been altered.

DNS (domain name system)

The method by which Internet addresses (such as mit.edu) are converted into computer-readable IP addresses (such as 182.156.12.24). The DNS is one of the most flexible and powerful technical features of the Internet, enabling computers to appear and disappear from the Internet without causing problems. It also makes sending messages much easier because it does not require a central repository of all names.

download

To copy a file from a remote system to your computer. Downloading files from anonymous FTP servers or Web servers is a popular way to get freeware and shareware files.

dweeb

See *geek.*

EFF (Electronic Frontier Foundation)

One of the first large groups concerned with Internet-related privacy and access issues. The EFF does extensive education and lobbying in Washington and often educates local law enforcement agencies about computer technology. The EFF is one of the strongest supporters of personal freedom on the Internet.

e-mail

Electronic mail. Internet users often use the term *e-mail* to differentiate those messages from postal mail.

encryption

Scrambling a message so that it is virtually impossible for other people to read unless they have a key. You use encryption to maintain privacy when sending messages and also to verify the identity of the sender of a message. Many different types of encryption are used on the Internet, none of them compatible with each other.

ERIC (Educational Resources Information Center)

Funded by the U.S. Department of Education, ERIC is a clearinghouse of general information for teachers. It sponsors AskERIC, an Internet site with many online teaching resources for K-12 teachers.

FAQ (Frequently Asked Questions)

A file that contains a list of questions that appear regularly on a Usenet newsgroup and the answers to those questions. FAQs are useful for preventing the same questions from being asked repeatedly by newcomers. The term FAQ has now moved beyond Usenet and is used for anything that answers the most common questions on a topic.

file

A group of characters stored electronically. Files can contain anything from text to pictures to programs to movies, and so on. Most programs refer to files by their names.

Finger

An Internet service that enables you to find out information about a user on a computer. Computers that run Finger servers tell you when a user was logged on last and give some information about the user.

flame

To attack someone in a discussion, usually with language much harsher than necessary. It is also used as a noun to describe the message(s) sent. Flames are usually personal even if the flamer is attacking ideas. The term comes from the concept of a "heated" debate.

freeware

Software you can use and copy with no obligation. People write freeware because it feels good or as a way to hone their programming and design skills. Although you can give it away, most freeware authors restrict you from selling or altering the program.

FTP (File Transfer Protocol)

The Internet's file transfer program. FTP is one of the older standards on the Internet. FTP is still an efficient way to transfer files between systems and to distribute information on request to Internet users.

FYIs (For Your Information files)

A subset of the Internet RFC files that give information to Internet beginners. FYIs are often much simpler to read and cover less technical information than other RFCs (see *Requests for Comments*).

gateway

A translator between two different interfaces. Many kinds of gateways exist, but on the Internet, the term is most commonly used to indicate a protocol gateway that converts between two Internet services. For example, a mail-to-Web gateway enables users who have only mail access to get files from the Web.

geek

A somewhat affectionate term for someone who is overly interested in computers. Similar terms of partial endearment/partial criticism include *nerd, dweeb,* and *weenie.*

GIF (Graphics Interchange Format) files

Graphics files stored using the GIF format. The GIF format was designed by CompuServe as a way of compacting images and making them easily viewable on many kinds of computers. The GIF standard has been widely adopted on the Internet.

Gopher

A service that enables you to navigate through Internet information easily, although without graphics. Gopher appeared about the same time as the Web but has pretty much fallen out of use.

home page

The initial page you see when you enter a Web site. The term is somewhat ambiguous because it is also commonly used as the page you see when you first start your Web browser.

host computer

Any computer on the Internet to which you can connect. Generally, a host computer is any computer to which you can send mail or that has a Web server, an FTP server, or something similar.

HTML (HyperText Markup Language)

The formatting language used by World Wide Web servers. HTML documents are text files with extra commands embedded into them.

HTTP (HyperText Transfer Protocol)

The protocol used for passing hypertext documents on the Web. HTTP has become popular as a result of its somewhat simple nature and the fact that you can easily write both client and server programs that can communicate with HTTP.

hypertext

A type of document that contains links to other documents. When reading a hypertext document, you can quickly jump to linked documents and then jump back whenever you feel like it. Hypertext enables you to organize the information you read into different formats.

IAB (Internet Architecture Board)

The group that oversees Internet technical issues. It oversees the IETF and the IRTF and acts as a liaison with other non-technical Internet bodies.

IETF (Internet Engineering Task Force)

The group that oversees the technical standards on which the Internet is based. The IETF is an all-volunteer organization and is heaven for computer geeks. The technical decisions made by the IETF affect how the Internet functions, how fast it operates, and how it will look in the future.

inline images

Pictures that appear in a Web page. An inline image is different from a regular picture that you may find on the Internet in that it appears as part of a Web document, not as a stand-alone image.

Internet Society (ISOC)

The main group that acts as a focal point for Internet building. The ISOC has been particularly active in bringing non-U.S. users onto the Internet and in coordinating other Internet-related groups.

IP (Internet Protocol)

The standard used by computers to transmit information over the Internet. IP defines how the information looks as it travels between computers, not what the computers do with it. IP also defines how Internet addresses work.

IRC (Internet Relay Chat)

A program for coordinating many people talking at the same time. Using IRC, you can talk with groups of people by typing. Using IRC is similar to being at a party while participating in many conversations at the same time.

IRTF (Internet Research Task Force)

The research arm of the IAB. The IRTF looks at issues that affect the Internet's future, such as what happens after the explosive growth that the Internet has been experiencing and how certain technologies will affect Internet traffic.

ISDN (Integrated Services Digital Network)

A digital form of data transfer over regular telephone lines. Using ISDN phone service enables you to have both voice and data on the same phone line. ISDN modems run about ten times faster than popular 14.4 Kbps modems, although they cost much more than regular modems. ISDN service from the telephone company is also usually more expensive than regular telephone service.

JPEG (Joint Photographic Experts Group) files

Graphics files stored in JPEG format. The JPEG format is an open industry standard that is used widely for storing photographs in a compact form. A few variations on the JPEG format exist, but most programs such as Communicator can read them all.

LISTSERV

A program used on some computers for handling mailing lists. LISTSERV has an arcane interface but has been around for more than a decade. Many important mailing lists are still run from LISTSERV computers. Many LISTSERV mailing lists also enable you to retrieve files related to the mailing list.

local area network (LAN)

A network of computers that are all in the same location, such as at an office or building. LANs have become much more common in the past few years as more companies have realized the importance of communication. Some LANs are attached to the Internet, giving each person on the LAN access to Internet resources.

Lynx

A character-based client program for accessing the World Wide Web. Although Lynx is not as flashy as other Web clients such as Communicator, it works well for the millions of Internet users who have only character-based access.

mail

Messages that are sent over the Internet by using the Simple Mail Transport Protocol. Internet mail is by far the most popular and most used feature of the Internet.

mailing list

A system of duplicating one message and sending it to many people. A single letter is sent to the mailing list host and a copy is sent to every person on the mailing list. Some mailing lists have thousands of people.

markup language

A method for specifying types of content and formatting in a text file. Markup languages enable you to enter text strings in your file to denote various features of the file, such as which words should be boldface and which words are part of the title.

Messenger

The portion of the Communicator package that handles Internet mail and Usenet news. Messenger has a single interface for both of these services.

MIME (Multipurpose Internet Mail Extensions)

The standard for enclosing binary files in Internet mail. MIME enables you to specify the type of attachment you are making to your Internet mail. Many non-mail programs, such as the World Wide Web, also use the MIME standard to make reading files easier for client programs.

mirror

A duplicate of an FTP site. Mirrors help reduce long-haul Internet traffic by enabling people to choose to download files from hosts that are closer to them. Usually, mirror sites are updated each night so that they have the same contents as the main site.

modem

A piece of hardware for connecting computers over telephone lines. Most personal computer users connect to the Internet over modems, although some have direct connections through company networks. The most common modems cost less than $100, although faster modems can cost much more.

MUD (Multi-User Dungeons)

A program that simulates a place where you can move around, talk to other users, and interact with your surroundings. Most are centered on fantasy themes such as dragons, science fiction, and so on. Many MUDs on the Internet enable you to not only interact but also create parts of the environment for others to interact with.

Navigator

The Web browser portion of Netscape Communicator. Navigator is also available as a separate product from Netscape.

Netcenter

A Web site created by Netscape that can be used for many things, such as searching the Web and finding news. Netcenter can be found at `home.netscape.com`.

netiquette

A play on the word *etiquette*, this term refers to the proper way to behave on the Internet. This includes respecting the rights and desires of others, setting an example of how you want strangers to treat you, and acknowledging that the Internet is very different from face-to-face communication.

Netscape

The name of the company that produces Communicator, the topic of this book. Netscape Communications also produces a number of other Internet software and services.

netstorm

The nastiness that happens when packets get lost or undelivered on the Internet. Netstorms have many causes and sometimes last only a minute or two. Sometimes, however, netstorms can last for days on small parts of the Internet.

newsgroups

Topical divisions of Usenet. A newsgroup generally has a single topic (such as the communications software for Microsoft Windows), but within that topic anyone can ask or answer questions. The term *news* is outdated; the majority of the discussion in newsgroups has to do with old items, not news. See also *Usenet*.

NSFnet (National Science Foundation network)

The network run by the National Science Foundation that was previously the backbone of the Internet. The NSFnet is now in transition, with most of its usefulness supplanted by commercial networks.

packet

A group of bytes going from one Internet host to another. Packets have variable lengths and can contain any kind of information.

plug-ins

Programs external to Communicator that can display different types of documents inside Communicator's window. Plug-ins are generally used to display formats that would be hard for Communicator to incorporate, such as page layout or animation formats. Some plug-ins are free; others are commercial.

POP (Point Of Presence)

A place you dial into to get Internet access. Many Internet service companies have POPs in many cities, although local Internet service providers often have only one POP with many modems.

POP (Post Office Protocol)

The most popular way to get Internet mail by using a mail client such as Messenger. When you have mail stored on a remote mail server, you use POP to see what the mail is and to download it to your personal computer.

port

A number that helps TCP identify what kind of service you are asking for from another computer. Most common Internet features such as HTTP have standard port numbers (for example, 80 for HTTP) that client software uses if you do not specify a different port number. The only time you need to know about ports is if a server requires that you use a nonstandard port number to communicate.

PPP (Point-to-Point Protocol)

A fast, reliable method for connecting computers on the Internet over serial lines, such as telephone wire. PPP has become more popular than SLIP in the past few years, and many Internet service providers offer PPP connections. Using PPP or SLIP, your personal computer can be directly connected to the Internet. See also *IP*.

protocol

A set of rules. On the Internet, protocols are generally considered to be the rules used for communicating between computers. Some common protocols are FTP, HTTP, and SMTP.

RFCs (Requests for Comments)

Documents that define the technical aspects of the Internet. Originally, these documents were used to get input from other technical users of the Internet before standards were set down, and many RFCs today still serve that purpose. Other RFCs are simply statements of reality.

root domains

The main domain names assigned by the root domain of the Internet. The main root domains in the U.S. are .com, .edu, .gov, .mil, .net, .org, and .us. The other root domains are the two-letter country codes, such as .ca (for Canada) and .jp (for Japan).

router

A device that connects two networks, enabling only certain traffic to pass through. Routers are used at almost every intersection on the Internet to both limit traffic going to smaller networks and help choose the most efficient way to get packets to their desired destination. Some routers cost less than $1,000; others cost more than $100,000.

server program

The program a host computer runs that communicates with users running client programs. Server software establishes a standard for communication, and all client programs must act in that standard fashion to work correctly. Many different client programs can interact with one server program.

service

The generic term for a communication protocol and the content that goes with it. Electronic mail, FTP, and HTTP, for example, are all services.

SGML (Standard General Markup Language)

The language from which HTML was spawned. SGML is much more flexible than HTML and is used by many large companies for creating structured text that can be searched and indexed. Many text purists feel that HTML has too many faults for real formatting and that SGML is the only way to go.

shareware

Software that you can freely copy and try before buying it. Shareware enables you to test software and pass it along to others without paying for it. If you continue to use the software for a specified amount of time, however, you must send the author money to license the software.

shell

A program that enables a user to interact with an operating system. Programs such as the MS-DOS command line and Microsoft Windows are shells to the MS-DOS operating system. Many popular shells run under UNIX, such as the c shell, Bourne shell, and so on.

SLIP (Serial Line IP)

A fast, simple method for connecting computers on the Internet over serial lines, such as telephone wire. PPP has become more popular than SLIP in the past few years, although many Internet service providers offer SLIP connections as well as PPP connections. Using PPP or SLIP, your personal computer is directly connected to the Internet. See also *IP*.

S/MIME (Secure MIME)

The standard for secure Internet mail. S/MIME is the most popular protocol used to send both encrypted e-mail and e-mail with digital signatures.

SMTP (Simple Mail Transfer Protocol)

The rules that govern how Internet mail moves from the sender's computer to the recipient's. Mail on the Internet is quite flexible, mostly thanks to the fact that SMTP has been around so long and is well understood by mail administrators. Messenger users need to know which SMTP host they can use to send mail from their accounts to other places on the Internet.

SSL (Secure Sockets Layer)

A protocol developed by Netscape to let all types of client software (not just Web clients) securely communicate with servers. Using SSL prevents someone who is watching a conversation going across the Internet from determining what is being said. It is thus useful for transmitting things like credit card numbers and other sensitive information.

tags

Text you add to an HTML document so that Web clients can format the document. In HTML, tags always begin with the < character and end with the > character. Tags often come in pairs, called *start tags* and *end tags;* for example, the tags <title> and </title> are a pair of start and end tags.

TCP (Transmission Control Protocol)

The standard used on the Internet to identify the kind of information in packets. TCP is almost always used with the IP standard, and you normally hear of them together as TCP/IP. TCP also makes sure that data is passed without any errors.

telnet

An Internet service that enables one computer to act as a terminal on another computer. Using telnet, you can type on another computer as if you were directly connected. In this way, telnet is somewhat like common communications programs (sometimes called *terminal programs*) for personal computers.

terminal program

Software that makes your computer act like an old-style computer terminal. Terminal programs are still useful because so many Internet hosts enable users to attach to them through terminals. Literally hundreds of terminal programs are available.

UNIX

The most common operating system for servers and hosts on the Internet. Almost any computer can be an Internet host, but since the early days, such computers more commonly run UNIX.

upload

To send a file to a remote computer. A few hosts enable anyone to leave files on the computer for others to read. About 99 percent of the people on the Internet, however, only download files and never upload them.

URL (Uniform Resource Locator)

The method for specifying the addresses of things on the Web. URLs are also starting to be used by non-Web client software as a way of identifying the location of files, mail addresses, and so on.

Usenet

A widely used Internet service that organizes people's comments by topic. These topics, called newsgroups, have their own structure with people commenting on previous comments, starting new threads of discussion, and so on. Usenet is probably the most popular Internet feature other than mail. It is sometimes incorrectly listed in all caps as *USENET*.

UUCP (UNIX-to-UNIX-Copy)

A common method used to communicate among computers that are connected to the Internet only part of the time. UUCP is a very old standard that enables mail messages, Usenet news, and files to be transferred from computer to computer. It has become less popular in recent years, although many bulletin board systems use it to pass mail.

VRML (Virtual Reality Modeling Language)

A language used to display three-dimensional information on the computer screen in a way that looks somewhat realistic. VRML programs often make it look like you're walking or flying around a scene and enable you to interact with objects in the scene.

WAIS (Wide Area Information Server)

A method for searching databases over the Internet. WAIS was once trumpeted as the next big thing on the Internet, but the free versions of WAIS server software and client software are not very easy to use, and few sites are running commercial versions. WAIS is also used by many Gopher and Web sites as a method for searching just within those sites.

wide area network (WAN)

A network of computers spread out across a great distance. Some of the connections in a WAN are typically through telephone lines or over satellites. WANs are often networks of networks, linking local area networks (LANs) into a single network.

Winsock

A standard that Microsoft Windows programs use to interact with the Internet and other TCP/IP networks. Winsock is short for "Windows sockets." Today, all Windows TCP/IP programs use standard Winsock interfaces.

workstation

A very high-powered personal computer. The line between the most powerful PCs and the least powerful workstations is blurry, but workstations usually have much more RAM and hard disk space and are much faster. Workstations are also often used as servers on the Internet.

World Wide Web (WWW)

An Internet service that enables users to retrieve hypertext and graphics from various sites (often just called "the Web"). The Web has become one of the most popular Internet services in the past few years. In fact, many Internet information providers are now publishing only on the Web.

XML (eXtensible Markup Language)

The XML is a method of tagging information that will probably become popular in the coming years. Many people expect XML to replace HTML for Web pages. XML is also useful for other kinds of data.

Index

• *Symbols* •

& (ampersand) in HTML, 296
< > (brackets) in HTML, 46, 268
!-- and -- HTML tags, 295
`<head>` HTML tag, 293
`<html>` tag, 293
`<title>` HTML tag, 294
404 error, 108–109

• *A* •

Activity monitor, 64
Address Book command (Communicator menu), 130
address books, 130—133
  address book card, 123
  vCards, 132
addresses. *See also* URLs
  e-mail, 125–126
  as FTP passwords, 83
  pinpoint addressing, 125
  IP addresses, 56
  Messenger, 148
  pinpoint addressing, 149
addressing area (Messenger), 148
administration costs of Web page maintenance, 256–257
Advanced option (Preferences dialog box), 82–84
advertising, 27–28
  banner ads, 28
  Internet keyword searches, 97
  Netcenter, 63
alabanza.com/kabacoff/Inter-links (Inter-Links), 178–180
alignment of images, 286
Amazon (www.amazon.com), 210–211
America Online (AOL), 323

anonymous FTP, 323
AnyWho (www.anywho.com), 192–194
AOL Instant Messenger, 166–168
Appearance option (Preferences dialog box), 77–79
Apple Web site www.apple.com, 224–225
applications (helper applications), 87
Archie servers, 323
Argus Clearinghouse (www.clearinghouse.net), 177–178
ARPAnet, 323
ASCII (American Standard Code for Information Interchange), 323
attachments to e-mail messages, 144, 151–152
attributes (HTML), 293
auctions (WebAuction), 206–207
automatically loading images, 82

• *B* •

Back button, 67
backing up, 67
banner ads, 28
baseline of text and image alignment, 286
BBSs (bulletin board systems), 52, 324
behavior online, 332
Bill's Lighthouse Getaway (zuma.lib.utk.edu/lights/), 313–314
bird watching (www-stat.wharton.upenn.edu/siler/birding.html), 321
BITNET, 324
bits per second (bps), 20
BizWeb (www.bizweb.com), 182
body of message (Messenger), 149–150
bookmarks, 101, 324
  adding, 103
  editing, 102, 105

folders, 104
importing, 106
moving, 104–105
organizing, 103–105
separators, 105
Bookmarks command (Edit menu), 102
Bookmarks menu, 103
Bookmarks window, 85, 102
book shopping online
Amazon, 210–211
BookWeb, 214
Computer Literacy Bookshops, 209–210
BookWeb (www.bookweb.org/), 214
bps (bits per second), 20
brackets <> and HTML, 46
broken pictures, 114
browsers, 324
buddhism (sunsite.unc.edu/zen/), 313–314
bulletin board systems. *See* BBSs
Business Web (www.bizweb.com), 182
business-related Web sites, 215–217
businesses
selling products, 258–259
Web page publishing, 257–260
buttons
Back, 67
Forward, 67
Home, 68
Reload, 69
Security, 88
Stop, 68–69
What's Related, 98

• C •

c shell, 324
caches, 83–84, 324
California state government Web site
(www.ca.gov/), 241–242
cameras, 307–308
Capital PC User Group (www.cpcug.org),
220
case of letters, 34
HTML, 291, 297

catalogs online, 27–28
CD-ROMs and Communicator distribution,
5
CEO Express (www.ceoexpress.com/),
215–217
CERT (Computer Emergency Response
Team), 325
certificate authority (CA), 90, 160–163, 325
certificates (security), 89, 160-163, 325
end-user, 161
personal certificates, 90
site certificates, 90
CGI (Common Gateway Interface), 325
character formatting (Composer), 273–274
character-based browsers and images, 288
character-based Internet connections, 21
chatting, 325
CIX (Commercial Internet Exchange), 325
client programs, 325
client-server software, 31, 326
clients, 31
clip art (newsgroups), 309
color preferences, 79
column headers in e-mail messages, 138
commands
Communicator menu
Address Book, 130
Composer, 270
Messenger, 135
Edit menu
Bookmarks, 102
Find in Page, 86
Preferences, 75, 121
File menu
Get New Messages, 137
Open Page, 69
Print, 72
Save As, 72
HTML. *See* tags
pop-up menu, 85–86
comments in HTML, 295
CommerceNet (www.commerce.net/), 215
communications cost (Web pages), 256
communications software, 20-21

Communicator, 1, 326
  acquiring, 4–5
  basics, 3
  CD-ROMs, 5
  downloading, 4
  installation, 62
  updating, 5
  versions, 62
Communicator menu commands
  Address Book, 130
  Composer, 270
  Messenger, 135
communities on the Web, 305–306
Component bar, 64-65
Composer
  Format menu, 273–274
  formatting, 272–277
    character formatting, 273–274
    pages, 276–277
    paragraph, 274–275
  headings, 275
  horizontal lines, 277
  HTML, 265
    editing source, 289–290
    tags, inserting, 292–293
  lists, 275–276
  printing Web pages, 280
  saving Web pages to hard drive, 280
  settings, 270
  starting, 270–272
  tables, 277–280
  word processor comparison, 266–267
Composer command (Communicator
    menu), 270
Composer option (Preferences dialog
    box), 81
CompuServe, 326
Computer Emergency Response Team
    (CERT), 325
Computer Literacy Bookshops
    (www.clbooks.com/), 209–210
Computer Professionals for Social
    Responsibility Web site
    (www.cpsr.org/), 249–250

computer requirements for
    Communicator, 19
computer-related newsgroups, 221
computer-related Web sites, 220–234
connections, character-based, 21
Contact host message, 112
content of Web page, 24–30
  reviews, 303
Content area, 64
conventions used in book, 2
cookies, 83
copying
  e-mail messages, 128, 142
  URLs, 70
  Web pages for practice in Composer, 272
cost of content, 29
CPCUG (Capital PC User Group) Web site,
    220
crafts groups, 190–192
crossword puzzles newsgroup, 319
Cryptographic Modules, 89
cryptography, 159
customizing toolbars, 85
cws.internet.com/ (Winsock Apps list), 234

• *D* •

daily news, 304, 308
DealerNet (www.dealernet.com/), 204–205
defining mail filters, 156–158
deleting
  addressees in messages, 148
  e-mail messages, 123
  folders in Messenger, 143
descenders in text, and image alignment,
    286
digital certificates, 160–163
digital signature (e-mail), 158, 163–164, 326
direct sales, 258–259
disks
  caches, 83
  hard disk space for e-mail, 129
  saving Web pages to, 72

displaying toolbars, 85
DNS (domain name system), 326
documents
  HTML, 268–270
    beginning and ending, 293–234
    parts, 293–294
    titles, 294
  hypertext, 44
  links within, 285
domain name system (DNS), 34, 55–56, 326
  root domains, 334
Done message, 112
downloading, 326
  Communicator, 5
  files, 73
  pages, stopping, 68–69
DSNs (Delivery Status Notifications), and
    e-mail, 129
Dummies series information, 2
dweebs, 326

• E •

e-mail, 327. *See also* messages; Messenger,
    331
  addresses, 125–126, 148–150
    as FTP password, 83
    pinpoint addressing, 125
  AOL Instant Messenger, 166–168
  attachments to messages, 144, 151–152
  body of message, 149–150
  column headers in messages, 138
  copying messages, 128
    to folders, 142
  daily news and entertainment, 308
  deleting, 123
  digital signature, 158
  DSNs (Delivery Status Notifications), 129
  filtering messages, 155–158
  folders, 128, 137
  fonts, 122
  formatting messages, 128
  forwarding messages, 126, 150–151
  IMAP server, 119–120

Internet mail, 118
  MDNs (Message Delivery Notifications),
    129
  moving messages between folders, 142
  offline mode, 48
  POP server, 119–120, 333
  reading messages, 140-141
  receiving messages, 137–141
  replying to messages, 150–151
  return receipt, 129
  searching for, 143
  security, 158–165
  sending messages, 150
  sound upon receipt, 122
  spelling in messages, 126, 152–153
  storing messages, 120
  word wrap, 126
EarthLink (www.earthlink.net/book/), 42
Edit menu commands
  Bookmarks, 102
  Find in Page, 86
  Preferences, 75, 121
editing
  bookmarks, 102, 105
  HTML source code, 289–290
education Web sites, 243–245
EFF (Electronic Frontier Foundation), 327
Electronic Frontier Foundation (EFF), 327
electronic magazines, 226–229
encoding, 78
encrypted messages, 158-159, 327
  sending/receiving, 164–165
end-user certificates, 161
entertainment (daily news and
    entertainment), 308
ERIC (Educational Resources Information
    Center), 327
  ericir.syr.edu/, 245–246
Error code 404, 108–109
errors, 107–114
  Contact host message, 112
  Done message, 112
  Host contacted. Waiting for reply
    message, 112

Looking up host message, 112
Transferring data message, 112
etiquette, 332
Exploratorium (www.exploratorium.edu/),
315

● *F* ●

FAQ (Frequently Asked Questions), 327
federal legislation (thomas.loc.gov/), 237
FedWorld (www.fedworld.gov/), 238–239
File menu commands
  Get New Messages, 137
  Open Page, 69
  Print, 72
  Save As, 72
files, 327
  downloading, 73
  HTML, 72–73
  opening in Navigator, 73
  text, opening in Navigator, 73
filtering messages, 155–158
Find in Page command (Edit menu), 86
Finger, 52, 327
fixed-width font, 122
flames (newsgroups), 328
folder list (Messenger window), 136
folders
  bookmarks, 104
  e-mail messages, 128
  Messenger, 137
    copying messages to, 142
    creating, 142
    deleting, 143
    moving messages between, 142
  Personal Toolbar Folder, 85
  subfolders, 136
fonts
  Composer, 273
  e-mail, 122
  preferences, 78
Format menu (Composer), 273–274
formatting
  Composer, 273
    character, 273–274

horizontal lines, 277
  page, 276–277
  paragraph, 274–275
  e-mail messages, 128
forms, 70–71
  HTML, 295
Forward button, 67
forward movement, 67
forwarding e-mail messages, 126, 150–151
freeware, 328
FTP (file transfer protocol), 48–49, 328
  anonymous, 323
  passwords, 83
ftp.netscape.com (Netscape), 4
FYIs (For Your Information files), 328

● *G* ●

games, 194–196
Games Domain (www.gamesdomain.com),
  195
gardening Web sites, 320, 322
GardenNet (www.gardennet.com/), 320
gateways, 53, 328
geeks, 328
Get New Messages command (File menu
  command), 137
GIF (Graphics Interchange Format) files,
  328
Go menu, 67
Gopher, 50–51, 53, 329
government Web sites, 235–250
  state and local, 241–243
graphics. *See* images

● *H* ●

hard disk and e-mail storage, 129
hardware requirements, 19
headings (HTML), 275
helper applications, 87
hiding toolbars, 64, 85
hierarchies in newsgroups, 145
Home button, 68

home pages. *See also* start page, 57, 173, 329
  creating. *See* Web pages, publishing
  Yahoo! Personal Page Web Site, 188–189
home.netscape.com/ (Netscape), 4, 62–63
Homebuyers's Fair (www.homefair.com), 213
horizontal lines in Web pages, 277
host computers, 34, 329
Host contacted. Waiting for reply message, 112
host names, 55–57
HotWired (www.hotwired.com/), 227–228
HTML (HyperText Markup Language), 45–46, 329
  < > (brackets), 46, 268
  attributes, 293
  comments, 295
  Composer and, 265
  documents, 267–270
  files
    opening in Navigator, 73
    saving, 72
  forms, 295
  headings, 275
  line length, 291–292
  lists, 275–276
  source
    editing, 289–290
    viewing, 289–290
  special characters, 296–297
  tags, 267, 290–297, 336
    head, 293
    html, 293
    title, 294
HTML For Dummies, 265
HTTP (hypertext transfer protocol), 40–46, 329
http:// in addresses, 69
hypertext, 45–46, 281–285, 329
  documents, 44
  links, 42–43
  multimedia, 41

• I •

IAB (Internet Architecture Board), 329
Identity (Mail & Newsgroups), 123
IETF (Internet Engineering Task Force)
  defined, 329
  Web site (www.ietf.org/), 230–231, 329
image maps, 295
images, 261-262
  alignment, 286
  as links, 287
  broken, 114
  character-based browsers and, 288
  downloadable, 285, 287
  GIF files, 328
  inline, 285, 330
  inserting in documents, 286
  JPEG files, 330
  loading automatically, 82
  newsgroups, 309
  saving, 72
  text flow, 286
IMAP server (e-mail), 119–120
importing bookmarks, 106
incoming mail servers, 124
Indigo Girls Web site, 197–199
information service, 304–305
Information Superhighway, 11
inline images, 285, 330
inserting images, 286
installing Communicator, 62
Inter-Links (alabanza.com/kabacoff/Interlinks), 178–180
Internet
  basics, 12–15
  introduction Web page, 15
  protocols, 14
  services, 14, 38–40
    e-mail, 47–48
    FTP, 48–49
    Gopher, 50–51
    names in URLs, 54–55
    non-Web, 52–53

Telnet, 51–52
Usenet news, 49–50
WAIS, 51
standards groups, 14
Internet Explorer (Microsoft), 30
Internet For Dummies, The, 12, 52
Internet keywords, 97–98
Internet keywords feature, 80
Internet mail, 118
Internet Mall (www.internet-mall.com/),
205–206
Internet service providers. *See* ISPs
Internet Shopping Network
(www.internet.net/), 208–209
Internet Underground Music Archive
(www.iuma.com), 197
IP (Internet Protocol), 330
addresses, 56
IRC (Internet Relay Chat), 330
IRTF (Internet Research Task Force), 330
ISDN (Integrated Services Digital Net-
work), 330
modems, 20
ISOC (Internet Society), 330
ISPs (Internet service providers), 5, 20
communications cost for Web pages, 256
EarthLink, 42

• *J* •

Java, 82, 89
JavaScript, 83, 89
JPEG (Joint Photographic Experts Group)
files, 330

• *K* •

key pairs (cryptography), 159
keywords (Internet keywords), 97–98
kindergarten through 12th grade Web
sites, 243–245

• *L* •

language preferences, 80
LANs (local area networks), 19
mail, 118
Larry's InfoPower Pages (www.clark.net/
pub/lschank/home.html), 183–185
LDAP (Lightweight Directory Access
Protocol), 132
legal guidelines to publishing Web pages,
263–264
legislation-related Web sites, 246–250
libraries
Sport Virtual Library, 196
virtual libraries, 174–185
WWW Virtual Library, 33–34
library.microsoft.com/ (virtual library),
182–183
lighthouses Web site (zuma.lib.utk.edu/
lights/), 313–314
line length (HTML), 291–292
links, 65–66, 281–285
hypertext, 42–43
images as, 287
locations, 284
moving backward/forward, 67
names, 282–283
pointers, 174
targets, 283–284
typing *versus* clicking, 69–70
underlined text, 65
within documents, 285
listening to the radio, 308
lists (HTML), 275–276
LISTSERV, 331
loading images automatically, 82
local area network (LAN), 19, 331
location toolbar, 63–66
Location: box, 62
Looking up host message, 112
lowercase letters, 34
Lynx, 331

• M •

Macintosh, Communicator and, 65
MacInTouch (www.macintouch.com/), 222
magazines, electronic, 226–229
magnetic poetry on the Web, 310
Mail & Newsgroups option (Preferences
    dialog box), 80, 121–129
mail servers, 123–125
mail. *See* e-mail
mailbox, 118
mailing lists (LISTSERV), 132-133, 331
maps (AnyWho), 194
markup language, 46, 331
MDNs (Message Delivery Notifications),
    and e-mail, 129
media of the Web, 26–27
memory caches, 83, 324
menus
  Go, 67
  pop-up, 85–86
Message area, 64, 66
message list (Messenger), 137
messages. *See* e-mail; Messenger
Messenger. *See also* e-mail, 117–134, 331
  address book, 130–133
  addresses, 148
  attachments to messages, 144, 151–152
  body of message, 149–150
  column headers, 138
  copying messages, 128
  creating messages, 147–150
  encrypted messages, 164–165
  deleting messages, 148
  filtering messages, 155–158
  folders, 137, 142–143
    copying messages to, 142
    creating, 142
    deleting, 143
    moving messages between, 142
  forwarding messages, 150–151
  mail security, 158–165
  mailing lists, 132–133
  message list, 137
  pinpoint addressing, 149

POP, 333
  reading messages, 140–141
  receiving mail, 137–141
  replying to messages, 150–151
  return receipt, 165–166
  searching for messages, 142, 143
  sending messages, 150
  spelling, 152–153
  subject line, 149–150
  threads, 139–140
  Usenet news
    creating messages, 153–154
    filtering, 158
    reading messages, 146
    subscribing to newsgroups, 145
  window settings, 127
Messenger command (Communicator
    menu), 135
Messenger window, 135–136
MetaCrawler search engine
    (www.metacrawler.com,
    www.metaspy.com), 310
Microsoft Web site (www.microsoft.com),
    223
Microsoft Internet Explorer, 30
Microsoft Library (library.microsoft.com),
    182–183
MIME (Multipurpose Internet Mail
    Extensions), 87, 332
mirror sites, 302, 332
modems, 19, 332
  ISDN, 20
  programs, 21
  speed, 20
    TCP/IP software, 21
Modems For Dummies, 20
MORE Internet For Dummies, 12, 52
moving
  bookmarks, 104–105
  e-mail messages between folders, 142
MUD (Multi-User Dungeons), 332
multimedia, hypertext and, 41
Music Boulevard (www.musicblvd.com/),
    207–208
music-related Web sites, 197–199, 309
  shopping, 207–208

• N •

names in links, 282–283
National Organization for Women Web
    site, 247–248
National Rifle Association Web site,
    247–248
National Science Foundation
    (www.nsf.gov/), 239–240
navigation toolbar, 63–64
Navigator, 3, 332
  logo, 62
Navigator option (Preferences dialog box),
    79–80
Navigator window, 63
Netcenter, 29–30, 62–63, 332
netiquette, 332
Netscape, 333
Netscape Communicator. _See_
    Communicator
Netscape Composer For Dummies, 265
Netscape Navigator. _See_ Navigator
netstorms, 113–114, 333
networks
  protocols, 39
  routers, 334
Newbie home page (www.newbie.net/
    Newbie-Pages/), 45
newciv.org/worldtrans/positive.html
    (Positive Vibrations), 318
newsgroups. _See also_ Usenet news, 49–50,
    308, 333
  computer-related, 221
  creating messages, 153–154
  filtering messages, 158
  flames, 328
  hierarchies, 145
  Mail & Newsgroups dialog box, 121
  photographs, 309
  puzzles, 319
  reading messages, 146
  rec.crafts.misc, 190–191
  rec.travel.misc, 189
  resources, 231–233
  servers, 125
  subscribing to, 145

newspapers on the Web, 304
  daily news and entertainment, 308
No Activity error, 111–112
No Response error, 110–111
Notepad (Windows), 237
Novell Web site (www.novell.com/),
    224–226
NOW (www.now.org/), 247–248
NRA (www.nra.org/), 247–248
NSFnet (National Science Foundation
    network), 333

• O •

offline mode (e-mail), 48, 140–141
Offline option (Preference dialog box),
    81–82
online services
  America Online (AOL), 323
  CompuServe, 326
Online/offline indicator, 64
Open Page command (File menu), 69
Open Page dialog box, 69
Oregon state government Web site
    (www.state.or.us/), 242–243
outgoing servers, 125

• P •

packets, 333
page formatting (Composer), 276–277
paragraph formatting (Composer),
    274–275
parents and teachers interests, 244–245
passwords (FTP), e-mail address as, 83
Peace Page (www.ccnet.com/elsajoy/
    index2.html), 317
People.yahoo.com, 192
Perl 5 For Dummies, 228–229
Perl programming language, 228–229
personal certificates, 90
Personal Toolbar, 63–64, 85
Personal Toolbar Folder, 85
Pete's Pond Page (reality.sgi.com/
    employees/peteo/), 322

photographs (newsgroups), 309
pictures. *See* images
pinpoint addressing (e-mail), 125, 149
plug-ins, 87, 333
Plugged In (www.pluggedin.org/), 316
poetry (magnetic), 310
pointers (links), 65, 174
POP (Point Of Presence), 333
POP (Post Office Protocol) server (e-mail),
    119–120, 333
pop-up menu, 85–86
portals, 29
ports, 40, 334
Positive Vibrations (newciv.org/
    worldtrans/positive.html), 318
post office, 118
PPP (Point-to-Point protocol), 334
preferences, 75–91
Preferences command (Edit menu), 75, 121
Preferences dialog box, 75
  Appearance, 77–79
  Mail & Newsgroups, 121–129
Print command (File menu), 72
printing Web pages, 72, 280
programs
  server programs, 335
  shells, 335
properties
  bookmarks, 105
  Composer, 276
proportional font, 122
protocols, 14, 334
  clients, 31
  HTTP, 40
  servers, 33
  TCP/IP, 38
proxies, 84
public key cryptography (security), 159
publications on the Web, 226–229
Publisher's Catalogues Home Page
    (www.lights.com/publisher), 28
publishing Web pages, 253–256
  businesses, 257–260
  Composer, 265–280
  software, 301–302

• R •

radio listening, 308
rec.puzzles.crosswords, 319
Reload button, 69
reloading pages, 69
replying to e-mail messages, 150–151
retain sales, 258–259
return receipt (e-mail messages), 129,
    165–166
reviewing content, 303
RFCs (Requests for Comments), 334
Roaming Access option (Preferences
    dialog box), 81
roaming server, 81
robots (searches), 94
root domains, 334
routers, 334
routing table, netstorms and, 113–114

• S •

S/MIME (Secure MIME), 159, 335
sampling music, 309
Save As command (File menu), 72
saving
  files
    downloaded, 73
    HTML, 72
  images, 72
  Web pages, 71–73, 280
science Web sites (National Science
    Foundation), 239–240
searches
  e-mail messages, 143
  FedWorld, 238–239
  Internet keywords, 97–98
  Netscape (home.netscape.com/escapes/
    search/ntsrchrnd-3.html), 95
  people, 192
  robots, 94–95
  spiders, 94
  text (Web pages), 86
  Web Robots page, 96
  WebCrawler (info.webcrawler.com/mak/
    projects/robots/robots.html), 95

What's Related button, 98
whole-Web, 304
MetaCrawler
  www.metacrawler.com/, 310
  www.metaspy.com/, 310
  Yahoo!, 176
Secure Sockets Layer (SSL), 336
security
  CERT, 325
  certificates, 90, 160–163, 325
  digital signature, 326
  forms, 70
  mail, 158–165
  preferences, 88–90
  S/MIME, 335
  warnings, 89
  Web sites regarding, 233
Security button, 88
Security indicator, 64
Security Reference Index
  (www.telstra.com.au/info/
  security.html), 233
Seidman's Online Insider
  (www.onlineinsider.com/), 226–227
selling items via the Web, 258–259
separators in bookmarks, 105
server programs, 335
servers, 33
  Archie, 323
  host computers, 34
  mail servers, 124–125
  name errors, 110
  roaming servers, 81
  SMTP (Simple Mail Transfer
    Protocol), 120
services, Web sites, 212–214
services, Internet, 14, 38–40
  e-mail, 47–48
  FTP, 48–49
  Gopher, 50–51
  names in URLs, 54–55
  non-Web, 52–53
  Telnet, 51–52
  Usenet news, 49–50
  WAIS, 51

SGML (Standard General Markup
  Language), 335
shareware, 335
shells, 335
shopping online, 28
  Amazon, 210–211
  Computer Literacy Bookshops, 209–210
  DealerNet, 204–205
  Internet Mall, 205–206
  Internet Shopping Network, 208–209
  Music Boulevard, 207
  WebAuction, 206–207
  Wits' End Antiques, 211–212
site certificates, 90
sizing
  Component bar, 64–65
  panes in Messenger, 136
slashes (/) in URLs, 58
SLIP (Serial Line IP), 335
Smart Browsing, 80, 97–99
SmartUpdate, 84
SMTP (Simple Mail Transfer Protocol),
  120, 336
software
  client-server, 326
  communications software, 20
  freeware, 328
  publishing in Web pages, 301–302
  shareware, 335
  TCP/IP, 21
  terminal emulation, 21
  Web clients, 30–32
sound (e-mail receipt), 122
source code (HTML), 5
  editing, 289–290
  viewing, 289
source documents, viewing, 72
spam (Usenet news), 49
special characters in HTML, 296–297
spelling in e-mail messages, 126, 152–153
spiders (searches), 94
spirituality Web sites, 317–318
Sport Virtual Library, 196
sports online, 194–196
SSL (Secure Sockets Layer), 125, 336

SSL version, 89
standards groups, 14
Star Trek: Voyager (www.paramount.com/
tvvoyager/), 199–200
start page. *See also* home page, 62–63, 68,
79, 173
starting Composer, 270–272
state and local government Web sites,
241–243
stock market, 310–311
Stop button, 68–69
stopping page download, 68–69
storing Web pages, 255–256
style sheets, enabling, 83
subfolders, 136
subject line (messages), 149–150
submitting forms, 70
subscribing to newsgroups, 145
sunsite.unc.edu/zen/ (Zen buddhism),
313–314
surfing, 172, 311
szym.com/cameras/, 307

• T •

tables (Composer), 277–280
tags (HTML), 267, 290–297, 336
< > (brackets), 268
head, 293
html, 293
title, 294
Talk, 52
targets (links), 283–284
TCP (Transmission Control Protocol), 336
TCP services, 40
TCP/IP (Transmission Control Protocol/
Internet Protocol), 38–39
software, 21
technical support Web sites, 222–225
telephone service via the Web, 305
television-related Web sites, 199–201
telnet, 51–52, 336
Terminal (software), 21, 336
terminal emulation programs, 21

text
baseline, 286
files, opening in Navigator, 73
flowing around images, 286
HTML, 45–46
hypertext, 41–46
markup language, 46, 331
searching for in Web pages, 86
underlined (links), 65
text editors, 267
THOMAS system, 237
threads (Messenger), 139–140
Tibet liberation (www.tibet.org/), 248–249
TLS (Transport Layer Security), 125
tone and intent of Web pages, 262–263
Tonight Show, The (www.nbc.com/
tonightshow), 200–210
toolbars
customizing, 85
hiding, 64
location, 63–64
navigation, 63–64
personal, 63–64, 85
topics for personal Web pages, 254–255
topics on the Web, 25
Transferring data message, 112
travel groups, 189–190
troubleshooting, 107–114
typing
links, 69–70
URLs in Open Page dialog box, 69–70

• U •

U.K. Government Information Service
(www.open.gov.uk/), 240–241
U.S. House of Representatives
(www.house.gov/), 236
underlined text (links), 65
UNIX, 337
updating Communicator, 5
uploading files, 337
uppercase letters, 34
URL requests, 57–58

URLs (Uniform Resource Locator), 337
    case of letters, 54
    copying, 70
    errors, 108–109
    location toolbar, 66
    message area, 66
    Open Page dialog box, 69
    service names, 54–55
    slashes (/), 58
URNs (Uniform Resource Names), 302–303
Usenet news, 49–50, 121, 337
    creating messages, 153–154
    information resources, 231–233
    reading messages, 146
    subscribing to newsgroups, 145
    threads, 139–140
UUCP (UNIX-to-UNIX Copy), 337

• V •

validity of content, 25
vCard, 132
versions of Communicator, 62
    SmartUpdate, 84
video cameras, 307–308
viewing
    HTML source, 289
    source documents, 72
virtual communities, 305–306
Virtual Fridge (magnetic poetry), 310
virtual libraries, 174–185
virtual software library, 32–33
vlib.stanford.edu/Overview.html (virtual
        library), 174
VRML (Virtual Reality Modeling
        Language), 337

• W •

WAIS (Wide Area Information Server), 51,
    337
WAN (wide area network), 338
warnings (security), 89
Web
    addresses. *See* URLs
    basics, 11–22
    media, 26–27

Web browser, 24
Web catalogs, 94–96
Web clients, 24, 30–32
Web pages
    administration costs, 256–257
    as e-mail attachments, 152
    attracting visitors, 259–260
    businesses (selling products), 258–259
    content, 260–261
    copying for practice in Composer, 272
    downloading, stopping, 68–69
    graphics, 261–262
    legal guidelines, 263–264
    non-existent, 108
    printing, 72, 280
    publishing, 253–264
    reloading, 69
    saving, 71–73, 280
    software publishing, 301–302
    spiritual, 317–318
    storage space, 255–256
    text, searching for, 86
    tone and intent, 262–263
    topics, 25
    viewing multiple, 73–74
    Web robots, 96
Web sites
    bird watching, 321
    buddhism, 313–314
    business-related, 215–217
    computer discussions, 229–234
    computer-related, 220–234
    education, 243–245, 315
    Exploratorium, 315
    games, 194–196
    gardening, 320, 322
    government, 235–250
    kids, 316
    legislation-related, 246–250
    lighthouses, 313–314
    maps, 194
    moving, 17
    music-related, 197–199, 207–208, 309
    Plugged In, 316
    publications, 226–229

radio listening, 308
searches, 176–180
security, 233
services, 212–214
shopping, 208–212
sports-related, 194–196
technical support, 222–225
television-related, 199–201
video cameras, 307–308
Web66 (web66.coled.umn.edu/), 244–245
WebAuction (www.webauction.com/),
206–207
WebRing (www.webring.org), 180–181
What's Related button, 98
whois, 52
whole-Web searching, 304
Windows
Communicator and, 65
Notepad, 237
windows
Bookmarks, 102
Messenger, 127, 135–136
multiple, 73–74
Winsock, 338
Winsock Apps List (cws.internet.com/),
234
Wired magazine, 227–228
Wits' End Antiques (www.tias.com/stores/
witsend/), 211–212
word processors compared to Composer,
266–267
word wrap in e-mail messages, 126
workstations, 338
World Wide Consortium (W3C,
www.w3.org/), 18
World Wide Web (WWW). *See also* Web,
338
World Wide Web Virtual Library, 174–175

X.500 directories, 52
XML, 46, 338

Yahoo! (www.yahoo.com), 25–26, 175–177
Yahoo! People Search
(People.yahoo.com/), 192
Yahoo! Personal Pages Web site, 188–189

• Z •

Zen Buddhism (sunsite.unc.edu/zen/),
313–314
zuma.lib.utk.edu/lights/ (lighthouses),
313–314

Notes

Notes

Notes

Notes

Get the Most from Your PC!

Every issue of PC World is packed with the latest information to help you make the most of your PC.

- Top 100 PC and Product Ratings
- Hot PC News
- How Tos, Tips, & Tricks
- Buyers' Guides
- Consumer Watch
- Hardware and Software Previews
- Internet & Multimedia Special Reports
- Upgrade Guides
- Monthly @Home Section

YOUR FREE GIFT!

As a special bonus with your order, you will receive the IDG Books/ PC WORLD CD wallet, perfect for transporting and protecting your CD collection.

SEND TODAY
for your sample issue
and FREE IDG Books/PC WORLD CD Wallet!

How to order your sample issue and FREE CD Wallet:

✉ Cut and mail the coupon today!
Mail to: PC World, PO Box 55029, Boulder, CO 80322-5029

☎ Call us at 1-800-825-7595 x434
Fax us at 1-415-882-0936

☛ Order online at www.pcworld.com/resources/subscribe/BWH.html

PC WORLD

YOUR ONLINE RESOURCE

WWW.DUMMIES.COM

Discover *Dummies*™ Online!

The *Dummies* Web Site is your fun and friendly online resource for the latest information about *...For Dummies*® books on all your favorite topics. From cars to computers, wine to Windows, and investing to the Internet, we've got a shelf full of *...For Dummies* books waiting for you!

Ten Fun and Useful Things You Can Do at www.dummies.com

1. Register this book and win!
2. Find and buy the *...For Dummies* books you want online.
3. Get ten great *Dummies Tips*™ every week.
4. Chat with your favorite *...For Dummies* authors.
5. Subscribe free to *The Dummies Dispatch*™ newsletter.
6. Enter our sweepstakes and win cool stuff.
7. Send a free cartoon postcard to a friend.
8. Download free software.
9. Sample a book before you buy.
10. Talk to us. Make comments, ask questions, and get answers!

Jump online to these ten fun and useful things at
http://www.dummies.com/10useful

SURF THE NET

WWW.DUMMIES.COM

For other technology titles from IDG Books Worldwide, go to
www.idgbooks.com

Not online yet? It's easy to get started with *The Internet For Dummies*,® 5th Edition, or *Dummies 101*®: *The Internet For Windows*® *98*, available at local retailers everywhere.

IDG BOOKS WORLDWIDE™

Find other *...For Dummies* books on these topics:

Business • Careers • Databases • Food & Beverages • Games • Gardening • Graphics • Hardware
Health & Fitness • Internet and the World Wide Web • Networking • Office Suites
Operating Systems • Personal Finance • Pets • Programming • Recreation • Sports
Spreadsheets • Teacher Resources • Test Prep • Word Processing

IDG BOOKS WORLDWIDE BOOK REGISTRATION

Register This Book and Win!

We want to hear from you!

Visit **http://my2cents.dummies.com** to register this book and tell us how you liked it!

- ✔ Get entered in our monthly prize giveaway.
- ✔ Give us feedback about this book — tell us what you like best, what you like least, or maybe what you'd like to ask the author and us to change!
- ✔ Let us know any other ...*For Dummies*® topics that interest you.

Your feedback helps us determine what books to publish, tells us what coverage to add as we revise our books, and lets us know whether we're meeting your needs as a ...*For Dummies* reader. You're our most valuable resource, and what you have to say is important to us!

Not on the Web yet? It's easy to get started with *Dummies 101*®: *The Internet For Windows*® *98* or *The Internet For Dummies*®, 5th Edition, at local retailers everywhere.

Or let us know what you think by sending us a letter at the following address:

...*For Dummies* Book Registration
Dummies Press
7260 Shadeland Station, Suite 100
Indianapolis, IN 46256-3945
Fax 317-596-5498

BESTSELLING
BOOK SERIES
FROM IDG